ECONOMIC AND SOCIAL COMMISSION FOR ASIA AND THE PACIFIC

Asian Population Studies Series No. 150

Gender Dimensions of Population and Development in South-East Asia

UNITED·NATIONS
New York, 1999

ST/ESCAP/1950

UNITED NATIONS PUBLICATION
Sales No. E.99.II.F.60
Copyright © United Nations 1999
ISBN: 92-1-119927-1

UNITED NATIONS
ECONOMIC AND SOCIAL COMMISSION FOR ASIA AND THE PACIFIC

Readership Survey

Publication: *Gender Dimensions of Population and Development in South-East Asia,* Asian Population Studies Series No. 150

It would be appreciated if you would complete this form and return it to us by air mail or fax, at the following address: Population and Development Section, ESCAP Population and Rural and Urban Development Division, United Nations Building, Rajadamnern Avenue, Bangkok 10200, Thailand. Fax no. 66-2-288-1009. Alternatively, you are invited to send your reply by e-mail to **huguet.unescap@un.org**

QUESTIONNAIRE

1. Please circle your rating of the quality of the publication on the following aspects:	Excellent	Very good	Average	Poor	Very poor
(a) Presentation/format	5	4	3	2	1
(b) Readability	5	4	3	2	1
(c) Timeliness of information	5	4	3	2	1
(d) Coverage of subject matter	5	4	3	2	1
(e) Analytical rigour	5	4	3	2	1
(f) Overall quality	5	4	3	2	1

2. Please circle your rating of the usefulness of the publication on the following aspects:	Very useful	Quite useful	Useful	Somewhat useful	Not useful
(a) Information	5	4	3	2	1
(b) Identification of issues	5	4	3	2	1
(c) Findings	5	4	3	2	1
(d) Recommendations	5	4	3	2	1
(e) Overall quality	5	4	3	2	1

3. Comments on the issues covered in the publication:

....

....

....

....

4. Suggestions for improvement of the publication:

....

....

....

....

Your name: ....

Affiliation: ....

Mailing address: ....

....

Thank you very much for your kind cooperation in completing and returning this questionnaire to us.

PREFACE

The Programme of Action adopted at the International Conference on Population and Development, held at Cairo in 1994, stated as a basic principle,

> *"Advancing gender equality and equity and the empowerment of women, and the elimination of all kinds of violence against women, and ensuring women's ability to control their own fertility, are cornerstones of population and development-related programmes. The human rights of women and the girl child are an inalienable, integral and indivisible part of universal human rights. The full and equal participation of women in civil, cultural, economic, political and social life, at the national, regional and international levels, and the eradication of all forms of discrimination on grounds of sex, are priority objectives of the international community."* (Principle 4 of the Programme of Action.)

The Programme of Action also stated that "Population-related goals and policies are integral parts of cultural, economic and social development, the principal aim of which is to improve the quality of life of all people." (Principle 5.)

The Programme goes on to state that, as a basis for action,

> *"The empowerment and autonomy of women and the improvement of their political, social, economic and health status is a highly important end in itself. In addition, it is essential for the achievement of sustainable development.... Achieving change requires policy and programme actions that will improve women's access to secure livelihoods and economic resources, alleviate their extreme responsibilities with regard to housework, remove legal impediments to their participation in public life, and raise social awareness through effective programmes of education and mass communication."* (Paragraph 4.1)

With these principles in mind, the ESCAP Population and Rural and Urban Development Division initiated a project on "Strengthening policy analysis and research on female migration, employment, family formation and poverty in Cambodia, Lao People's Democratic Republic, Myanmar and Viet Nam". The project is funded by the United Nations Population Fund. It focuses on those countries because they are the four least developed countries in South-East Asia.

Under the auspices of the project the volume, *A Demographic Perspective on Women in Development in Cambodia, Lao People's Democratic Republic, Myanmar and Viet Nam,* Asian Population Studies Series No. 148, was prepared and published by the ESCAP secretariat. That report draws on existing census and survey data in order to provide general descriptions of the role of women in development in those countries.

That volume and similar reports prepared by experts for other countries of South-East Asia provided the basis for discussion and recommendations for further actions at the Policy Seminar on Gender Dimensions of Population and Development in South-East Asia, held at Bangkok from 1 to 4 September 1998. The chapters of the present report on Indonesia, Malaysia, the Philippines, Singapore and Thailand were prepared for the Policy Seminar and the policy recommendations contained in chapter I were adopted by the Policy Seminar.

The Population and Rural and Urban Development Division is grateful to Ms. Naushin Mahmood for editing the papers in this volume and for preparing chapter I.

CONTENTS

CONTENTS *(continued)*

LIST OF TABLES

LIST OF TABLES *(continued)*

LIST OF TABLES *(continued)*

LIST OF FIGURES

I. GENDER DIMENSIONS OF POPULATION AND DEVELOPMENT

Introduction

Achieving equality and equity between men and women in different spheres of life is essential for the attainment of sustainable development goals. In this context, the need for enhancement of women's participation in national development programmes and their full integration into the development process has been widely recognized in various global and regional forums. The World Population Plan of Action adopted at Bucharest in 1974 and the declaration of the United Nations Decade (1976-1985) for Women: Equality, Development and Peace were major achievements in this direction (United Nations, 1995b).

More recently, the Programme of Action adopted by the International Conference on Population and Development at Cairo in 1994 reaffirmed and elaborated the role of women in national development, and endorsed a new strategy that emphasizes gender equality, equity and empowerment of women. In this context, the Programme of Action recommends that countries should act to empower women and should take steps to eliminate inequalities between men and women by providing them with more choices through expanded access to education and health services, skill development and employment, and eliminating all practices that discriminate against women (United Nations, 1995a).

Pursuant to these principles, the present study examines the gender dimensions of population and development with a particular focus on the current role of women in development, and the issues and concerns that confront them and warrant future action toward improving the situation of women. The issues discussed in the study, despite being common in nature and base, vary among countries, cultures and ethnic groups, and affect men and women differently. In this context, it is important to identify the behavioural attitudes and practices conditioned by the social construction of gender roles in different societies and to take them into account in future policies and programmes.

This study includes five countries in South-East Asia, namely Indonesia, Malaysia, Philippines, Singapore and Thailand which have exhibited a rapid pace of economic growth and structural transformation during the past two decades. The socio-economic changes in these countries have provided significant opportunities for utilizing the potentials and energies of the young population, women in particular, who have not only contributed to but also substantially benefited from the overall national development programmes. For example, a high rate of economic growth has provided greater options for many young women to benefit fully from educational and employment opportunities, particularly in industry, thus providing a measure of autonomy and gender equity, which eventually has affected their reproductive choices and goals.

Given that the demographic transition is well under way in all of these countries, it is of interest to examine these changes from a women-in-development perspective. Recognizing the importance of the family as the basic social unit, women's role in the family may be seen as acting as agents of change in many aspects of life, including the adoption of fertility control and family planning, the provision of health care for children and the acquisition of an independent economic livelihood. Thus, information on such indicators helps to assess the status and role of women in development relative to men and to women in other countries. The measures of literacy and educational attainment, headship, employment, fertility, migration, etc., which are largely estimated from data in censuses and demographic surveys and have rather standard demographic concepts, definitions and methods of analysis, provide the possibility of making generally valid comparisons between the sexes as well as among countries.

In other areas, however, such as legal rights, equal pay, treatment in the labour force and decision-making power, where there is a less precise relationship between women's status and level of development, measures of gender equality depend more upon the political and the socio-cultural setting in which women live. While the five countries included in this study are quite similar in terms of social and economic status of women, there are significant political, cultural and ethnic differences which distinguish them on issues of gender roles and equity. In each country, women have equally and actively participated in economic and social spheres of life and have traditionally not been subjected to any formalized discrimination in the family. It appears, however, that underlying socio-cultural practices and sex-based biases during the socialization process have restricted women's role in many ways, which has resulted in an unequal distribution of productive and familial roles between men and women. Although the State laws and the national governments ensure equal rights and obligations for all, the available evidence suggests that a lot more needs to be done to improve the situation of women, particularly the poor, the rural, the elderly and those in minority ethnic groups.

A. Demographic perspective

This section gives a brief description of the demographic situation of women in the five selected countries and compares the findings on key indicators in order to assess their role in demographic change and its implications for development.

Each country has undergone a rapid fertility transition since the 1970s with moderate to high levels of urbanization and modernization. The proportion of population living in urban areas is about 31 per cent in Thailand and 37 per cent in Indonesia compared with 47 per cent in the Philippines, 57 per cent in Malaysia and 100 per cent in Singapore (table 1). Hence, the structure of labour force varies from being mostly agricultural in Indonesia and Thailand and to relatively more formal and industrialized in the other three countries. Recognizing that Singapore is basically an urban metropolis with explicit state policies and programmes, the important sectors of the economy are manufacturing, construction and services. Agriculture plays a negligible part, and this is a feature that distinguishes Singapore from other countries where the agricultural sector makes a major contribution to the economy and a large proportion of women are engaged in rural-based occupations and activities.

As a result of steady decline in fertility, the proportion of children under 15 years of age has substantially declined over the past two decades. On the other hand, the share of those 65 years and above has risen, being around 7 per cent in Singapore and Thailand and about 4 per cent in Indonesia and Malaysia (table 1), implying an ageing of population in these countries. The overall sex ratio in each country is fairly balanced, except for Thailand where women constitute a larger proportion than men in total population. There are, however, some variations in sex ratios by age. As indicated by the elderly sex ratio (age 60 and above), women outnumber men owing to their longer life expectancy.

In accompaniment with socio-economic development, there have been significant changes in patterns of marriage and family formation in all of these countries. Although marriage remains nearly universal and has great relevance for family life, women tend to marry at somewhat later ages, between 24 and 26 years, on average. Thus the proportion of never-married women in the younger age groups has substantially increased. For example, the proportion of women reported single among those aged 20-24 years is as high as 78.5 per cent in Singapore, compared with 40 per cent in Indonesia and 48 per cent in Thailand. Among those aged 25-29 years, 39 per cent in Singapore, 25.3 per cent in Thailand and 15.2 per cent in Indonesia have remained single (table 2). The evidence suggests that a decline in teenage and arranged marriages in Indonesia has brought a steady decline in divorce rates, whereas an increasing trend in the divorce rate is noted for Thailand, where the incidence of remarriage among younger women is also increasing. It is suggested that greater access to education and employment opportunities and exposure to urban living have contributed significantly to delaying marriage among women and to changing patterns of family formation in these countries.

Closely related to delayed marriage is the process of fertility decline which has occurred rather rapidly in all these countries. The decline is particularly noteworthy in Indonesia and Thailand because of their moderate level of socio-economic development. Currently, the total fertility rate (TFR) is estimated at 3.2 in Malaysia with notable variation by ethnic group; near the replacement level in Indonesia and Thailand, with TFR of 2.8 and 2.0, respectively; and below replacement level in Singapore with TFR of 1.7 in the 1990s (table 2). With the acceptance of a small-family norm by a majority of women in these societies, the contraceptive prevalence rate (CPR) is as high as 72 per cent in Thailand, 65 per cent in Singapore, about 55 per cent in Indonesia and 50 per cent in Malaysia (table 2). Women's contribution to fertility decline has been significant as they have been targets of strongly

Table 1. Population, per cent urban and sex ratios, selected countries

	Indonesia 1990	Malaysia 1995	Philippines 1990	Singapore 1996	Thailand 1990
Total population (in million)	179.24	20.69	60.56	3.04	54.55
Per cent urban	37.00	57.00	47.00	100.00	31.00
Per cent population in age group:					
0-14	37.00	35.00	38.30	23.00	28.80
15-64	59.20	61.00	58.40	70.00	64.00
65+	3.80	4.00	3.30	7.00	7.20
Sex ratio*					
All ages	99.50	102.00	101.10	101.20	98.50
Age 60 and above	90.50	–	88.40	86.10	86.00

Sources: Following chapters and ESCAP (1995), (1996) and (1998).

* Number of males per 100 females.

Table 2. Selected indicators of fertility, marriage and family formation

Indicator	Indonesia 1995	Malaysia 1993-1995	Philippines 1993-1995	Singapore 1990-1996	Thailand 1990-1995
Total fertility rate	2.8	3.2	3.9	1.7	2.0
Contraceptive prevalence rate (%)	54.7	50.0	46.0	65.0	72.0
Proportion never married					
20-24 years	40.1	–	–	78.5	48.0
25-29 years	15.2	–	–	39.2	25.3
30-34 years	5.5	12.0	–	20.9	14.1
Female headed households (%)	12.7	–	14.0	–	20.1

Sources: Following chapters and ESCAP (1995), (1996) and (1998).

state-supported and -controlled family planning programmes. In fact, women's role as both the recipients and providers of family planning services is widely recognized as contributing to the success of the family planning programme in Thailand.

The demographic changes in concurrence with the process of socio-economic development have affected women's family life and levels of living in many ways. The evidence from Indonesia, the Philippines and Thailand indicates that household size, on average, has declined and the share of single and small households consisting of 3-4 persons has risen. Although a majority of households are headed by men, the share of women-headed households has increased to 13 per cent in Indonesia with an average of 2.9 members, 14 per cent in the Philippines with average of about 3 persons and 20 per cent in Thailand with 3.2 persons, on average (table 2). Young women household heads (aged 10-24 years) are more likely to be single and, as women become older, the probability of becoming household heads rises owing to increase in widowhood. The statistical evidence indicates that over 60 per cent of women household heads are widowed in Indonesia, the Philippines and Thailand, and a majority of them are concentrated in older age groups (50 years and above). This may largely be reflected in the low elderly sex ratios and the higher life expectancies for women than men in these countries. As a consequence, most female heads, with low levels of education and income,

face difficult circumstances in caring for their families.

As an expected outcome of the development process and a steady decline in fertility in the five countries, mortality and expectation of life of both men and women have substantially improved. The infant mortality rate, an important indicator of health care availability and development, is as low as 4 per 1,000 live births in Singapore, 12 in Malaysia, 29 in Thailand and 36 in the Philippines, and is the highest at 53 in Indonesia (table 3). Among the five countries, Indonesia appears to have gained the least improvement in maternal and child health care indicators, despite its noteworthy achievements in fertility decline. The highest maternal mortality ratio was estimated to equal 390 per 100,000 live births in Indonesia in 1994, compared with only 80 in Malaysia, 180 in the Philippines and 100 in Thailand in 1993. In contrast, the key health indicators in Singapore are comparable to other developed countries and clearly reflect the advanced and accessible health care facilities.

The demographic measures discussed above reflect the status of women in the five countries in terms of their position as household heads who are responsible for the well-being of their families; as objects and targets of fertility control programmes which have played an important role in reducing family size; as independent workers in the labour market who have made significant contributions to

Table 3. Selected mortality and health status indicators for five countries, 1990-1996

Indicator	Indonesia	Malaysia	Philippines	Singapore	Thailand
Infant mortality rate (per 1,000 live births)	53	12	36	4	29
Maternal mortality ratio (per 100,000 live births)	390	80	180	–	100
Expectation of life at birth (in years)					
Male	61	69	67	74	70
Female	65	74	70	80	75
Percentage pregnant women aged 15-49 with anaemia	74	36	48	–	48
Percentage births attended by trained personnel	36	94	53	–	71

Sources: Following chapters and ESCAP (1995), (1996) and (1998).

productive activities; and as being elderly and widowed and thus an important component of the ageing population that faces hard social and economic circumstances in life.

B. Social and economic conditions

As part of the development process, women have substantially benefited from the expanding education and employment opportunities in the five selected countries. On the one hand, enhancement in women's level of education has directly affected fertility levels, health of their children and their participation in gainful employment. On the other hand, improved education has indirectly prepared women to recognize their rights and abilities to participate equally and actively in all aspects of development.

Given the equality in access to education, nearly universal primary education has been achieved and the gender gap in school enrolment has disappeared in all these countries. The evidence indicates that by the year 1990, virtually equal proportions of boys and girls aged 6-15 years were attending school (table 4). Although female enrolment at tertiary levels has increased markedly, some gender differences are still evident at post-secondary levels in

Indonesia, the Philippines and Thailand. It also appears that women mostly choose the fields of study traditionally considered more suitable for them such as fine arts, education, science and humanities, whereas men are more concentrated in the fields of business, engineering, architecture, accounting, sciences, etc.

Educational disparities between urban and rural areas also exist, particularly for secondary and higher levels where most women have left school either to enter the labour market or matrimony. Thus, policies and programmes are required to involve those women fully in development by reaching rural areas and the disadvantaged groups of women.

The economic expansion and increase in the educated workforce have led to a structural shift in the labour market from the agricultural to industrial and service sectors since the 1980s. Although labour force participation rates remain higher for males than females in all of these countries, it appears that a larger proportion of women workers have begun to play a significant role in traditionally male-dominated occupations and industries. The statistics show that women's participation in work has markedly increased in all age groups in Singapore, especially among young women aged 20-29

Table 4. Percentage of population aged 6-24 years attending school by age group and sex, selected countries: 1990-1994

Level of school and sex	Indonesia 1994	Philippines 1993	Thailand 1990
Primary	(7-12 years)	(6-10 years)	(6-11 years)
Male	91.2	76.9	80.8
Female	91.7	79.0	81.0
Lower secondary	(13-15 years)	(11-15 years)	(12-17 years)
Male	67.9	86.9	47.6
Female	62.6	89.5	45.7
Upper secondary	(16-18 years)	(16-20 years)	
Male	39.6	48.9	–
Female	32.9	49.1	–
Tertiary	(19-24 years)	(21-24 years)	(18-24 years)
Male	13.3	14.9	11.3
Female	8.6	11.2	11.1

Sources: ESCAP (1995), (1996) and (1998).

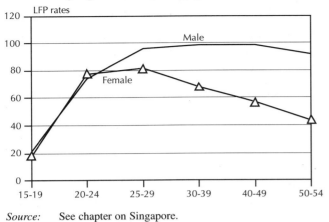

Figure 1. Labour force participation rates by age and sex, Singapore 1996

Source: See chapter on Singapore.

where eight out of ten women are reported working in 1996. However, work participation rates drop quickly after age 30 (figure 1), when women confront the issue of balancing two roles – that of a mother and a worker in the labour market (see the chapter on Singapore). The argument put forward to explain this phenomenon is that when women experience stress over the competing demands of jobs and child rearing, they tend to compartmentalize or separate their two main roles by joining the labour force when they are young, single or childless and withdraw when they have other responsibilities later in the life cycle. Although there is clear indication that women in Singapore are moving away from the sole role of homemakers to a dual-role ideology, the occupational distribution shows that there is still an inclination towards taking up lower-level clerical and secretarial jobs. Hence, despite women's increased participation in work, they still need to make inroads into the full spectrum of occupations and employment in the formal sector.

Economic activity rates by age among the other four countries have a similar pattern (figure 2). Thailand shows the highest proportion of women participating in work (71.5 per cent in 1990). With the predominance of agriculture in the economy and low educational skill among women, a large number of them are working on farms as unpaid family

workers or in low-paid jobs in the trade, industry and service sectors. As a result, many women are restricted from fully participating in the development process.

In Indonesia, 44.5 per cent of women are reported as participating in the labour force in 1994 with 36 per cent in urban and 49 per cent in rural areas. The evidence, however, suggests that greater dynamism and gains in economic activities have been experienced by urban women, especially those between the ages of 15 and 30 years, who have actively participated in the expanding trade and industrial sectors of the economy and have benefited more from the formalization of the labour market.

In Malaysia, in a similar fashion, rapid economic growth and structural transformation have resulted in greater gains for women than men, especially in terms of their expanded employment in manufacturing and electronics industries. The statistics show that the percentage of women workers increased from 8 per cent to 24 per cent in manufacturing, and from 16 per cent to 21 per cent in the service sector between 1970 and 1990. Despite such gains, more than 60 per cent of women in Malaysia are still working in the informal sector as own account workers and unpaid family workers. Even for women with high levels of education and full employment, the dual-role burden of being mothers and workers is an issue confronting women where the concept of gender equality is not well-accepted in all sections of the society. Thus, policies and programmes for easing the conflicts between formal employment, child care and household responsibility need to be given more attention. In this context, it is important to incorporate and emphasize issues of male responsibility in plans to promote women's development.

The overall distribution of employed persons in different occupations shows some variations among these five countries. Agriculture is the dominant occupation for both men and women in Indonesia and Thailand.

6

Figure 2. Labour force participation rates by age group and sex

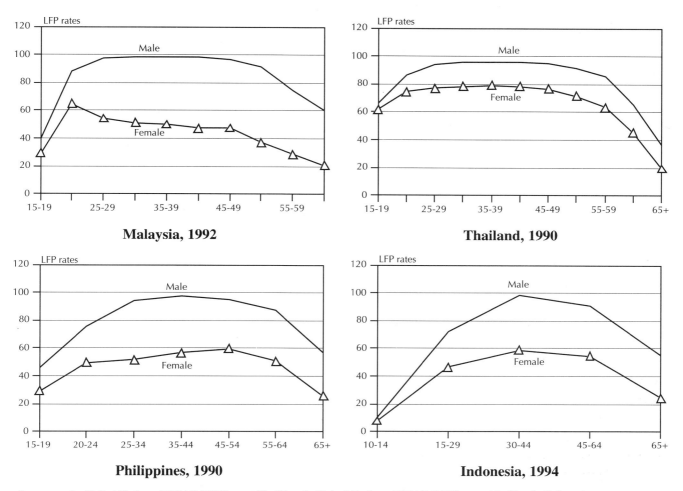

Malaysia, 1992

Thailand, 1990

Philippines, 1990

Indonesia, 1994

Sources: 1. United Nations, ESCAP (1995) see table 27; 2. United Nations, ESCAP (1995) see table 53; 3. Indonesia paper.

In other countries, most women are employed either as service and sales workers or in clerical and related jobs. It is, however, interesting to note that the small proportion of women employed in the professional and technical occupations outnumber men in each of these countries, whereas men are mostly concentrated in administrative and managerial work or in production-related occupations (table 5).

Women's enhanced role in the development process has also increased their mobility, both domestically and internationally. Women in Indonesia not only dominate the overseas labour market, but also show high migratory movements between provinces within the country, mostly for seeking better employment opportunities. In Malaysia also, internal migration trends are high for women.

Overall, men tend to migrate more than women over longer distances, whereas women outnumber men in rural-to-urban intra-state and urban-to-urban inter-state movements. There is also increasing evidence of single and young women (15-29) migrating to other areas for economic reasons. Female migration in Malaysia is characterized by two distinct groups. One comprises young females between 15 and 24 years of age with less education but high levels of labour force participation in service and production-related occupations. The other comprises relatively older women, mostly aged of 25-34 years, who are highly educated and have found employment in professional and administrative jobs. In Thailand, when the demand for industrial labour increased because of the economic boom during the past two decades, female migrants outnumbered male

Table 5. Percentage distribution of employed persons by major occupation groups, selected countries

Occupation category	Indonesia 1990		Malaysia 1995		Philippines 1990		Singapore 1996		Thailand 1993	
	Male	Female	Male	Female	Male	Female	Male	Female	Male	Female
Professional, technical and related workers	3.3	4.4	8.4	13.5	3.6	10.8	18.7	24.8	3.6	4.7
Administrative, managerial, executive workers	0.3	0.1	4.4	1.9	1.3	0.9	12.5	6.0	3.1	1.0
Clerical and related workers	6.0	3.0	7.3	17.6	3.1	6.6	4.5	27.9	3.1	4.2
Service and sales workers	14.2	26.0	20.8	24.7	13.4	39.0	14.0	13.8	10.9	18.2
Agriculture, forestry, fishermen workers	50.4	48.9	20.9	15.8	52.3	30.9	–	–	56.3	57.6
Production, transport operators and labourers	25.4	16.4	38.2	26.5	25.8	11.3	20.9	13.5	23.0	14.3
Others/not stated	0.4	1.2	–	–	0.5	0.5	29.4*	14.0*	–	–

Sources: Following chapters and ESCAP (1995), (1996) and (1998).

Note: Includes labourers, assemblers in others category.

migrants. However, a large number of female migrants have moved to big cities without any basic skill or training and are engaged in low-status and low-paid jobs.

Besides increased mobility in domestic labour markets, the evidence indicates the departure of a significant number of women from Indonesia, the Philippines and Thailand for employment abroad, mostly as contract workers and in service-related occupations. Although overseas migration can serve to provide financial gains and temporary relief from unemployment, the issue of social and psychological costs of such movements makes those women workers vulnerable to adverse consequences of global economic trends and the difficult times they have to face being away from home and their families.

C. Prospects for women's development

Based on the available evidence, it is apparent that women's participation in productive employment has increased substantially in the five selected countries. There is, however, growing concern about many disadvantaged groups of women with relatively lower social and economic status who are restricted from full participation in development activities.

With the sudden economic downturn and financial crisis in Indonesia, Malaysia, the Philippines and Thailand since 1997, the future prospects for the attainment of gender equality, maintenance of equal rights and participation of women in the labour force are uncertain. With the limited available evidence on the situation, it is feared that women are likely to be more affected by the adverse consequences of economic crisis and will be the first ones to lose their jobs. The estimated open unemployment rate in Indonesia is higher for women than men, indicating that women will be relatively more deprived than men in obtaining new jobs or retaining the existing ones. In Thailand, a large number of female workers who are unskilled or semi-skilled would be at high risk of being laid off from work. As a result, more women are expected to opt for the informal labour market or housekeeping.

In the context of Singapore, where women seem to be striving for coherence in the midst of conflicting role ideologies, the analysis suggests that contradictory social trends and conflicting roles of women are likely to continue in future as long as the State policy continues fostering tradition in peoples' values and productivity continues as an essential force of economic development. The issue of shared-role ideology, however, remains as a question of concern for a majority of women and needs to be explored further.

D. Policy recommendations

The five papers included in this study were presented in the Policy Seminar on Gender Dimensions of Population and Development in South-East Asia organized by the Population and Rural and Urban Development Division, ESCAP in September 1998. The papers focussed on the role of women in productive and reproductive spheres and on existing government policies and programmes on women's development. Besides, representatives of governments from each country also participated and described their policies on gender and development issues. Taken together, the five papers mapped out many of the major issues of interest to researchers and policy makers concerned with gender dimensions of population issues and offered a number of policy recommendations relevant to the current situation in the region.

The Policy Seminar reaffirmed its support for and adherence to the Programme of Action adopted at the International Conference on Population and Development held in Cairo in 1994 and the Platform for Action adopted at the Fourth World Conference on Women held in Beijing in 1995. Since those Conferences, the countries represented at the Seminar had adopted national plans of action to promote the status of women. The Seminar also endorsed those plans and urged their thorough implementation. The recommendations below adopted by the Policy Seminar were intended to emphasize certain actions within those plans, to elaborate some points within those plans, or to deal with the financial and economic crisis that had begun in Asia in 1997.

Policy context

1.   Policies and programme interventions designed to deal with gender aspects of population and development need to be specific to the culture and economic circumstances of the target population, as these varied greatly within the region and within countries.

2.   Governments should adopt an analytical framework in order to determine if population and development policies and programmes are responsive to gender equality, equity and the empowerment of women and families, and if they are responsive to reproductive health needs throughout the life cycle.

3.   Governments should create favourable conditions for women's participation at all levels of decision-making concerning reproductive health.

4.   In anticipation of the growing number and proportion of the elderly in countries in the ESCAP region, governments should develop or strengthen and expand policies and programmes for the elderly, especially for elderly women in rural areas.

5.   Governments should provide improved health services, especially in rural areas, where needed.

Data and research

6.   Governments and other organizations should make greater efforts to strengthen monitoring and evaluation systems and the collection of demographic data, with special consideration given to gender disaggregation, and the coverage and reliability of statistics. To ensure a better understanding of the nature of women's and men's social and economic issues, the development of gender-sensitive indicators, especially on reproductive health, should be emphasised.

7.   All governments, with the support of relevant organizations, should make efforts to collect and publish data to assess gender

equality, including on wages/salaries of women and men by occupation as an indicator of gender equality in the labour force and employment. In this context, particular attention should be given to the implementation of wage laws and social-equity goals with a view to eliminating gender-based disparities in income.

8.   Research should be conducted on gender and population issues, and the results widely disseminated. Such research should cover different cultural and economic contexts. Research and programmes should take into account that gender perceptions and definitions are culture-specific and vary within regions and countries and by socio-economic group, ethnic group and life-cycle stage.

9.   Ways to promote male participation and responsibility in family life and population programmes should be explored, including by operational research. Research on gender issues should employ qualitative methods, including focus-group discussions. One aim of such research should be to improve communication between the sexes and an understanding of their shared responsibilities. Men and women should be equal participants in and beneficiaries of reproductive health programmes. Governmental and other organizations should seek ways to promote male responsibility and participation, including through the use of positive male role models and peers.

10.   Responsible sexual behaviour among adolescents, both boys and girls, should be inculcated from an early age onwards through various channels, such as schools, parents, family life, the media, religious organizations and peer groups.

11.   Governments should give emphasis to the study of the socio-economic causes and consequences of international migration of both women and men. Special attention should be given to the issues of foreign domestic workers, entertainers and those involved in sexual trafficking, including the implications on reproductive health, in order to devise special programmes and interventions for migrant workers. Special emphasis is also needed to assess the impact of international migration on families left behind and on the welfare of families and children. Governments should strengthen the implementation of laws protecting migrants, especially women and children.

12.   Government should assess micro-credit policies and programmes for women and their impact on the financial independence, reproductive choices and health of women.

Economic crisis

13.   In developing strategies to mitigate the negative effects of the current economic crisis, countries should not reduce budget allocations for the health and education sectors, as these would be crucial for long-term development. Reproductive health, including family planning and sexual health, should remain a priority area. Expanded technical, vocational and non-formal education programmes for women and men, especially those in poor families, should be incorporated in the strategies for individuals to cope with the crisis.

14.   Employers, in formulating retrenchment policies, should be gender-sensitive, especially concerning employees in female-headed households and single-parent households.

15.   Governments should assist people to weather the economic crisis by instituting job-creation programmes, particularly in building infrastructure, as this provides income to workers and benefits the long-term development of the country. Job-creation programmes should be designed for women as well as men.

16.   Different departments and governments at all levels should improve their coordination and cooperation with each other in order to promote the efficient mobilization and use of resources to mainstream gender concerns in population policies, programmes and projects.

17. Governments at all levels should explore innovative ways of maintaining effective programmes in the face of declining resources. To do this, they should promote greater cooperation and partnerships with civil society organizations, including NGOs, community-based organizations, religious groups, voluntary groups, foundations and the private sector in order to maximize the efficient use of existing physical, organizational and human resources. Cooperation with women's NGOs should be strengthened in this process.

18. International organizations and national governments should rely to the extent possible on local organizations, leaders, consultants, materials and other resources for programme implementation, while emphasising the potential for gender equality, equity and empowerment of women in this approach.

19. A gender perspective should be central to all research conducted on the social impact of the Asian economic crisis.

REFERENCES

Economic and Social Commission for Asia and the Pacific (ESCAP) (1995). *Women in the Philippines: A Country Profile*. Statistical Profiles No. 3. New York: United Nations.

_____ (1996). *Women in Thailand: A Country Profile*. Statistical Profiles No. 5. New York: United Nations.

_____ (1998). *Women in Indonesia: A Country Profile*. Statistical Profiles No. 14. New York: United Nations.

United Nations (1995a). *Population and Development: Programme of Action adopted at the International Conference on Population and Development, Cairo, 5-13 September 1994*. ST/ESA/SER.A/ 149. (United Nations publication, Sales No. E.95.XIII.7).

_____ (1995b). *Review and Appraisal of the World Population Plan of Action: 1994 Report*. ST/ESA/SER.A/152. (United Nations publication, Sales No. E.95.XIII.27).

II. WOMEN IN DEVELOPMENT: DEMOGRAPHIC PERSPECTIVES IN INDONESIA

Mayling Oey-Gardiner, Djoko Hartono and Soewartojo *

A. Social context

The economic and socio-political upheavals that led to the downfall of the Soeharto government in Indonesia on 21 May 1998, may not have had any observable impact on the country's demographic trends of the past two and a half decades. Demographic patterns of change have benefited from past rapid economic and social development. After the change of government in 1996, when Soeharto took over the presidency from Soekarno, the government orientation changed radically. Soekarno, who became the first president of Indonesia after its independence from the Netherlands in 1945, was primarily concerned with nation building. In his drive to place Indonesia on the map, Soekarno neglected the economy. Towards the end of his reign, inflation had reached as high as 650 per cent and social and economic services had broken down. Hungry stomachs forced Soekarno out of office. After about three decades or so, the basic story has repeated itself. Hunger has also led to uprisings against Soeharto. As of August 1998, the economy continues to deteriorate and reversals in demographic achievements are also feared.

Soeharto, who took over from Soekarno as Indonesia's second president in 1966, gave a completely new direction to his government. Economic development with stability became the goal of Soeharto's government. When Soeharto took office, rapid population growth was considered a major impediment to development. As Indonesia embarked on her path of economic development, the government adopted anti-natalist policies. Family planning was adopted as a national programme with strong government support. The National Family Planning Programme has been very successful in rapidly reducing fertility, which, combined with continuing and even accelerating economic and social development, has affected and has been affected by other demographic parameters as well. In the case of Indonesia, where the most common fertility control devices are those used by women, it can appropriately be said that women played an important role, as both cause and effect, in the development process. The development theme (with stability), carried through by the "New Order Government" of Soeharto, in fact, placed women as the central agents and, to a much lesser extent, the beneficiaries of the development process. Women have been the objects of development in fertility reduction.

Traditional social structures and modern administrative structures have placed men as the head of the family and society. Indonesian society as well as its government have reinforced this view in the 1974 Marriage Law, *UU Perkawinan No.1/1974*, which basically states (paragraph 31) that men's roles are mainly as the heads of households and family providers while women's roles remain as wives and mothers. While it may be true that men spend more time in formal social and religious affairs, and are major decision-makers in the community, it is equally true that women tend to play a major role in household affairs, in household resource allocation and in household consumption patterns. Women are also active and independent income generators. As such, this has tended to give them greater influence over household economies. Also, as more women become income earners and assume the position of household head, they are more likely to control household affairs and maintain their involvement as independent income earners.

---

* *Insan Hitawasana Sejahtera*, Jakarta.

Cumulatively, women play a major role in changing the make-up of the nations socio-economic development.

This paper aims to canvass the many demographic changes relating to the role of women in the development process. Of interest shall be an examination of the demographic transition from a women in development perspective. More specifically, the study shall focus on such demographic and social parameters as the age and sex structure, household formation, fertility, mortality, women's role in the labour market, gains in education, and the magnitude of their migration.

B. Profile of Indonesian women

1. Age and sex structure

As the bearers and guardians of future generations, fertility control was exercised through a strongly state supported and controlled programme of contraception targeted at women. As a result of women's participation in the National Family Planning Programme, fertility has declined substantially. The effects are reflected in the age and sex structure of the population.

Following the experience of the demographic transition of other populations, Indonesia's population pyramid has slowly changed from being flat and wide towards a bell-shape, narrowing at the base. In 1971, the younger the age group, the larger the size of the cohort. By 1990, however, the share of the youngest under 5-year age group had become substantially smaller than the next 5-year age group, aged 5-9 years (figure 1).

As a result of the fertility control programme, the Indonesian population is ageing. The proportion of the young (0-14 years) has declined, from 44 per cent in 1971 to 41 per cent in 1980 and to only 37 per cent in 1990. At the other end of the spectrum, the share of those aged 65 years and above has risen, albeit much more slowly, from 2.5 per

Figure 1. Population by age and sex, 1971, 1980 and 1990

(in millions)

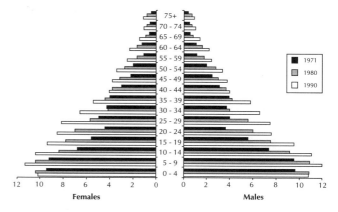

Source: BPS, 1971, 1980 and 1990 Population Censuses.

cent in 1971 to 3.2 per cent in 1980 and 3.8 per cent in 1990 (BPS, various years).

Accepting that during the wars of independence, many more men had lost their lives, another way of observing women's contribution to population changes is in declining sex ratios. The dip in the age groups of 20-34 years in 1971, especially among men, has been attributed to the loss of lives during the wars of independence and the consequent reduced fertility (Iskandar, 1970). In a reaction similar to many other societies after Second World War, fertility rose sharply thereafter. Besides, apparently better coverage of males in consecutive censuses, fertility rises seem to have also contributed to declining sex ratios, as measured by the number of females over 100 males. In 1971, the sex ratio was 103, in 1980 it was 101, and in the latest census of 1990, it was 100.5 females per 100 males.

The above description of the age and sex structure is, of course, a result of substantial changes in a variety of demographic parameters, a number of which are closely related to women and their role in society. Over the development process, as women have been the object as well as the subject of development, life styles have changed having their effects on the patterns of family formation.

2. Household formation

In order to understand how the development process in Indonesia has effected household formation, the next section begins with some observations with regards to age at first marriage and household conditions, both of which are assumed to have a positive impact on women's socio-economic status.

(a) Age at first marriage

The household life cycle is generally considered to begin with the marriage of a couple and ends at the time of death of the last surviving spouse. Marriage, in particular the timing of first marriage, is a prime indicator of women's exposure to the risk of pregnancy and, therefore, is important for understanding fertility patterns. Theoretically, age at marriage affects the number of years a woman is exposed to the chance of having a child. Women who marry early tend to have more children than those who marry late. Age at first marriage may be used, to some extent, to reflect processes of modernization that eventually affects women's status. Economic advancement that resulted in the increased chances for women to pursue their education is associated with late entry into matrimony. Social change has brought opportunities to women to play adult roles outside the family in the public sphere, and this, in turn, has created categories of women for whom late marriage is an acceptable or even a desirable option.

In Indonesia, the legal limitation on age at marriage is based on the 1974 Marriage Law, *UU Perkawinan No.1/1974*, which sets minimum ages of 16 years for women and 19 years for men. At that time, 16 years for girls was a relevant lower age limit to enter into matrimony, as many parents wanted to marry off their daughters in their early teens for fear of having 'old maids', daughters who were not *laku*, not in demand. Besides, early age at first marriage was accompanied by high divorce, which was followed by remarriage as there is generally no stigma to being a divorcee. In fact, in some areas frequency of marriage is an indication of being *laku*, in demand. If the first marriage was a child marriage, usually arranged by the parents, then divorce and remarriage can be the couples' own choice.

It is generally observed that very early marriage is associated with poverty. As the development process progressed and poverty was reduced, so did the need for parents to marry off their daughters at very early ages. Daughters were no longer only liabilities but also assets when the labour market, especially the formal labour market, opened widespread employment opportunities for young and 'educated' women. Parents were equally willing to invest in their daughters' education as access to employment opportunities increased with education. These factors have contributed to significantly delaying marriage, even though marriage remains practically universal.

Thus, the proportions ever married for given age groups have continued to decline but eventually most women enter matrimony (table 1). The percentage of ever-married children in the age group of 10-14 years declined from 2.3 per cent in 1971 to only 0.1 per cent in 1995. As table 1 shows, during the past two and a half decades, the sharpest decline in the proportions ever married occurred

Table 1. Percentage of women ever-married by age group, 1971-1995

Age	1971	1980	1985	1990	1995
10 - 14	2.3	0.8	0.1	0.3	0.1
15 - 19	37.4	30.1	18.8	18.2	14.3
20 - 24	81.5	77.7	70.3	64.3	59.9
25 - 29	95.0	92.6	91.1	88.8	84.8
30 - 34	97.8	96.6	95.9	95.5	94.5
35 - 39	98.6	98.1	97.5	97.3	97.2
40 - 44	99.0	98.6	98.3	98.0	97.9
45 - 49	99.0	98.8	98.6	98.5	98.1
50 - 54	99.1	98.9	98.9	98.7	98.5
Total	**69.1**	**65.7**	**62.3**	**62.1**	**61.0**

Sources: BPS, *1971, 1980,* and *1990 Population Censuses* and *1985* and *1995 SUPAS.*

14

among those aged 15-19 years, from 37 to 14 per cent (a decline of 23 percentage points) and among those aged 20-24 years, from 82 to 60 per cent (a decline of 22 percentage points). Yet in 1995, among those aged 25-29 years, about 15 per cent had not been married. Another striking phenomenon to note in table 1 is that at the beginning of the New Order Government in 1971, universal marriage was almost achieved before age 35 years, with 98 per cent of those aged 30-34 married. Today marriage is still practically universal though somewhat delayed. Most women are married by age 40 years.

Delays in marriage has also meant relatively fewer child marriages, i.e. prior to reaching the minimum legal age at marriage. The trend of a rising age at marriage was already observable from the results of the 1980 population census. For example, starting with the age group 30-34 and older, about one-third of women were married before reaching age 16, and this proportions declined to 20 per cent among those aged 20-24 years[1] (table 2). For the same age group of 20-24 years in 1995, only 9 per cent were married before age 16 years. As such, the minimum legal age at marriage seems no longer relevant, and would be better if it were raised.

In fact, the important changes in age at first marriage are at the lower and the upper age groups (table 3). As we can see from the table, the proportion of ever married women aged 10-54 years who were married before age 16 declined by about one-third, from 32 per cent in 1980 to 22 per cent in 1995 (or 10 percentage

---

[1] As the proportion married before reaching age 16 can still rise among those aged 15-19, the better example is the age group 20-24 years. On the other hand, due to inconsistencies, we rather not rely on a cohort analysis. For instance, those aged 15-19 years in 1980, were 20-24 years old in 1985 and 30-34 years old in 1995. While it can be expected that the proportion married by age 16 would have risen between 1980 and 1985 for that cohort, it is rather doubtful that the rise would have continued to 1995.

Table 2. Percentage of women married before reaching age 16 years by age group, Indonesia, 1980-1995

Age	1980	1985	1990	1995
10 - 14	0.8	0.1	0.2	0.1
15 - 19	10.7	5.1	5.5	4.6
20 - 24	20.2	13.2	11.5	9.0
25 - 29	26.3	19.1	17.5	15.1
30 - 34	32.4	21.5	21.3	18.9
35 - 39	33.3	23.2	23.1	22.0
40 - 44	33.7	24.6	26.6	23.2
45 - 49	33.1	25.7	26.9	25.4
50 - 54	35.2	27.2	29.2	27.6

Sources: BPS, *1980* and *1990 Population Censuses* and *1985* and *1995 SUPAS.*

Table 3. Percentage distribution of ever-married women aged 10-54 by age at first marriage, 1980-1995

Age at first marriage	1980	1985	1990	1995
<16	31.9	23.1	23.4	21.5
16 - 17	27.1	28.6	26.5	25.0
18 - 19	19.1	21.8	21.4	21.8
20+	21.9	26.5	28.7	31.7
Total	**100.0**	**100.0**	**100.0**	**100.0**

Sources: BPS, *1980* and *1990 Population Censuses* and *1985* and *1995 SUPAS.*

points). On the other hand, the proportion of those entering matrimony at age 20 years or older has risen from 22 to 32 per cent over the same period. It is this delayed marriage that has demographic implications. For instance, analysis of the results of the first World Fertility Survey (Caldwell, McDonald and Ruzicka, 1980) show that due to sub-fecundity, rising age at marriage of teenagers has little effect on fertility, and only when substantial proportions enter matrimony beyond age 20 are there observable effects on fertility.

(b)   Divorce

Early age at first marriage has been closely related to high divorce. In fact, the World Fertility Survey results showed Indonesia (more specifically the data referred to Java and Bali only) to have the highest divorce rate at that time (Caldwell, McDonald and Ruzicka, 1980). As age at first marriage rose, divorce ratios have been steadily declining[2] (figure 2). The impact of the marriage bill has been quite significant. While enacted in 1974, the bill took effect only in 1975. The divorce ratio took a sharp plunge thereafter in 1976 when for every 100 marriages there were 11 divorces, while earlier the ratio was around 4 to 1. Since then, has been a decline in divorce ratio to less than 10 per 100. Marriages have become more stable as marriages have become more likely to be based on self selection rather than arranged by parents.

Figure 2. Divorce ratios 1974-1995

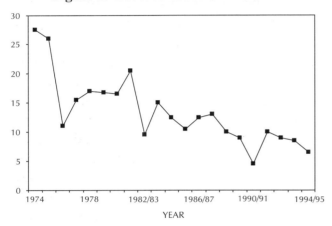

Sources: BPS, *Statistical Yearbook of Indonesia,* several years.

Notes: Divorce ratios have been calculated from data reported by the Ministry of Religious Affairs on many Islamic marriages, divorce and reconciliations (as marriages involving persons of other religious are usually registered at the civil registry). Divorce ratios are measured as the ratio of marriages and reconsiliations over the number of divorces.

(c)   Household size

Another related demographic parameter of late entry into marriage is household size. Households have become smaller, from an average of 4.8 persons in 1980 to 4.3 persons in 1995 (table 4). Part of the decline in household size is a result of a rise in the

---

[2] Even though these data refer only to the followers of the Islamic faith, they cover the majority of the Indonesian population (according to the 1990 Population Census, 87 per cent of the population had Islam as religion).

Table 4. Percentage composition of household size and average household size, 1980-1995

Household size	1980	1985	1990	1995
1	4.7	4.9	5.3	5.6
2	11.5	11.3	12.0	12.0
3 - 4	33.5	35.4	38.1	41.7
5 - 6	28.0	28.9	28.4	28.4
7 - 8	18.9	16.7	14.1	11.0
10+	3.5	2.8	2.1	1.3
Total	**100.0**	**100.0**	**100.0**	**100.0**
Average household size	4.8	4.7	4.5	4.3

Sources: BPS, *1980* and *1990 Population Censuses* and *1985* and *1995 SUPAS.*

percentage of single households, from 4.7 per cent to 5.6 per cent. Similarly there was a rise in the share of households consisting of 3 to 4 persons, from 33 per cent in 1980 to 42 per cent in 1995. These are usually the 1-2 child families. On the other hand, a major decline has occurred in the share of large households of 7 or more persons, from 22 per cent to 12 per cent over the same period. Consistent with the fact that one hardly hears about large families anymore, i.e. some 10 or more children, so large households soon be facts of the past, only experienced by those cohorts currently aged 50 or more. If socio-economic progress were not disrupted by the crisis, one would expect further declines in the incidence of large households and a simultaneous rise in the share of single and small households.

(d)   Gender and age of household heads

The situation of household size can be further examined in terms of gender and age of household heads. There are a number of basic differences in households headed by women and men. Households headed by women are substantially smaller than those headed by men. While the overall average household consists of 4.3 persons those headed by men are substantially larger than those headed by women, which consist of only 2.9 persons, on average. This difference is a function of

Figure 3. Household size by age and sex of household head, 1996

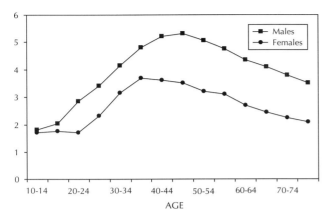

Source: BPS, special tabulations from SUSENAS 1996.

socio-demographic differences between male and female household heads.

There is a striking difference in the relation between age and household size by sex of household head (figure 3). Households headed by men follow the usual household life cycle pattern where household size changes with age of household head due to birth of children and their departure. Their households grow in size, up to ages 40-44 mostly due to birth of children and also taking in of relatives and household help, but a decline in household size occurs until they are about 50 years or older when their offspring leave households. On average, households start to expand beyond

couples, when household heads are in their 20s (average household size for those age 20-24 years is 2.6 persons) and continue growing to an average of 5 persons when household heads are in their 40s. Thereafter, households contract in size to an average of 3 persons in households where the heads are 75 years and over.

Households headed by women reflect different life histories than those headed by men. They do not reflect life cycle histories of households of growth and decline, but rather one of changing marital status. This demographic phenomenon is better explained by simultaneously examining composition of household heads by sex, age and marital status (table 5). Young women household heads are more likely to be single, and as they become older, their probability of widowhood and their chances of being household heads rises. When women are household heads in their youth (10-24 years), they are most likely single (83 per cent). On the other hand, men are most likely to be married (70 per cent), and relatively far fewer men establish households on their own when they are single (30 per cent). When women household heads are between ages 20 and 40 years, their households expand. The difference in size of households headed by women and men is about 1 person. This implies the absence of a man in the household. In the

Table 5. Percentage distribution of household heads by age, sex and marital status, 1996

Sex and age	Single	Married	Divorced	Widowed	Total	Number (millions)
Males						
10 - 24	30.1	69.5	0.2	0.2	100	1.2
25 - 39	2.7	96.4	0.5	0.4	100	15.9
40 - 54	0.5	97.5	0.6	1.5	100	13.7
55+	0.3	92.8	0.8	6.1	100	8.7
Total	**2.3**	**95.1**	**0.6**	**2.0**	**100**	**39.6**
Females						
10 - 24	82.8	11.0	4.7	1.6	100	0.3
25 - 39	16.0	26.3	27.6	30.1	100	0.9
40 - 54	2.5	12.7	17.6	67.2	100	1.8
55+	1.2	6.8	7.4	84.7	100	2.8
Total	**8.5**	**11.8**	**13.4**	**66.2**	**100**	**5.8**

Source: BPS, special tabulations from *SUSENAS 1996*.

age group of 20-39 years, the proportion of single household heads is much smaller (16 per cent) than those who are ever married (26 per cent are married and therefore *de facto* household heads, 28 per cent are divorced and 30 per cent widowed). As widowhood becomes increasingly dominant among women household heads when they are aged 40 years and above, their households contract, not only due to the absence of a man but also as offspring depart to establish their own households.

Thus, the factors behind households headed by men and women are essentially different. While households headed by men appear to move smoothly as they age, households headed by women are subject to truncation as women move in and out of being household heads when they switch marital status. Most male household heads are married (95 per cent), with only small proportions are either single (2 per cent) divorced (0.6 per cent) or widowed (2 per cent). In contrast, most female household heads are widowed (66 per cent), a relatively smaller proportion is single (9 per cent), and slightly larger proportions are either married (12 per cent) or divorced (13 per cent).

Closely related to the difference in marital status of female and male household heads is the difference in their age composition. Female household heads tend to be older than male household heads (table 6). As about two-thirds of women household heads are widowed, almost half of them are aged 55 years and over compared to only 22 per cent of men in the same age group. About 40 per cent of male household heads are in the productive ages of 25-39 years compared with only 15 per cent of female household heads in the same age group.

(e) Women household heads

Returning now to an examination of trends, the interesting phenomenon is that while the percentage of women household heads at older ages is increasing, this is not the case with

male household heads (table 7). A good indicator is the proportion aged 55 years and over. In 1980, almost 38 per cent of female household heads were 55 years and above while in 1995, about half (50.2 per cent) were in this age group. This phenomenon is most probably related to declining mortality, not just for women but also for men, thereby lengthening the marital duration and delaying widowhood for women. For men, there has been little

Table 6. Percentage distribution of household heads by marital status and age, 1996

Sex and age	Single	Married	Di-vorced	Wid-owed	Total
Males					
10 - 24	41.5	2.3	1.3	0.3	3.1
25 - 39	48.3	40.7	32.3	7.4	40.2
40 - 54	6.9	35.5	34.7	26.1	34.7
55+	3.2	21.5	31.7	66.3	22.0
Total	**100.0**	**100.0**	**100.0**	**100.0**	**100.0**
Number (m)	*0.9*	*37.7*	*0.2*	*0.8*	*39.6*
Females					
10 - 24	56.2	5.4	2.0	0.1	5.8
25 - 39	27.9	33.4	30.6	6.8	14.9
40 - 54	9.3	33.7	40.9	31.7	31.2
55+	6.6	27.6	26.5	61.4	48.1
Total	**100.0**	**100.0**	**100.0**	**100.0**	**100.0**
Number (m)	*0.5*	*0.7*	*0.8*	*3.8*	*5.8*

Source: BPS, special tabulations from *SUSENAS 1996.*

Table 7. Percentage distribution of household heads by age and sex, 1980-1995

Age	1980	1985	1990	1995
Males				
10 - 24	6.5	4.9	5.4	4.2
25 - 39	40.8	42.4	44.1	41.6
40 - 54	34.3	32.6	30.7	33.4
55+	18.5	20.0	19.9	20.8
Total	**100.0**	**100.0**	**100.0**	**100.0**
Females				
10 - 24	3.9	4.0	6.4	6.3
25 - 39	17.9	15.5	15.5	15.3
40 - 54	39.7	35.5	35.5	28.2
55+	38.5	45.0	45.0	50.2
Total	**100.0**	**100.0**	**100.0**	**100.0**

Sources: BPS, *1980* and *1990 Population Censuses* and *1985* and *1995 SUPAS.*

change in the age composition as household heads as the proportion of elderly, 55 years and older, remained 19 per cent and 21 per cent in 1980 and 1995, respectively.

On the other hand, the pattern for young adults between the sexes is reversed. While the share of young adult female household heads rose from 4 per cent to 6 per cent between 1980 and 1995, the proportion of male household heads actually declined from 7 per cent to 4 per cent in the same period. This phenomenon is related to the fact that women are increasingly delaying marriage and becoming single heads of households. Delayed marriage for women does not mean that when they are in their teens and twenties they continue living with their parents. As shall be discussed later, development has also meant increased mobility, also for young women. As young women increasingly leave their parental homes, they establish their own households while still single.

Contrary to popular belief, the incidence of women headed households is not on the rise. Instead, the share of households headed by women declined slightly over time, from 14 per cent in 1980 to 13 per cent in 1995 (table 8). This phenomenon is related to various other demographic changes occurring in the society. Earlier, we discussed the household composition in relation to the rise in age at first marriage and the decline in divorce rates. However, declining mortality has also contributed to the change in household composition. Declining mortality means that men too live longer, thereby postponing and also reducing the

Table 8. Percentage of female household heads by age, 1980-1995

Age	1980	1985	1990	1995
10 - 24	9.0	11.0	15.3	18.0
25 - 39	6.8	5.2	5.6	5.1
40 - 54	16.1	14.1	14.2	10.9
55+	25.6	25.3	25.1	25.9
Total	**14.2**	**13.1**	**13.3**	**12.7**

Sources: BPS, *1980* and *1990 Population Censuses* and *1985* and *1995 SUPAS.*

incidence of widowhood for women, the main reason for women to be household heads. All these opposing forces have resulted in a constant share of about one-fourth of women household heads among ages 55 and over. The earlier cited phenomenon among the youth, 10-24 years, concerns the freedom of young adult women to establish their own households. As a result, the share of female household heads in this age group has doubled over the same period, from 9 per cent to 18 per cent.

(f)   Summing up

A number of changes in household formation and conditions have been examined. Some highlights include the following. With socio-economic developments or modernization, parents, girls and women themselves, choose to delay matrimony. This delay has not only meant declines in child marriages, i.e. before the legal minimum age at marriage of 16 years, but most significantly, the proportions marrying in their 20s has risen substantially. Besides, even though marriage remains a practically universal phenomenon, this too is achieved at a later age, more likely by the time a cohort reaches 40 years or more. As child marriages, which are mostly arranged, have declined so has the divorce rate declined.

Related to delayed marriage is the contraction in household size from 4.8 in 1980 to 4.3 persons in 1995. Two factors have contributed to this decline. On the one hand, the share of large households, i.e. 7 persons or more has declined from 22 per cent to 12 per cent, and on the other hand, a more slowly rising share of single households from 4.7 per cent to 5.6 per cent.

A further examination by sex of household heads shows that households headed by women are substantially smaller than those headed by men, 2.9 compared to 4.3 persons on average in 1996. This is partly a function of a larger percentage of women household heads being single (9 per cent) compared with male household heads (2 per cent). As it is widely said that men are usually not capable of taking care of themselves, most male household heads are married (95 per cent), whereas women, become household heads mainly as a result of widowhood (66 per cent). Women household heads are substantially older than male household heads as only 22 per cent of male household heads are aged 55 years and over compared with 48 per cent of female household heads. Overall, it is observed that the share of female household heads has shown a slight decline over time, from 14 per cent in 1980 to 13 per cent in 1995. Part of the explanation lies in declining mortality, which has affected men also. As men live longer, so do couples and therefore affecting entrance into widowhood for women.

3. Fertility

Closely related to changes in household size is the fertility decline. The demographic transition occurred in a relatively short period in Indonesia. Fertility decline in Indonesia has been claimed as the most striking demographic transition in modern history (Gertler and Molyneaux, 1994). Unlike the experiences of many other populations, the initial decline in Indonesian fertility occurred in spite of widespread poverty. The total fertility rate (TFR) declined from 5.6 to 2.8 children over

a period of about three decades (table 9). Women of all ages wanted to have fewer children, but it was among the youngest, the teenagers, that fertility declined the fastest. Young teenage women, who are increasingly becoming better educated, simply do not yet want to untake the burdens of child rearing and prefer to enjoy their friends' company and work for monetary rewards allowing new horizons in consumerism. Consequently marriage is delayed beyond 20 years.

As table 9 shows, the fastest decline in fertility occurred among the youngest age group. For example, the age-specific fertility rate among those age 15-19 years declined from 155 in the late 1960s to 61 births per 1,000 women (60 per cent decline) in the early 1990s. There was also a substantial decline in fertility among women aged 20-24 years, from 286 to 147 births per 1,000 women (47 per cent decline) over the same period. Age-specific fertility rates of women between the ages of 30 and 49 years all declined by about one half.

Rather striking has been the considerable flattening of the age-specific fertility curve. This pattern occurred as a result of sharp declines in fertility of women aged between 20-34 years (figure 4). These are the same age groups which experienced sharp declines in proportions ever married (table 6). The small

Table 9. Age-specific and total fertility rates, 1967-1994

Age	1971 Census 1967-1970	1976 SUPAS 1971-1975	1980 Census 1976-1979	1985 SUPAS 1980-1985	1990 Census 1986-1989	1995 SUPAS 1991-1994
15 - 19	155	127	116	95	71	61
20 - 24	286	265	248	220	179	151
25 - 29	273	255	232	206	171	146
30 - 34	211	199	177	154	129	105
35 - 39	124	118	104	89	75	63
40 - 44	55	57	46	37	31	27
45 - 49	17	18	13	10	9	8
TFR	5.605	5.200	4.680	4.055	3.326	2.802

Source: CBS (1997), *Estimation of Fertility, Mortality, and Migration Based on the 1995 Intercensal Population Survey.*

Notes: TFR = total fertility rate
Estimates based on own children method.

Figure 4. Age-specific fertility rates, 1967-1997

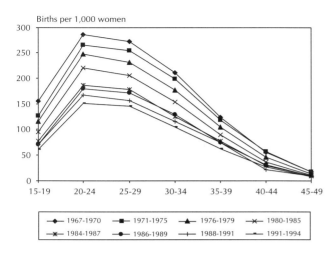

Births per 1,000 women

Legend:
- 1967-1970
- 1971-1975
- 1976-1979
- 1980-1985
- 1984-1987
- 1986-1989
- 1988-1991
- 1991-1994

Source: Based on table 9.

and happy family norm promoted by The National Family Planning Coordinating Board (BKKBN) seems to have gained wide acceptance among women as they bear, on average, between 2 and 3 children only (Adioetamo, 1993).

The age pattern of fertility has also changed over time, reflecting a change in the reproductive behaviour of Indonesian women. Early in the transition, about 18 per cent of fertility decline was experienced by the youngest age group of 15-19 years (table 10). This is primarily a function of increased age at marriage. During in the latter half of the 1970s, sharp declines were also experienced by older

women (19 per cent among women age 40-44 years and 28 per cent among women age 45-49 years), suggesting reductions in martial fertility. These patterns are indicative of a tendency toward behavioural changes to limit fertility among women in all age groups.

More importantly, the pace of fertility decline accelerated during the first two decades of the New Order Government, and somewhat slowed down during the early 1990s. Table 10 shows that total fertility rate declined by 7 per cent between the late 1960s to early 1970s, by 10 per cent between the early 1970s to late 1970s, by 13 per cent between the late 1970s to early 1980s, and by 18 per cent between the early and late 1980s. As fertility had already reached a rather low level given Indonesia's level of development at that time, the total fertility rate stalled and showed a decline by only 16 per cent during the late 1980s to early 1990s.

The causes of fertility decline have been widely studied. Studies conducted in Indonesia have shown that fertility reduction is primarily a function of dramatic increases in contraceptive prevalence, as intermediate cause of fertility change. It has been suggested that improvements in the structure and organization of the family planning programme have contributed to increased contraceptive prevalence (Freedman *et al.,* 1981; Hugo *et al.,* 1987; Hull *et al.,* 1977 cited in Gertler and Molyneaux, 1994:34).

Others have suggested that modernization factors affecting women have contributed even more to this decline. Gertler and Molyneaux (1994:60) who used combined demographic and economic approaches to evaluate the impact of the family planning programme on fertility in Indonesia, suggested that the Indonesian family planning programme inputs in themselves had a limited effect on fertility decline. A 75 per cent fertility decline observed between 1982 to 1987 was attributed to increases in contraceptive use, which was largely a result of changes in

Table 10. Percentage decline in age-specific fertility rates, 1967-1994

Age	1967-70 to 1971-75	1971-75 to 1976-79	1976-79 to 1980-84	1980-84 to 1986-89	1986-89 to 1991-94
15 - 19	18.1	8.7	18.1	25.3	14.1
20 - 24	7.3	6.4	11.3	18.6	15.6
25 - 29	6.6	9.0	11.2	17.0	14.6
30 - 34	5.7	11.1	13.0	16.2	18.6
35 - 39	4.8	11.9	14.4	15.7	16.0
40 - 44	-3.6	19.3	19.6	16.2	12.9
45 - 49	-5.9	27.8	23.1	10.0	11.1
TFR	7.2	10.0	13.4	18.0	15.8

Source: Based on table 9.

education levels and wages. This study suggests that the success of development programmes, especially those related to improvement in female's education and labour force participation, have contributed significantly to fertility reduction in Indonesia.

The role of female education in reducing fertility has long been studied. It has been documented that there is a strong negative association between women's schooling and fertility (Cleland and Rodriguez, 1988). Hatmadji and Suriastini (1995) reported a similar observation. The authors have noted, in general, a negative relation between education and fertility, except for the lowest education categories. In fact, those who have no formal schooling have slightly lower fertility than those who have completed primary school (table 11).[3] At the same time, women who have no education are experiencing a faster decline in fertility than women who have some schooling.

Table 11. Total fertility rate by education of mother

Education	NICPS 1987 (1984-1987)	IDHS 1991 (1988-1991)	IDHS 1994 (1991-1994)
No education	3.7	3.3	2.9
Some primary	3.7	3.5	3.2
Completed primary	3.4	3.1	3.0
Some secondary+	2.4	2.6	2.6
Total	**3.3**	**3.0**	**2.8**

Sources: 1987 National Indonesia Contraceptive Prevalence Survey, and the 1991 and 1994 Indonesia Demographic and Health Survey.

We support the arguments put forth by Gertler and Molyneaux (1994) on the socio-economic advancements made by Indonesian women over the past few decades. During the development process, when Indonesia was enjoying strong economic growth and social services were expanding, women also benefited

substantially from investments in education. Due to a lower base at the outset, women appear to have benefited slightly more than men. Besides, since the mid-1980s, deregulation measures were introduced that have led to a more active private sector investments in labour-intensive and export-oriented industries. As a result, like women in other parts of East and South-East Asia, Indonesian women benefited from expansion in formal sector employment. Rising education and paid employment opportunities for women have changed their life styles, including the desire to have fewer children. The expansion of paid employment opportunities have, in many cases, resulted in young girls opting to move away from home, gain freedom and reject early motherhood.

In the context of the current crisis and due to acknowledged breakdowns in overall social and economic services, an important question of concern is whether the past trends will be maintained. The media often reports on rising retrenchments and school drop-outs. This is a severe challenge to the national family planning programme, that due to rapid achievements in fertility decline had already looked for other direction and activities, such as those factors beyond family planning. In particular, the agency had already spread its wings to deal with poverty. However, the current fears are that the prospective reductions in contraceptive supplies, and further exacerbated by declining purchasing power of the masses, may lead to inaccessibility and limited availability of contraceptive supplies, thereby raising fertility. The experience of other societies suggests the opposite. In the light of declining welfare, parents are reluctant to expand their families. This has been the history of the West during the depression.

4. Family planning

Fertility decline has been attributed to a dynamic and innovative Family Planning Programme launched throughout the country

---

[3] This phenomenon had been noted much earlier when the general belief was a negative relation between class and fertility. Hull (1977) refuted this almost "gospel" based on her study using Indonesian data.

(Hull, Hull and Singarimbun, 1977; Warwick, 1986; Adioetomo *et al.*, 1990). A dramatic rise in contraceptive prevalence and an increase in age of marriage are the two major proximate determinants of such rapid fertility decline (Adioetomo, 1993; Adioetomo *et al.*, 1990; Hull and Hatmadji, 1990 cited in Gertler and Molyneaux, 1994: 36).

In Indonesia, efforts to lower fertility by the family planning programme were formally established in 1970. At the initial stage of implementation, programme activities set up under the National Family Planning Coordinating Board (BKKBN) were based mostly on a "clinical approach", and focused on the islands of Java and Bali. The second stage began in 1974 and covered most of the provinces in Sumatra, Kalimantan, and Sulawesi (outer Java-Bali I). At this stage, the "political commitment approach" was developed to obtain greater support from various parties in the community. The third stage was launched in 1979 and covered the remaining provinces of Jambi, Bengkulu, Riau (in Sumatra); East and Central Kalimantan, and Eastern Indonesian Islands (outer Java-Bali II). At this stage, a "community participation approach" was cultivated in order to promote and maintain existing family planning acceptors/users and to increase the number of new family planning participants (*Kantor Menteri Negara Kependudukan*/BKKBN, 1996:21).

The State Guidelines for National Development (GBHN) in 1973 mentioned that the purpose of the family planning programme was to increase maternal and child health by controlling births. In the GBHN 1978, the aims of the family planning programme were expanded further to increase mother and children prosperity within the framework of realizing small, happy and prosperous families. This was the foundation for achieving the objective of prosperous families, i.e. by controlling births, and thus assuring control of population growth in Indonesia (*Kantor Menteri Negara Kependudukan*/BKKBN 1996: 55).

The importance of family planning to the health of women and children has been recognized for many years. Mothers and children lead healthier lives if women have the means to control their own fertility. This will allow postponement of the first birth until after adolescence, spacing of subsequent children at least two years apart, and lowering fertility among older women with many children. Although the health benefits of family planning have been recognized, demographic concerns remained the major driving force behind the policies. Hence, the final indicators of success of the national family planning programme are usually expressed in terms of fertility reduction.

Increased rates of contraceptive prevalence may be used as intermediate outputs of the programme. According to the BKKBN data, contraceptive prevalence rose impressively from the beginning of the programme to the end of *Pelita III*, the third 5-year development period, from 2.8 per cent in 1971-1972 to 59 per cent in 1983-1984 (figure 5). For the last 10 years, however, since the mid-1980s to the mid-1990s, the programme could no longer claim such rapid rises in contraceptive prevalence rates. The curve has, in fact, flattened (Appendix I). These results support the earlier cited study by Gertler and

Figure 5. Contraceptive prevalence rates (per cent of current users among eligible couples), 1971-1972 to 1995-1996

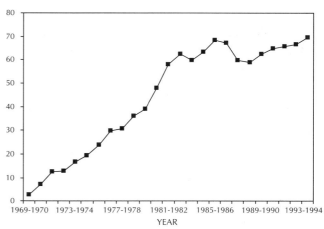

Source: BKKBN (1997), *Basic Information: Family Planning Movement and Prosperous Family Development*, p. 185.

Molyneaux (1994) that fertility decline in Indonesia, which continued until the mid-1990s, appears to have occurred irrespective of outreach of the national family planning programme. The trend had already set in by that time and hence, motivation was already strong to control fertility, irrespective of activities of the programme. Thus, the programme may no longer be as effective as it was the beginning and hence, a shift in the pursuits of the Board, i.e. towards beyond family planning measures seems an appropriate alternative reason for its existence.

As elsewhere, the Indonesian National Family Planning Programme is extremely female biased, where women simply have been the objects of the programme. The National Family Planning Programme relies strongly on modern methods which are considered far more effective. The 1994 Indonesia Demographic and Health Survey (IDHS) has recorded that about 95 per cent of users are relying on modern methods (table 12). This is true whether measured in terms of ever-married or currently married women. Male contraceptives, condoms and male sterilization, account for less than 3 per cent of all current users of contraception.

As previously noted, fertility decline in Indonesia has been largely attributed to increases in contraceptive use. Rising contraceptive use[4] has, in turn, been attributed to rising education and income earning opportunities for women (Gertler and Molyneaux, 1994:60). It has also been noted earlier that from the mid-1980s onward, contraceptive prevalence rate has not risen much (even BKKBN estimates show less than 10 percentage points increase). A combination of all these factors seem to suggest that the

Table 12. Percentage distribution of current users by contraceptive method
(March 1995)

Method	Ever married women	Currently married women
Any method	51.0	54.7
Modern methods		
Any modern method	48.5	52.1
Pill	15.9	17.1
IUD	9.5	10.3
Injection	14.1	15.2
Condom	0.8	0.9
Norplant	4.5	4.9
Female sterilization	2.9	3.1
Male sterilization	0.6	0.7
Traditional methods		
Any traditional method	2.5	2.7
Periodic abstinence	1.0	1.1
Withdrawal	0.7	0.8
Other methods	0.8	0.8
Not currently using	49.0	45.3
Total	100.0	100.0
Number of women	28 168.0	26 186.0

Source: CBS et al., *IDHS 1994*, 1995: Table 5.1: 73.

recent changes in socioeconomic development played a much more important role than did the changes in the family planning programme inputs. However, this point does not suggest that the cumulative influence of previous investments in family planning infrastructure and services is unimportant. The large increase in demand could not have led to large increases in contraceptive prevalence without a highly responsive supply of contraceptive devices.

The above findings also suggest that improvements in socioeconomic conditions, together with efforts to increase demand for contraceptives through information, education, and communication programmes would be relevant for settings in rural areas with limited local resources and relatively low contraceptive prevalence.

Efforts to combine the improvement of service delivery and community self-reliance in adopting family planning is thought to be important in achieving programme targets.

---

[4]   Available statistics on current use of contraception vary substantially. Programme statistics from the BKKBN suggest about two-thirds of eligible couples using any birth control devices, while the IDHS recorded slightly more than half of ever married or currently married women were current users of contraception.

A study conducted in Thailand in 1982 aimed at evaluating the impact of community development programmes on the family planning programme, suggests that family planning users who accepted a development input show consistently higher proportions still continuing to practise family planning. This also suggests that other development programmes have contributed towards the maintenance of contraceptive use.[5] In Indonesia, efforts to improve family prosperity, especially in relation to the family planning programme, have been initiated since 1996 coupled with the implementation of a Prosperous Family Economic Movement through a Presidential Decree, *Kepres No.3 of 1996*. This movement is basically developed within the framework of alleviating poverty. Prosperous Family Savings (*Takesra*) and Prosperous Family Business Loans (*Kukesra*) are some of the programmes aimed at improving family economic capabilities. Since the problem of contraceptive use maintenance is central to the success of all family planning programmes, the integration of development programmes such as the Prosperous Family Economic Movement with family planning programmes should be encouraged.

5. Mortality

Mortality, and particularly infant mortality, has long been used as an indicator of health status and level of care available to both mothers and babies in a given population. This indicator has also been used as a proxy measure of a country's stage of socio-economic development. In Indonesia, infant mortality estimates are usually based on survey and census data because registration data are still not reliable. Infant mortality based on census data is estimated indirectly using information on numbers of children ever born and still living, whereas direct estimates using survey data, such

as the Demographic and Health Survey, are based on birth history data.

Closely related to earlier discussed social indicators is infant mortality. Infant mortality has declined substantially over Indonesia's development process to date, from 142 per 1,000 live births in 1971 to 57 in 1994, reflecting a decline of about 60 per cent. Yet, this level appears high compared with Indonesia's neighbouring countries.

While achievements in fertility decline through a strongly government supported family planning programme have been hailed internationally as a noteworthy achievement, Indonesia has done less well on the health front. On practically all mortality and survival indicators, Indonesia is well behind ASEAN countries such as Thailand, Malaysia, Philippines and even Viet Nam (table 13). Sri Lanka appears to be an anomaly considering its level of development, and also among countries in the subcontinent. As a nation, they are known for giving highly priority to female education and, as has been widely noted, it is female education that is highly correlated with health and mortality. Hence, Sri Lanka is characterized by rather low infant, child and maternal mortality. Almost all births (95 per cent) in Sri Lanka are attended by trained health personnel. The Indonesian health sector has not paid sufficient attention to the needs of women, as only 36 per cent of births are attended by trained health personnel. Not surprising, Indonesia has recorded the highest maternal mortality in the region (650 per 100,000 live births, table 13)[6], an indicator of the poor health status of Indonesian women and mothers.

In Indonesia, efforts have been made to overcome the barriers to access of maternal and child health services, including the provision of mobile health services and monthly opening of a *Posyandu* (integrated village health post)

[5]   Stoeckel *et al.,* Increasing family planning acceptance through development programmes: An experimental study in Northeastern Thailand (1984:28).

[6]   Based on the 1994 IDHS, MMR for the early 1990s was estimated at 390 per 100,000 live births.

Table 13. Mortality and survival indicators for selected countries

Human Development Index (HDI) rank and country	IMR (per 1,000 live births) 1994	q_5 (per 1,000 live births) 1995	MMR (per 100,000 live births) 1990	% Pregnant women aged 15-49 with anaemia 1975-1991	% Births attended by trained health personnel 1990-1996
High HDI rank					
59 Thailand	29	32	200	48	71
60 Malaysia	12	13	80	36	94
Medium HDI rank					
91 Sri Lanka	16	19	140	..	94
98 Philippines	36	53	280	48	53
99 Indonesia	**53**	**75**	**650**	**74**	**36**
121 Viet Nam	41	45	160	..	95
High HDI rank					
138 India	74	115	570	88	34
144 Bangladesh	85	115	850	58	14

Source: UNDP (1997) *Human Development Report 1997.* New York: Oxford University Press, table 12: 174-75.

organized by the local community with the assistance of the local health centre. In 1988, a village-based midwifery service, *Polindes*, was launched. *Polindes*, which is primarily staffed by a *bidan di desa*, a village-based midwife, was initiated by the government as part of the effort to increase maternal welfare. The introduction of *Polindes* is a crucial step in providing services close to the people in need. This is particularly the case for pregnant women who cannot afford to use private or government-based maternal health services, such as *Puskesmas* (health centre). Further development of currently promoted village-based maternity services (*Polindes*) has also been encouraged with the Mother Friendly Movement (*Gerakan Sayang Ibu*). This movement, together with *bidan di desa* programme has bridged the gap between the formal health care delivery system and informal health delivery practices such as traditional birth attendants (Cholil, Iskandar, and Sciortino, 1998). The effectiveness of these programmes in reducing maternal mortality has, however, not been tested.

In the final analysis, the main reason for relatively poor health among the Indonesian population, in general, and mothers in particular, is attributable to low spending on health.

Indonesia spends less on health than other countries at similar levels of development in the Asian region (Prescott, 1997). Total health spending (public and private) comprised only 1.9 per cent of GDP in 1993. China spent 2.9 per cent of GDP in 1993 and Thailand 5.4 per cent in 1992. With regards to public spending, Indonesia also compares poorly. As a share of GDP, it remained at less than 0.9 per cent between 1984/85 and 1994/95, which is substantially less than the next lowest spender in ASEAN, the Philippines, which spends 1.3 per cent of GDP on public health (World Bank, 1997:79). During *Repelita V* (1989-1993), both public and private health care expenditures constituted only 2.8 per cent of GDP, which is roughly half of that spent in other countries with comparable per capita incomes (UNICEF 1996:5). To further reduce mortality, the government inevitably will have to weigh alternative levels of health expenditure against other pressing demands on the national budget.

In addition to the lower level of government expenditure on the heath sector, the provision of health care services are biased toward hospital-based, urban focused services, and rely on costly modern technology. To date, urban hospitals represent the core of the system, and a substantial proportion of total funds are poured into them, despite their accessibility to only a small proportion of the population. In order to effectively tackle health care problems in the light of current budgetary and manpower constraints, a more dramatic political breakthrough is needed, especially in times of crisis as now experienced.

6. Schooling and work participation

As earlier alluded to, changes in Indonesian women's life style and aspirations, in particular with regard to delayed marriage and increasingly allowing women to establish their own households, have affected the patterns and trends in fertility decline. This has been achieved in conjunction with improvements in access to social and economic services in the areas of school and work. As mentioned earlier, girls and women have benefited disproportionately from expanding education and employment facilities and opportunities, especially in the formal sector.

As a result, women have continued to be affected by social transformation, and have increasingly contributed to the development process. This process has brought about changes in the employment structure. The changes in job opportunities and employment structure have also raised the status of women, reflecting that women have been both the object as well as the beneficiaries of development.

The development orientation of the New Order Government was to shift from agriculture to industrialization. Consequently, the role of agriculture, in both GDP and labour absorption has declined. Between 1983 and 1993, for instance, the share of agriculture in GDP declined from 23 per cent to 18 per cent, while the share of manufacturing rose from 13 per cent to 21 per cent (World Bank, 1998: table 6). Similarly, overall labour absorption in agriculture has continued to decline, from 66 per cent in 1971 to 41 per cent in 1997, while the share of manufacturing workers rose from 7 per cent to 13 per cent (BPS, 1971 Population Census and *SAKERNAS*, 1997).

This structural shift in the labour market came about as the work force became better educated. In just 8 years between 1986 and 1994, the share of the working age population (10 years and above) with little or no schooling declined from 50 per cent to 38 per cent and the share of those who completed primary schooling rose from 31 per cent to 35 per cent (table 14). The decline in the percentage of the working age population with primary schooling or less was slightly sharper for females than for males. For females, the decline was from 86 per cent in 1986 to 77 per cent in 1994 or some 9 percentage points, while for males the decline was from 78 per cent to 72 per cent or 6 percentage points. Thus, females have gained relatively more than males from expanding

Table 14. Percentage distribution of the working age population (10+) by education and sex, 1986, 1990 and 1994

Education	1986			1990			1994		
	Total	Females	Males	Total	Females	Males	Total	Females	Males
No school and some primary	50.5	56.5	44.4	44.3	49.7	38.7	38.3	42.8	36.6
Primary	31.3	29.2	33.5	33.5	31.9	35.2	34.8	34.1	35.5
Lower secondary	10.1	8.6	11.6	11.6	10.1	13.1	12.9	11.6	14.1
General – upper secondary	4.2	2.9	5.4	5.7	4.5	6.9	7.5	6.2	8.9
Vocational – upper secondary	3.1	2.3	3.8	3.7	3.0	4.4	4.5	3.8	5.3
Tertiary	0.9	0.5	1.3	1.3	0.9	1.7	2.0	1.5	2.5
Sum	**100.0**	**100.0**	**100.0**	**100.0**	**100.0**	**100.0**	**100.0**	**100.0**	**100.0**

Source: Oey-Gardiner and Suleeman (1997): 22, based on special tabulations from the respective *SAKERNAS*.

education opportunities, thereby contributing significantly to the overall development process of the nation.

These achievements are attributable to widespread investments in public primary schools through the *SD Inpres* programme (special primary school programme), which targeted at least one school per village. In addition, school fees at the primary level were abolished as the government introduced the *programme wajib belajar 6 tahun* (6 years compulsory education programme). As a result, schools have been brought closer to home, thereby inducing parents to send their children to school, especially their daughters. Besides, incentives also came from investments into export-oriented industries which created large numbers of paid employment opportunities, again often favouring women.

As the formal sector has remained rather limited in Indonesia,[7] most workers have to find their income earning activities in the

---

[7] And has contracted much more since the crisis.

non-formal, including agricultural, sector. In light of the preceding discussion, it is surprising to find that in fact, based on the *SAKERNAS* series, female labour force participation has remained fairly constant (table 15). This phenomenon can be explained in terms of the urban-rural distribution. Regardless of cursory observations in and around Jakarta, which suggest fairly advanced levels of modernization, Indonesia's population is, in fact, not that urbanized. In 1995, most of the population still resided in rural areas (64 per cent according to the *1995 SUPAS* or Intercensal Population Survey). Hence, total statistics continue to be weighted in favour of levels reflecting conditions of the rural population.

Earlier observations on betterment and development of women, in the market in general, and the labour market in particular, reflect more of the urban environment, or an urban bias. Consequently, labour force participation has remained fairly stable among rural residents of different ages, for women as well as for men (table 15). Dynamism has,

Table 15. Economic activity rates by residence, age group and sex, 1986, 1990 and 1994

Age and type of area	1986			1990			1994		
	Total	Females	Males	Total	Females	Males	Total	Females	Males
Total	**57.3**	**44.4**	**70.5**	**57.3**	**44.0**	**70.9**	**58.0**	**44.5**	**72.0**
10 - 14	12.9	11.5	13.8	11.1	9.1	12.9	9.2	7.9	10.5
15 - 29	58.0	46.1	71.2	57.2	45.0	70.4	58.8	46.8	72.0
30 - 44	79.2	59.8	98.5	78.6	59	98.4	78.4	58.8	98.1
45 - 64	73.9	56.7	91.3	74.5	57.2	91.6	72.9	54.9	91.0
65+	38.3	22.9	55.3	40.2	24.7	56.9	39.1	24.5	55.4
Urban	**44.4**	**29.5**	**59.5**	**46.9**	**32.7**	**61.4**	**50.4**	**36.1**	**65.1**
10 - 14	2.6	3.1	2.1	3.3	3.4	3.1	3.1	4.1	3.2
15 - 29	42.2	31.2	53.9	44.8	35.5	54.7	54.7	41.4	60.8
30 - 44	69.3	40.7	97.6	69.7	42.1	97.6	97.6	46.2	97.7
45 - 64	60.2	38.1	82.8	63.5	42.4	84.5	84.5	40.2	85.4
65+	23.8	13.7	35.0	27.7	17.5	39.0	39.0	16.0	39.5
Rural	**62.1**	**49.9**	**74.6**	**61.9**	**49.1**	**75.1**	**62.2**	**49.1**	**75.8**
10 - 14	16.4	14.3	18.4	14.2	11.5	16.7	12.1	9.9	14.2
15 - 29	64.8	52.3	78.8	63.6	49.8	78.5	64.1	50.3	79.5
30 - 44	82.6	68.5	98.8	82.3	66.2	98.7	81.8	65.5	98.4
45 - 64	78.5	63.0	94.0	78.7	62.9	94.4	77.4	61.4	93.6
65+	42.7	25.7	61.3	44.7	27.4	63.3	44.3	28.1	62.6

Source: Oey-Gardiner and Suleeman 1997:34, based on special tabulations from the respective *SAKERNAS*.

instead, mostly been experienced by urban residents, where both women and men of all ages have gained. Still, the most favoured have been young adults between the ages 15 and 29 years in the mid-1990s. This is the cohort born and raised during the New Order, experiencing most of the benefits of rapid growth and development. These young adults are the ones who benefited from the introduction of wide ranging development programmes. In the social arena, they have been the beneficiaries of education programmes, and in the economic arena, they have benefited from the introduction of a variety of deregulation measures initiated since the mid-1980s, which have set the economy in rapid motion.[8] Most of those young adults have delayed marriage and a good proportion has introduced new norms of establishing individual households, as they are better educated and some of them have well paying jobs.

Whether these statistics will prevail in spite of the crisis and the aftermath of El Niño is highly questionable. The media widely publishes continuing retrenchments. The first hit of the crisis was on construction in late 1997. This was followed by manufacturing, in particular textiles, garments and leather goods, electronics, metal products and machinery, as the Rupiah continued to weaken and factories reduced production or eventually discontinued operations altogether. Even though formally approved[9] mass retrenchments number less than 200,000, statements by government officials, especially by labour union leaders on the numbers unemployed are quite substantial, well over 10 million to as high as 30 million.[10]

Given that no data are as yet available on the impact of the crisis on the labour market,[11] projections have been made on the basis of past trends. Following a model proposed by Islam (1998) and combining data on recently announced contraction of the Indonesian economy by BPS (*Jakarta Post*, 8 July 1998), and using the labour force from the 1997 *SAKERNAS* with gender and sector specific elasticities computed by the World Bank (1998), estimates have been made on numbers of remaining job holders and job losses (Oey-Gardiner and Dharmaputra, 1998). The results indicate that from 82.3 million workers in mid-1997, 4.7 million would have lost their jobs by mid-1998. Of the total workers, 31.2 million or 38 per cent are females and of those losing jobs, 1.8 million or 39 per cent would be females (Oey-Gardiner and Dharmaputra, 1998:19). These results suggest that while in absolute terms fewer women are expected to have lost their jobs,[12] in relative terms women are slightly over-represented among those having to give up their jobs. Irrespective of gender, large numbers of workers are expected to have lost their jobs so far.

In this situation, the next related question concerns the number and level of open unemployment. These estimates derive from a number of projections, and therefore, are based on different assumptions used in these projections. As a first step, there is a need for population projections, the results of which depend on assumptions of fertility and mortality, which have continued to decline. Available population projections have also changed,

---

[8] In 1998, we are experiencing also the deep abyss of economic turmoil with bankruptcies, widespread unemployment and rapidly rising inflation.

[9] Approval for mass retrenchment is obtained from the Ministry of Manpower (more detailed discussions on this issue can be found in Oey-Gardiner and Dharmaputra, 1998).

[10] Compared to a 1997 labour force of around 91.3 million, and the projected 1998 labour force of 92-94 million.

[11] One population survey series, the *SUSENAS* is conducted annually in the month of February. These results should be published in the near future. The preferred series on the labour force is the annual *SAKERNAS*, which is usually conducted in the month of August. Due to the financial crisis faced by the government, however, this survey had not yet gone in the field in mid-August 1998, but was scheduled for implementation.

[12] Because there are simply fewer women in the work force.

usually because those projections have been more conservative in their estimates of fertility and mortality declines. The next step concerns assumptions on labour force participation. Using a conservative assumption of constant 1997 age and sex specific pattern of labour force participation, applied to two population projections, we arrive at the following results.

The impact of the projected population and hence the labour force is rather substantial on the number of unemployed as well as unemployment rate. As fewer women join the labour market, fewer are expected to be unemployed. But, the estimated open unemployment rate is higher for women than men (table 16), indicating that women shall be relatively more deprived than men in obtaining or retaining jobs. According to these estimates, the number of openly unemployed shall be between 10 and 12 million, and open unemployment rates for females shall be in the order of 13 or 12 per cent, and for males 12 or 10 per cent. Given the non-formality of the labour market, however, it can be expected that even these estimates are on the high side. The poor can simply not afford to be openly unemployed. One should probably not expect such a sweeping shift into open unemployment, especially among the newly emerging poor, but rather a shift from formal to non-formal sector activities. This may include the likelihood of returning to agriculture and petty trade, the sectors from which they came not long ago.

Moreover, given the non-formality of the Indonesian labour market,[13] one can expect even lower open unemployment estimates simply because a good proportion may well opt to drop out of the labour market. A much larger proportion of men may, however, become discouraged job seekers and hence, when asked about their economic activity during the week preceding the survey, they may respond that they had no activity and would therefore be categorized into "others". Women have two options. Some women will either similarly become categorized as others, or we can also expect a larger proportion of women to opt for "housekeeping". Only time will tell as we wait for the next round of labour force data to become available.

Moreover, as other quarters argue, the problem in Indonesia's economy today is less of open unemployment but rather one of low productivity. While wages were rising during the early half of the 1990s, the 'big bang' of the economic crisis has substantially reduced purchasing power of workers and the general public at large. Before the crisis, regional minimum wages set by the government for Jakarta had already reached Rp.172,500 per month (*Jakarta Post*, July 1, 1998), which in July 1997 was worth almost US$ 72. Effective

---

[13] Which, even before the crisis, was characterized by a labour surplus and hence predominantly engaged in non-formal sector activities.

Table 16. 1998 Unemployment estimates by sex, using 2 population projections

	Projection A			Projection B		
	Females	Males	Total	Females	Males	Total
Labour force (m)	36.1	58.2	94.3	35.5	57.1	92.5
Workers (m)	31.2	51.1	82.3	31.2	51.1	82.3
Unemployed (m)	4.8	7.1	12.0	4.3	6.0	10.2
Unemployment rate (%)	13.4	12.3	12.7	12.0	10.4	11.0

Source: Oey-Gardiner and Dharmaputra (1998): 21.

Notes: Projection A is based on BPS (1997), *Proyeksi Penduduk Indonesia per Propinsi 1995-2005*, Seri S7 SUPAS 95; Projection B is based on the estimated age and sex specific population distribution and growth of *SAKERNAS* 1994, 1996 and 1997, and labour force participation rates in the 1997 *SAKERNAS*.

from August 1, 1998, the regional minimum wage for Jakarta was set at Rp.198,500 (*Jakarta Post*, July 1, 1998), about 11 per cent higher than before. In the meantime, in mid-August 1998, the US$ exchange rate was between Rp.12,000 and Rp.13,000, and inflation had reached 47 per cent by July 1998.

Given the problems faced by workers, the government has made attempts to ameliorate their suffering. Regrettably, however, it has been the visibility of men and invisibility of laid off women, which has resulted in the introduction of gender blind policies that are extremely discriminatory against women.

The earliest mass retrenchments started towards the latter part of 1997 and affected mostly the property, real estate and construction industries, all representing very masculine sectors. Many of the construction workers are migrants, coming from rural areas. These men remained in the major cities after retrenchment in the hope of finding another job. At that time they were often found huddled together under bridges and along main roads. This has made them visible and created fears of social unrest among policy makers who are mostly males. As the crisis continues, however, manufacturing and services industries also started laying off their workers, including large numbers of women workers. Following social norms, unless destitute, idle women do not hang around or sit on road sides. As many of these women factory workers had come to the city for work, they went back home to their villages when there was no work thus making them invisible.

In response to widely discussed unemployment of large numbers of workers, the government introduced a gender blind labour intensive employment programme for the remaining three months of fiscal year 1997-1998, which ended in March 31, 1998. The activities were mainly of the public works types, digging city ditches and irrigation canals. Participants were expected to work for 5 hours

a day and were paid Rp.7,500 per person-day.[14] These jobs were accessible to men only. At that time there was no recognition that thousands of women workers had been laid off from manufacturing industries. It was only after the Lotus Foundation, an NGO concerned with women's rights as human rights, called on the government and the President of the World Bank to draw their attention to the issue, that the government conceded to allocate at least 20 per cent of jobs to women (*Kompas* and *Suara Pembaruan*, 5 February, 1998 and *Kompas* 12 February, 1998).

Given the worsening economy and the general pessimistic atmosphere of the political economy, it is hard to judge where we stand today and even more difficult to suggest where we should go. The government has introduced a variety of social safety net programmes and subsidies, including employment creation for the masses while reducing *KKN* (*Korupsi, Kolusi dan Nepotism*). While gender sensitivity has been written into the public sector programmes (especially those funded by foreign donor agencies), its implementation may still be questionable. The government apparatus remains strongly male dominated with little understanding of the differential needs and constraints faced by women and men. For instance, (unconfirmed) observations suggest that for the first time in the 1990s, enrolment in elementary and secondary school is lower for girls than boys in Jakarta. This phenomenon is not surprising, but feared by women activists, as parents have always tended to favour sons under conditions of financial limitations. Gender sensitivity in public policies on education on this matter has not been forthright. The same is true of employment creation and income generating policies. Only time will tell the effects of current policies to help the public, and especially the poor.

---

[14] Which was substantially higher than the going daily wage rate of almost Rp.6,000 per day for 8 hours.

7. Migration

This section will discuss the already touched upon issue of mobility. As development expanded and brought about changes in people's socioeconomic conditions, opportunities widened while mobility constraints were at times dampened. Increasingly, numerous positive and negative incentives affecting push and pull factors were operating to induce mobility.

(a) Internal migration

In light of the women's perspective taken in this paper, published migration data by sex is only available from the 1990 Population Census and the 1995 SUPAS or Intercensal Population Survey.[15] In order to identify trends in migratory movements, a comparison of these data suggests the need to question the validity of the implied trends of volume of migration. For instance, the implied volume of recent migration (i.e. 5 years ago) declined from 5.1 million persons to 4.2 million according to these two data sources (table 17). Such a trend is

[15] Household members are those who usually live in a particular household regardless of their location at the time of enumeration. A person was no longer regarded as a member of his or her former household if the person had been absent from home for six months or longer, or had left home for the purpose of moving away even when the six-months limit had not been reached. On the other hand, a guest who had stayed for six months or more, or even for less than six months but intended to move in was recorded as a household member.

Table 17. Numbers of recent in- and out-migrants by province and sex, 1990 and 1995

| Province | 1990 | | | | 1995 | | | |
| | Males | | Females | | Males | | Females | |
	In-migrants	Out-migrants	In-migrants	Out-migrants	In-migrants	Out-migrants	In-migrants	Out-migrants
Aceh	31	27	24	22	15	23	13	26
N Sumatra	60	153	47	125	50	104	53	95
W Sumatra	70	94	56	79	73	72	63	73
Riau	133	53	109	40	75	72	72	54
Jambi	74	36	61	28	31	32	26	21
S Sumatra	113	111	96	88	68	102	60	86
Bengkulu	46	16	37	12	35	20	31	16
Lampung	115	77	93	59	58	85	56	81
Jakarta	367	525	453	469	257	429	335	399
W Java	695	253	643	242	565	226	545	223
C Java	210	572	170	588	186	341	161	392
Yogyakarta	83	61	77	60	81	54	84	57
E Java	189	341	131	306	218	204	187	207
Bali	38	32	27	24	30	22	28	23
W Nusa Tenggara	20	22	15	15	20	19	17	16
E Nusa Tenggara	14	28	10	18	13	25	12	19
W Kalimantan	26	25	17	20	25	19	18	15
C Kalimantan	46	21	31	16	21	25	25	28
S Kalimantan	51	42	45	34	33	34	34	23
E Kalimantan	105	40	85	28	69	42	69	34
N Sulawesi	19	26	14	25	12	24	9	24
C Sulawesi	38	16	30	12	31	14	32	14
S Sulawesi	64	91	49	70	75	75	55	74
SE Sulawesi	39	21	31	16	32	19	25	20
Maluku	32	23	35	16	12	23	11	23
Irian Jaya	39	19	31	13	29	16	24	10
Total	**2 736**	**2 736**	**2 428**	**2 428**	**2 127**	**2 217**	**2 056**	**2 053**

Sources: BPS, *1990 Population Census* and *1995 SUPAS.*

Notes: Recent migration refers to different places of residence at the time of the census/survey and five years before the census/survey.

32

rather questionable as all other economic and social indicators suggest the contrary. These results may well be due to differences in sample size. Characteristics in population censuses have usually been obtained from a sample of around 5 per cent of households, about 2 million households. The 1995 SUPAS data are obtained from about 200,000 households. For one reason or another, as was the case with earlier SUPAS (1976 and 1985), the 1995 SUPAS results have often not been comparable with other data sources to reflect trends.

While trend analysis on absolute numbers, such as volume of mobility suggests questionable results, inter-provincial differences are still worth highlighting. For instance, contrary to popular belief, there are more out-migrants from Jakarta than in-migrants to Jakarta, both among men and women, in 1990 and still in 1995. These statistics are consistent with the process of suburbanization of the Jakarta population, as until the economic crunch, new developments attracting the Jakarta population, are centred around the capital city proper, into the adjacent province of West Jakarta. Thus, migration into West Java has been substantially higher than migration out of the province. On the other hand, among both men and women, migration out of Central Java is also consistent with cursory observations that the Jakarta work force is becoming more Javanese.[16]

The provinces of North Sumatra and, to a lesser extent, West Sumatra have historically been out-migration areas, and continue to be so. Riau, on the other hand, where Batam Island is located, which has been developed as an industrial area and export processing zone, has attracted more in-migrants than losing out-migrants in the period 1985-1990. During the next five-year period, however, the difference in the numbers of in- and out-migrants is less

striking, but more substantial for women than men.

East Kalimantan continues to attract migrants from other provinces as a result of dynamism in the economy resulting from wood-based industries, in particular the plywood industry. As investments into this industry have expanded and jobs are created, thousands of Indonesians from other provinces have come to work and settle here. Even though others have left the province in search for work or a better life, there are, on balance, more in- than out-migrants from this province.

A further question of interest in this regard concerns comparisons between women and men. Consistent with cursory observations, in particular around major industrial areas, mobility has become increasingly more feminine. Overall, the sex ratio (females per 100 males) has risen, from 89 to 97 women per 100 men (table 18). By the middle of the last decade, women have become almost as mobile as men. Women no longer only follow their husbands and fathers but increasingly single women are moving away from parental homes and known environments[17] in search of better lives and maybe freedom, especially from marriage and household responsibilities, including child rearing.

We would, thus, like to call attention to the following striking change in sex composition of the migration streams. Women dominate the migration scene into and out of larger numbers of provinces. As table 18 shows, or the earlier period of 1985-1990,

---

16 This is the ethnic group originating from Central and East Java, while the ethnic group originating from West Java are called Sundanese.

17 The difficulties in enticing the poor to join the transmigration programme away from their homes on Java used to be explained in terms of a Javanese saying "*mangan ora mangan asal ngumpul*" (whether we eat or not does not matter as long as we stay together). As not just men but also thousands of Javanese women are reported to be on the move, this saying is no longer mentioned or used to explain social phenomena. Obviously economic factors, rather than social or cultural, are stronger incentives, including incentives to leave familiar surroundings into the unknown and unfamiliar.

Table 18. Sex ratios of recent in- and out-migrants by province, 1990 and 1995

Province	1990		1995		Index of feminization	
	In-migrants	Out-migrants	In-migrants	Out-migrants	In-migrants	Out-migrants
Aceh	78	83	86	113	110	136
N Sumatra	78	81	104	91	134	111
W Sumatra	81	84	86	102	106	121
Riau	82	76	96	74	117	98
Jambi	82	77	84	65	102	84
S Sumatra	85	79	88	84	104	106
Bengkulu	80	75	88	82	110	110
Lampung	81	77	97	95	119	122
Jakarta	123	89	130	93	106	104
W Java	92	96	96	99	104	103
C Java	81	103	87	115	108	112
Yogyakarta	92	98	103	107	112	109
E Java	69	90	86	101	125	113
Bali	71	74	92	102	131	138
W Nusa	76	69	83	83	109	121
Tenggara	74	64	97	75	132	118
E Nusa Tenggara	59	25	84	81	143	317
W Kalimantan	66	79	73	81	111	103
C Kalimantan	68	78	117	114	173	145
S Kalimantan	88	80	103	68	117	84
E Kalimantan	81	71	100	81	124	116
N Sulawesi	75	97	72	97	96	100
C Sulawesi	79	78	101	103	128	132
S Sulawesi	77	77	74	98	96	128
SE Sulawesi	80	77	79	102	98	132
Maluku	111	71	92	104	83	147
Irian Jaya	79	70	85	65	108	93
Total	**89**	**89**	**97**	**97**	**109**	**109**

Sources: BPS, *1990 Population Census* and *1995 SUPAS*.

Note: Recent migration refers to different places of residence at the time of the census/survey and five years before the census/survey.
Sex Ratio = (Females/Males) x 100;
Index of feminization is expressed as the ratio of sex ratios of 1995/1990.

sex ratios of in- and out-migration exceeds 100 only in three provinces. Women dominate the migration stream (sex ratios of more than 100) into Jakarta and Maluku and out-migration stream from Central Java. For the next 5-year period, women dominate migration into 7 provinces and out of 10 provinces. These indicators further strengthen our earlier proposition that mobility in Indonesia is becoming increasingly female.

The process of feminization of mobility can also be expressed in terms of a ratio of sex ratios of in- and out-migration between two dates, in this case 1990-1995/1985-1990. An index of 100 means that the sex ratio of women over 100 men has remained constant over the period. The process of feminization of migration is indicated by an index exceeding 100. Noticeably, feminization of the migration process has occurred in most provinces. In 15 of 27 provinces, the in-migration process has exceeded the average for the nation, and with regards to out-migration, the feminization process has occurred in 17 out of 27 provinces (table 18).

The important phenomenon to be emphasized here is that, relative to men, Indonesian women are not really less willing to move. Instead, we suggest that women's propensity to move is more likely a function of their constraints and incentives, many of which seem to have been increasingly lifted and expanded. Women have become increasingly more mobile, not just socially and economically, but also geographically.

(b) *International migration*

Indonesian women's horizons are not limited to places only within the national boundaries. Instead, they stretch their wings to far off countries, where there is work for them. Even before the crisis, and especially in these difficult times, overseas employment remunerated in foreign currency, is regarded as the panacea for many families. Many are willing to risk their lives and go overseas for work. Some go legally, i.e. with approval and through government channels, and many more go illegally. The most recent widely reported hardships are those suffered by Indonesian migrant workers returned from countries experiencing their own economic downturn.

For many poor households, women working overseas are the only source of hope. During the latter half of the 1990s, more than twice as many women as men went legally overseas in search of work, leaving their families behind (table 19). Noticeably, the impact of the economic crisis has also affected opportunities for overseas work, not just in the Asia-Pacific region but also in the Middle East. After reaching a peak in 1996/97, when more than half a million Indonesian workers went overseas legally, of which women constituted 56 per cent, the numbers have declined substantially. The following year, during fiscal 1997/98, less than half as many managed to obtain legal overseas employment, mostly

Table 19. Number of Indonesian overseas workers deployed by region of destination and sex during *Repelita VI* of 1994-1998
(April 1, 1994 - May 20, 1998)

Year and Sex	Asia-Pacific	America	Europe	Middle East	Total
1994/95					
Males	28 772	4 007	1 705	8 349	42 833
Females	41 961	29	3	91 361	133 354
Total	70 733	4 036	1 708	99 710	176 187
1995/96					
Males	29 261	3 600	1 051	5 190	39 102
Females	38 626		3	43 165	81 794
Total	67 887	3 600	1 054	48 355	120 896
1996/97					
Males	218 544	1 080	456	8 357	228 437
Females	161 825		28	126 979	288 832
Total	380 369	1 080	484	135 336	517 269
1997/98					
Males	28 232	1 187	697	9 193	39 309
Females	73 411	2	12	122 541	195 966
Total	101 643	1 189	709	131 734	235 275
1998/99					
Males	2 899	261	136	1 403	4 699
Females	18 217			16 945	35 162
Total	21 116	261	136	18 348	39 861
Total					
Males	307 708	10 135	4 045	32 492	354 380
Females	334 040	31	46	400 991	735 108
Total	641 748	10 166	4 091	433 483	1 089 488

Source: Ministry of Manpower.

women (83 per cent). From April 1, to May 20, 1998, less than 40,000 managed to obtain overseas contracts, again dominated by women who constituted 88 per cent of the total. Legal overseas employment is increasingly becoming more available for women. Not surprising, the headline of a newspaper report states "*Pengiriman TKW Kian Marak*" (Sending of overseas women workers increases, *Suara Pembaruan*, August 19, 1998). Sending daughters, wives, or mothers is increasingly becoming a household strategy.

C. Conclusion

The discussion on mobility, and in particular female mobility, has brought the story to a full circle. Indonesian women have more often been the objects rather than the beneficiaries of development, both at the state and macro level as well as at the micro household level. Directly and also indirectly, women have been the key targets of the most important population control policy, i.e. through the birth control programme, and population growth has slowed down. As rapid population growth had been hailed as one of the major impediments of development, women's role in the development process in this context should, therefore, not be underestimated.

Indirectly women have also benefited from the development process. Women's education has risen relatively faster than men's education. While women's share in the labour market has not increased, again women have benefited more from formalization of the labour market. Work in the public sphere for women has also meant increased mobility, not only domestically but also internationally. While women dominate the international migration labour market, the domestic labour market has been more feminized.

All these factors are intertwined, simultaneously and mutually reinforcing, and they have contributed to rapid changes in the demographic front. Most demographic indicators have shown positive improvements as living standards have been improving until the crisis hit the shores and Indonesians continue grappling with the new realities of life.

Poverty, not only at the individual level, but also nationally and experienced by the government, has introduced fears of returning to the situation three decades ago, when poverty was widespread and social and economic services were practically broken down. This situation raises some basic demographic question. Will women, unable to prevent unwanted births for lack of birth control devices, end up with more children? Will morbidity and mortality also rise again? Will more or fewer burdens be placed on women's shoulders as a result of the crisis? Only time will tell.

REFERENCES

Adioetomo, Sri Moertiningsih (1993). *The construction of a small-family size norm in Java*, Ph.D. thesis, Australian National University, Canberra.

Adioetomo, Sri Moertiningsih, Ayke S. Kiting and Salman Taufik (1990). Fertility transition in Indonesia. Trends in poximate determinants of fertility, in *Population Studies in Sri Lanka and Indonesia based on the 1987 Sri Lanka Demographic and Health Survey and the 1987 National Indonesia Contraceptive Prevalence Survey*, New York: Population Council and DHS/IRD.

Biro Pusat Statistik (1975). *Sensus Penduduk 1971, 1980 and 1990, Penduduk Indonesia* (Population of Indonesia). Seri D. Jakarta.

_____ (1983). *Penduduk Indonesia Hasil Sensus Penduduk*. Population of Indonesia, results of the 1980 Population Census. Series S2.

_____ (1987). *Penduduk Indonesia, Hasil Survei Penduduk Antar Sensus*. Population of Indonesia, results of the 1985 Intercensal Population Survey. Series SUPAS No. 5.

_____ (1992). *Penduduk Indonesia, Hasil Sensus Penduduk*. Population of Indonesia, results of the 1990 Population Census, Series S2, Jakarta.

_____ (1996). *Penduduk Indonesia, Hasil Survei Penduduk Antar Sensus*. Population of Indonesia, results of the 1995 Intercensal Population Survey, Series S2, Jakarta.

_____ (1998). *Keadaan Angkatan Kerja di Indonesia Agustus*. Labour Force Situation in Indonesia August 1997.

Caldwell, John C., Peter F. McDonald and Lado T. Ruzicka (1980). *Interrelationships between nuptiality and fertility: the evidence from the World Fertility Survey*, Department of Demography, the Australian National University. Prepared for the World Fertility Survey Conference, London 7-11 July.

Central Bureau of Statistics, National Family Planning Coordinating Board (1992). *Indonesia Demographic and Health Survey 1991*. Ministry of Health and Macro International, Jakarta *Indonesia Demographic and Health Survey 1994*. Jakarta: CBS.

Central Bureau of Statistics, National Family Planning Coordinating Board (1995), *Indonesia Demographic and Health Survey 1991*. Ministry of Health and Macro International, Jakarta *Indonesia Demographic and Health Survey 1994*. Jakarta: CBS.

Central Bureau of Statistics (1997). *Estimation of Fertility, Mortality, and Migration Based on the 1995 Intercensal Population Survey*. Jakarta: CBS.

Cholil, A., Meiwita B. Iskandar, R. Sciortino (1998). *The Life Savers: the Mother Friendly Movement in Indonesia*. Jakarta: State Ministry for the Role of Women, RI.

Cleland, John and G. Rodriguez (1988). The effect of parental education on marital fertility in developing countries, *Population Studies*, 42(3): 419-442.

Coale, Ansley J. (1992). Age of entry into marriage and the date of the initiation of voluntary birth control, *Demography* 29(3): 333-341.

Freedman, R., S. Kho and B. Supraptilah (1981). Use of modern contraceptives in Indonesia: A challenge to the conventional wisdom, *International Family Planning Perspectives* 7(1): 3-15.

Gertler, Paul J. and John W. Molyneaux (1994). How economic development and family planning programmes combined to reduce Indonesian fertility, *Demography* 31(1): 33-63.

Government of Indonesia and UNICEF (1988). *Situation Analysis of Children and Women in Indonesia*. Jakarta: GOI and UNICEF.

Hatmadji, Sri Harijati and Diah Widyawati (1994). *Transformasi Ekonomi dan Produktivitas Tenagakerja Wanita, Demografi*, No.2: 29-34.

Hatmadji, Sri Harijati and Ni Wayan Suriastini (1995). *Kecenderungan dan Perbedaan Fertilitas*, in Aris Ananta, ed., *Kecenderungan dan Faktor Penentu Fertilitas dan Mortalitas di Indonesia* Trends and fertility and mortality determinants in Indonesia, Jakarta: *Kantor Menteri Negara Kependudukan/ BKKBN*.

Hugo, G.J., T.H. Hull, V.J. Hull and G.W. Jones (1987). *The Demographic Dimension in Indonesian Development*. Singapore: Oxford University Press.

Hull, T. and S.H. Hatmadji (1990). *Regional fertility differentials in Indonesia: causes and trends*. Ph.D. Thesis, Australian National University, Canberra.

Hull, Terence H., Valerie J. Hull and Masri Singarimbun (1977). Indonesia's family planning story. Success and challenge, *Population Bulletin*, 32(6):4-51.

Hull, Valerie J. (1977). The relation of economic class and fertility: An analysis of some Indonesian data, *Population Studies*, 30(1), March.

Indonesian Ministry of Health (1997). *Indonesia Health Profile 1996*, Jakarta: the Ministry of Health.

Iskandar, N. (1970). *Some Monographic Studies on the Population in Indonesia. Lembaga Demografi, Fakultas Ekonomi,* Universitas Indonesia.

Islam, Rizwanul (1998). *Indonesia: Economic Crisis, Adjustment, Employment and Poverty*. Issues in Development, discussion paper 23, Development Policies Department, ILO, Geneva.

Jakarta Post (July 8, 1998). *Economy shrinks for the first time in 30 years.*

_____ (July 1, 1998). *Minimum wages raised by 15%.*

Kompas (February 5, 1998). *Padat karya untuk wanita, mengapa tidak?* (Labour intensive activities for women, why not?).

_____ February 12, 1998). *Dibuka, padat karya untuk wanita* (Opened, labour intensive work for women).

_____ (April 27, 1998). *TKI, mafia, dan lemahnya perlindungan* (Indonesian workers, mafia, and weak protection); and *mereka yang dipulangkan dari Malaysia* (those sent home from Malaysia).

_____ (July 2, 1998). *Inflasi masih berkutat dengan urusan perut* (Inflation continues to deal with the stomach).

Kantor Menteri Negara Kependudukan/BKKBN (1996). *Informasi Dasar Gerakan KB Pembangunan Keluarga Sejahtera*. Jakarta.

Prescott, N. (1998). *Economics of health reform in East Asia*, paper delivered at Science and Health: Opportunities for the twenty-first Century International Conference, Feb. 1-5. Bangkok, Thailand.

Oey, Mayling (1974). Differential fertility among female-centered social groups in Indonesia, 1971, *Majalah Demografi, Indonesia* 1(2), 46-69.

Oey-Gardiner, Mayling and Soedarti Surbakti (1991). *Strategi Kehidupan Wanita Kepala Rumah Tangga*. Jakarta: Biro Pusat Statistik.

Oey-Gardiner, Mayling and Evelyn Suleeman (1997). *Gender Differentials in Schooling and Labour Market Implications*, report prepared for the Asian Development Bank. Jakarta: Insan Harapan Sejahtera.

Oey-Gardiner, Mayling and Nick Dharmaputra (1998). Gender differential impact of the crisis on Indonesian's labour market, paper prepared as part of an AIT-ILO joint research on *Gender Dimension of the Economic Crisis in Southeast and East Asia*. Jakarta, *Insan Hitawasana Sejahtera*.

Shane, Barbara (1997). *Family Planning Saves Lives*. Washington DC: Population Reference Bureau.

Standing, Guy (1982). Labour Force, *International Encyclopedia of Population*, New York: Macmillan and Free Press: pp. 391-398.

Stoeckel, John, Andrew A. Fisher, Mechai Viravaidya, and Rachita Na Pattalung (1984). *Increasing Family Planning Acceptance through Development Programmes: An Experimental Study in North Eastern Thailand*. Bangkok: The Population Council. Regional Office for South and East-Asia.

Suara Pembaruan (February 5, 1998). *Diusulkan 20 persen dana padat karya untuk kaum wanita*, (Proposed 20 per cent of the labour intensive programme funds for women).

_____ (August 19, 1998). *Pengiriman TKW kian marak*. (Sending of overseas women workers increases).

Tsui, Amy O., Judith N. Wasserheit, and John G. Haaga (1997). *Reproductive Health in Developing Countries. Expanding Dimensions, Building Solutions*, Washington DC: National Academy Press.

UNDP (1997). *Human Development Report 1997*. New York: Oxford University Press.

UNICEF (1996). *The Situation Analysis of Children and Women in Indonesia 1995*, Jakarta: UNICEF.

Warwick, Donald (1986). The Indonesian family planning programme: government influence and client's choice, *Population and Development Review*, 12(3), 453-490.

World Bank (1997). *Indonesia, Sustaining High Growth with Equity*. Report No. 16433-IND.

_____ (July 16, 1998). *Indonesia in Crisis, a Macroeconomic Update*.

Appendix I. Contraceptive prevalence rate, *Pelita* I to the second year of *Pelita* VI

Development period and fiscal year	Number of eligible couples (E) (millions)	Number of current users (U) (millions)	Contraceptive prevalence (U/E %)
Pelita I			
1971-1972	13.0	0.4	2.8
1972-1973	13.8	1.0	7.5
1973-1974	13.5	1.7	12.4
Pelita II			
1974-1975	19.2	2.5	12.8
1975-1976	19.2	3.2	16.7
1976-1977	19.6	3.8	19.4
1977-1978	19.0	4.6	24.1
1978-1979	18.6	5.5	29.7
Pelita III			
1979-1980	21.2	6.5	30.7
1980-1981	21.6	7.8	36.1
1981-1982	22.6	8.8	38.9
1982-1983	23.3	11.2	48
1983-1984	24.5	14.4	58.8
Pelita IV			
1984-1985	25.1	15.7	62.6
1985-1986	25.6	15.3	59.8
1986-1987	26.2	16.7	63.7
1987-1988	26.8	18.3	68.4
1988-1989	27.3	18.5	67.7
Pelita V			
1989-1990	30.9	18.5	59.9
1990-1991	31.7	18.8	59.3
1991-1992	32.3	20.3	62.6
1992-1993	32.9	21.4	64.9
1993-1994	33.4	21.9	65.7
Pelita VI			
1994-1995	34.3	22.8	66.6
1995-1996	34.8	24.2	69.6

Source: *Basic Information: Family Planning Movement and Prosperous Family Development*, 1997, p. 185.

III. WOMEN IN DEVELOPMENT IN MALAYSIA

Jamilah Ariffin*

Introduction

The aim of this paper is to discuss the position of Malaysian women in the development process and to ascertain their status. Wherever possible, comparison is also made with women in other Asian countries to see if there are any differences in women's status across societies in the region.

The paper begins with an introduction on the Malaysia nation and its general socio-economic characteristics. The ensuing discussion is divided into five main sections covering women's status and position in different aspects of life. The approach undertaken is to compare the position of women vis-à-vis men and to determine whether women's position has been improving or deteriorating over the years. Wherever possible, the main intervening gender issues which affect women's quest towards gender equality are also highlighted. The five main areas discussed are as follows:

1. Demographic profile including family formation, fertility, family planning and mortality.

2. Educational attainment.

3. Labour force participation.

4. Migration.

5. Economic and cultural issues.

A. Socio-economic background

Malaysia is a land of opportunities with abundant natural resources. Labour is cost-effective and industrial land is ample. Basic infrastructure in Malaysia is well developed, and its currency has been strong

until recently. All these assets have been utilized by the government to the nation's advantage and the country has shown a steady rate of economic growth (more than 7 per cent for the last five years until 1998). Now, together with many Asian countries, Malaysia is facing a sudden economic downturn. Thus far, the government has invested effectively in health and education, which has made Malaysia one of the leading nations in the ASEAN region in terms of its socio-economic development.

Located in the tropics, Malaysia straddles the South-China Sea and measures 329,758 square kilometres. It is comprised of three major territories, namely Peninsular Malaysia, Sabah and Sarawak. Peninsular Malaysia is at the tip of South-East Asia while the states of Sabah and Sarawak are on the island of Borneo. Malaysia was formerly under British colonial rule from 1876 to 1957. Today, it is a rapidly developing independent nation, governed as a parliamentary democracy with a constitutional monarchy. Current estimates indicate that the Malaysian population increased at an average annual rate of 2.7 per cent during the period 1991-1995, and reached 20.69 million in 1995. The total population comprises the indigenous people (i.e. the Malays, Ibans, Kadazans, Orang Asli etc.) who form about 61.7 per cent of the total and those of migrant origins, being mainly Chinese (27.3 per cent) and the Indians (7.7 per cent), who first came to Malaysia as labourers, artisans and businessmen during the British colonial period. The Malay language is the national language but English is widely spoken. Islam is the State religion but there is complete freedom of worship.

Until the recent economic crisis, Malaysia's per capita income was steadily rising. The mean monthly gross household income increased from RM 1,167 in 1990 to

---

* Senior Research Fellow, Institute Sultan Iskandar, University of Technology, Malaysia, Johor.

RM 2,007 in 1995 with an average growth of 9.5 per cent per year. The inflation rate is less than 5 per cent and has been at this level for the past seven years. The foreign exchange rate of the Malaysian currency, Ringgit Malaysia (RM) in the international market in 1997 was RM 2.30 for one US Dollar and RM 3.6 to one pound sterling but now, in 1998 due to the sudden economic downturn, it is about RM 4.20 for one US dollar and RM 7.00 to one pound sterling (as of July 1998).

B. Basic demographic features

This section draws heavily from Peng (1993) and analyses recent demographic trends and the health status of Malaysian women in comparison with their male counterparts. The data obtained from population censuses provide information on the size of the population, classified by gender (sex ratio), age, and ethnic groups. Statistics on births, deaths and life expectancy are obtained from the annual vital statistics reports. The information on fertility level, morbidity, contraceptive use and health status is derived from data collected in household surveys, Health Management Information System (HMIS), official documents and other published reports.

1. Age, sex and ethnic distribution of the population

During the period 1991-1995, the Malaysian population increased at an average annual rate of 2.7 per cent to reach 20.69 million in 1995. In 1990, the female population size was 8.9 million and it increased to 10 million in 1995, indicating a growth rate of 2.4 per cent per year. At present, women account for about one half of the Malaysian population.

According to the 1980 population census of Peninsular Malaysia, the Malays and the indigenous people constituted 55.3 per cent of the total population, the Chinese 33.8 per cent, the Indians 10.2 per cent and others 0.7 per cent.

According to the 1991 population census of Malaysia as a whole, the Malays and the indigenous people constituted 61.7 per cent of the total population, the Chinese 27.3 per cent, the Indians 7.7 per cent and the rest were "others". While it is generally known that there has been a substantial influx of immigrants in recent years (many of them illegal), the actual magnitude of migrant population cannot be determined with any precision. Unpublished reports state that it was over 5 million in 1995.

As a consequence of the declining fertility and mortality rates, the median age for the female and male population has risen from 18.2 and 18.4 years, respectively, in 1970, to 22.4 years and 20.3 years, respectively, in 1990. The proportionate share of the youngest age group in the population has declined over time, with a corresponding increase in the working age population. In terms of absolute numbers, there are about 5.8 million women in the working group indicating a potential pool of women's labour supply. It is estimated that if female labour force participation could be raised to be equivalent to that of the males (85.3 per cent in 1990), women would contribute an additional 2.2 million workers to the Malaysian labour force.

The issue of an ageing population is not yet a serious matter in Malaysia when compared to countries like Singapore or Japan. However, the absolute number in the elderly age group (65 and above) is projected to increase rapidly from about 660,000 in 1990 to more than a million by the turn of the century, and by a further one million by 2020. Currently, there are about 0.4 million women aged 65 years and over, and more than 80 per cent of these women are either widowed or divorced.

Overall, it is estimated that there are 102 males per 100 females in the country. The proportion of males is higher than females in the youngest age group, and less in the oldest age group.

2. Fertility, nuptiality and family planning

The level of fertility in Malaysia has declined gradually. Overall, the crude birth rate (CBR) has declined from 36.1 per thousand population in 1957 to 28.2 per thousand in 1993. The three main ethnic groups, however, show different rates of fertility change. The CBR for the Chinese declined rather rapidly from 29.8 in 1970 to 19.5 in 1990, as compared with the Indians from 29.6 in 1970 to 23.4 in 1990. On the other hand, the Malay fertility fell much more gradually, and even showed an increase between 1980 and 1985, before resuming it's downward trend. Malay women tend to have the largest family size, followed by the Indians and the Chinese. Based on the estimates of fertility in 1990, a Malay woman, on average, would produce about 4.1 children in her lifetime, as compared with 2.3 for a Chinese and 2.6 for an Indian woman.

The average number of children born to a woman at the completion of childbearing age fell from 6.7 in 1957 to 3.3 in 1993 for the country as a whole, indicating a decline by half in the total fertility rate (TFR). Fertility decline has taken place in both urban and rural areas. However, the 1988 Malaysian Family Life Survey (MFLS) indicates that rural women have, on average, a larger family size than their urban counterparts. Women's education is by far the most important determinant of fertility, as shown by the sharp differentials in the number of children ever born to women of different education levels. Women with more than 12 years of schooling have, on average, 1.8 children ever born as compared with 4.9 for those with no schooling. As primary education is becoming universal in Malaysia and more women are pursuing higher education, family size can be expected to drop further, thereby reaffirming the established pattern in the developed Western countries.

Owing to the declining trends in fertility, the proportions of women with a large family size has declined substantially over the years.

For example, between 1974 and 1988, the proportion of women with 7 or more children declined from 22.3 per cent to 8.3 per cent. During the same period, the proportion with 1-3 children increased from 40.2 per cent to 52.7 per cent, indicating larger proportions of women resorting to having small number of children.

Taking cognizance of the recent demographic trends, the Malaysian Government promulgated a population policy in 1980, seeking to slow down the rate of fertility decline in order to achieve a larger population of 70 million by the year 2100. In line with this policy, some pro-natalist measures, such as increased maternity benefits and child allowance from income tax deductions were introduced so as to encourage couples to have at least five children. However, the effects of all these policy measures on individual fertility behaviour have not yet been ascertained and studied in detail.

3. Marriage and contraceptive use

(a) Marriage and fertility

The present trend of fertility decline is largely the result of rapid socio-economic development in the country, with its positive effects on age at marriage and use of contraception. The data from population censuses and household surveys show that the overall singulate mean age at marriage (SMAM) of Malaysian women increased from 22.3 years in 1970 to 25.3 in 1991. Among the three ethnic groups, the singulate mean age at marriage is the highest among the Chinese (about 26 years), and the Indians (26 years), followed by Malays (24 years). The SMAM for women in other parts of Malaysia, i.e., Sabah and Sarawak, is about 1-2 years lower than for their counterparts in Peninsular Malaysia.

The census data also show that the proportion of women who remained unmarried has also increased. For example, in 1970, of those aged between 30-34 years, about 5.6 per cent had never been married. This proportion increased to 11.4 per cent in 1988 and to 12 per cent in 1991. The highest proportion was among the Chinese women (14.6 per cent), followed by the Indians (11.8 per cent) and then the Malays (9.1 per cent). It is observed that women with high levels of education are more likely to remain unmarried as compared with those with little or no schooling.

Due to cultural dictates, women in Malaysia tend to marry men who are older than themselves. The 1988 Malaysian Family Life Survey (MFLS) showed that 47 per cent of the respondents had married men at least five years older than themselves. As the data show, Malay women are on average about 5.9 years younger than their husbands. The corresponding figures for the Chinese and Indian women were 3.8 years and 5.0 years, respectively.

(b)   Contraceptive use

Since the inception of the family planning programme in 1966, contraceptive use has shown a rising trend. For example, it increased from about 9 per cent in 1966 to 16 per cent in 1970, to 36 per cent in 1974 and then up to nearly 50 per cent between 1984 and 1988. However, contraceptive use varies widely by ethnic groups. It is estimated to be 36 per cent among the Malays as compared with more than 60 per cent among the Chinese and the Indians. It has been found that contraceptive use is strongly and positively related with the level of women's education and with urbanization.

Data from the MFLS indicate that in 1988, about 65 per cent of current users were using a modern method and the remaining 35 per cent were using a traditional method. The pill is by far the most widely used method (30.3 per cent), followed by sterilization (14 per cent), condoms (11.5 per cent) and then the IUD (7.2 per cent). It is interesting to note that tubal ligation accounts for almost all of contraceptive sterilization and male sterilization is the least chosen method among couples. These data

further indicate that 14.4 per cent of all current users were employing the rhythm method, and 8.8 per cent the withdrawal method, while herbs (*akar kayu, majun* and *jamu*) were used by 7.8 per cent of all current users.

Among the currently married non-pregnant women in the reproductive age group, the proportion who had been sterilized ranged from a low of 2 per cent among Malay women to a higher level of 13 per cent among Chinese and 23 per cent among Indian women. Regarding use of the pills, the findings showed that use was higher among Malay women (23 per cent) than the Chinese (10 per cent) and the Indian women (7 per cent). The use of herbs was more common among the Malays than the non-Malays.

The majority of women were using contraceptive methods for purpose of spacing rather than for limiting births, as more than 85 per cent of the family planning acceptors had indicated a desire to have additional children.

The 1988 MFLS also showed that about 41 per cent of all currently married women had expressed an unmet need for modern contraception, with 19.4 per cent having unmet need for terminating child-bearing and 21.2 per cent for birth spacing. The extent of these unmet needs were highest among Malay women (45.6 per cent), followed by the Indian (37.8 per cent) and the Chinese women (29.5 per cent).

4. Mortality trends and differentials

The crude death rate has declined for both males and females in all ethnic groups. However, the death rate among the female population has remained consistently lower than that of the male population. The estimates show that mortality decline has been mainly for the young and old age groups.

(a)   Maternal mortality rates

The maternal mortality rate in Peninsular Malaysia has also declined from 0.7 per thousand live births in 1970 to 0.2 in 1994. The decline in maternal mortality has occurred in all ethnic groups, indicating a reduction of at least 66 per cent during the twenty-year period.

(b)   Life expectancy

Life expectancy is a good indicator of the level of mortality and health status in a country. Estimates from various sources have indicated a significant improvement in life expectancy over time. Data obtained from Vital Statistics show that between 1957 and 1995, life expectancy at birth of males increased from 55.8 years to 69.3 years, a gain of 13.5 years, while female life expectancy at birth increased from 58.2 years to 74 years, indicating a gain of 15.8 years over the same period. In each ethnic group in Peninsular Malaysia, women live longer than men, with a difference of 3.4 years for the Malays, 5.5 years for the Chinese and 4.9 years for the Indians. Peng (1993) noted that while Indian women's life expectancy was lower than that of their male counterparts in 1957, their gain has been more substantial and in 1970 they showed a higher average life expectancy than the Indian males.

C. Educational attainment

It is universally agreed that the attainment of formal education is a vehicle for upward social mobility and for getting better employment opportunities than those without any educational qualifications. It is also well established that education is a strong measure for uplifting the status of women. Various demographic studies have confirmed that the more highly educated the women the lower will be their fertility. Higher educational attainment provides the basis for getting highly paid jobs and better means of living. With greater economic independence, women are more likely to make their reproductive decisions or choose to marry or remain single.

Women's entry into the formal schooling system started in the 1930s with the implementation of British colonial rule in Peninsular Malaysia. However, due to an elitist approach towards the distribution of schools and the culturally influenced attitudes against education for women, schooling became the privilege of those women who mostly came from urban and economically well-off families. Women from low-status economic groups such as the poor Indian estate and Malay peasant families remained disadvantaged and deprived of educational attainment.

In the traditional social structure of Malaysia, there were separate and more schools for boys than girls. This formed the basis for female population to be left behind in education relative to males in later years.

By the end of the Second World War Period (1942 onwards), the negative attitudes towards women's participation in education started losing ground. As such, the percentage of girls in primary and secondary school increased notably and have continued to grow.

After political independence in 1957, formal education in schools was made more accessible to all individuals irrespective of sex or ethnic group. The Malay Muslim community, which had been against formal schooling for their daughters, were now convinced of the importance of education for all and keeping up with other ethnic groups. As such, they encouraged their women to be educated and to gain formal employment. All these factors led to an enormous leap in women's educational participation rates in the 1960s.

However, women's participation at the tertiary level still remained very low. For instance, when the first university was established in 1959, women's enrolment was only 19.8 per cent of the total, but this rose to 28.7 per cent by the end of the 1960s. Female enrolment continued to increase, especially in primary and secondary education. In 1979, females constituted 48.7 per cent of the total enrolment in primary and secondary schools. In 1986, females formed 49.2 per cent of total enrolment and in 1988 it increased to 51.2 per cent, hence confirming that females had attained an equal position with males at least in the secondary school general education.

It must be pointed out that since the 1970s, the Malaysian government has encouraged bright and prominent Malaysian students to go abroad for their university education in order to compensate for the past neglect. There was no discrimination against women in the granting of government scholarships. Many Malaysian women were sent abroad to study, but male students were still larger in number. Children from rich and well-off families were also sent by their parents to study abroad for attaining higher education and skills. However, there are no sex-segregated data on their specialized fields of study at university level.

During the 1980s, there was a marked increase in female enrolment in local universities. In 1983, female enrolment was 38.8 per cent of the total in the six universities. In 1986, when another new university was also established, female enrolment rose to 40.8 per cent and then to 41.2 per cent of the total in 1987.

Despite these impressive statistics, it must be noted that the bulk of women's participation was still confined to the Arts and General Education streams. In particular, there were still very few women in the engineering, science and medicine fields when compared with male students. It is, however, noteworthy that female students tend to top the list in examination results in many faculties proving that qualitatively and selectively, female students can be better if not equal to their male counterparts.

D. Labour force participation

1. Patterns and trends of women's labour force participation

Malaysian women have progressed a good deal since the country achieved political independence in 1957. There are three main factors which have contributed to the advancement in their economic status. The first is the rapid expansion of educational facilities, and the equal access of males and females to all levels of formal education. As a result of modernization and greater opportunities to acquire higher educational qualifications, women have developed positive attitudes towards having full-time careers. The second is the rapid pace of economic development and industrialization in Malaysia since the 1970s. This process has created many new employment opportunities for women in the urban areas, especially in the service sector and the labour-intensive industries. The third is the implementation of the New Economic Policy in 1970, which encouraged the participation of the rural Malays in the modern and formal sector including the government service. Due to this policy, there has been transition from unpaid rural economic activities to wage employment in the urban-industrial sector particularly among Malay women.

This section examines trends in the labour market of Peninsular Malaysia in terms of changes in the occupational distribution and employment status by gender. These trends are examined in three main scenarios:

(a) Structural changes in the Malaysian economy since 1970.

(b) Labour force participation patterns, 1970-1995.

(c) Employment structure of the economically active population.

(a)   Economic growth and structural changes

Malaysia has achieved rapid economic growth during the last three decades accompanied by substantial structural changes in production and employment patterns. During the 1960s and 1970s, agriculture was the leading sector contributing to the economy. This was reflected by its contribution to Gross Domestic Product (GDP) averaging 33.7 per cent in the 1960s, and 27.8 per cent in the 1970s.

Moreover, until the late 1970s, 50.5 per cent of the total labour force was engaged in agricultural activities. When the country embarked on its export-oriented industrialization programme in the 1970s, the employment pattern began to change gradually. The Malaysian Government took various measures to develop the manufacturing sector, and provided several incentives such as tax-free holidays for industrial enterprises located in "free-trade zones". It also embarked on a strong industry promotion drive overseas to attract foreign investment for the establishment of industrial factories in Malaysia.

The implementation of strategies for industrialization led to the rapid growth of the manufacturing sector. As a result, the manufacturing industries' contribution to GDP increased from 21.2 per cent in 1981 to 29.8 per cent in 1988. It also resulted in the rapid growth of employment in the industrial sector. While the percentage of employed persons in the agricultural sector declined from 42 per cent in 1975 to 22 per cent in 1990, the manufacturing sector, on the other hand, experienced an increase from 15 per cent in 1975 to around 17 per cent in 1985 and 22 per cent in 1990.

The declining level of employment in the agricultural sector was intensified by the heavy out-migration of the younger population (age group of 15-24 years) from agricultural employment to relatively more urbanized occupations which offered better earning prospects and a higher standard of living. Rural-to-urban migration trends were further

accelerated by the rapid growth of urban-based industrial jobs created in the mid-1970s and 1980s. Consequently, an increasing proportion of rural women migrated to urban areas in order to enter wage employment. Many of them found jobs in the growing textile, garment and electronics industries. It is pertinent to point out that the labour market of these industries is gender-segmented since the majority of the jobs offered are for women rather than for men. Hence, women constitute the majority of workers in these industries.

Overall, the Malaysian economy recorded impressive economic growth rates until 1998 and this trend has provided ample employment opportunities for all Malaysians, irrespective of race and gender. As table 1 indicates, there has been a steady increase in employment rates and a decline in unemployment during the period 1980-1995. For example, unemployment rate declined from 6 per cent in 1990 to 4.5 per cent in 1995, and other sources show it to be as low as 3 per cent in 1997. However, with the sudden economic depression in the recent past, it is expected that unemployment rates will rise again.

Before the economic downturn in 1998, there were severe labour shortage in some sectors, particularly in the electronics and textile industries and the construction and the plantation sectors. In order to overcome these problems, the government encouraged the hiring of male migrant labour, mainly from Indonesia and Bangladesh, to fill the jobs in the construction and plantation sectors, and female migrant labour mainly from the Philippines and

Table 1. Population, labour force and employment, Peninsular Malaysia, 1980-1995

Year	1980	1985	1990	1995
Population ('000)	11 426.2	15 864.0	18 010.2	20 262.7
Labour force ('000)	6 558.6	6 030.1	7 046.5	8 114.0
Employment ('000)	6 204.4	5 624.6	6 621.0	7 752.3
Unemployment ('000)	354.2	414.2	425.5	361.7
Unemployment rate (%)	5.4	6.9	6.0	4.5

Sources: Malaysia, *Sixth Malaysia Plan: 1991-1995,* Kuala Lumpur, Government Printers and Fadzim Othman (1997).

Indonesia as domestic helpers. Thai labour was also welcomed in the restaurant industry and as seasonal workers in the padi-growing areas. With the continuation of economic crisis and rising unemployment rates in all sectors, the present policy of the Malaysian government is to repatriate all foreign workers except those needed by some essential sectors. In order to reduce the number of Indonesians migrating to Malaysia, the Malaysian Government is now providing development assistance to the Indonesian Government for the socio-economic reconstruction of the domestic economy.

(b)   Labour force participation, 1970-1995[1]

Within the Malaysian context, the labour force includes all persons in the age-group 15-64 years old who are either employed or actively and inactively unemployed. It excludes persons in the same age group reported as either not in work, without jobs, or not wanting to work. Employed, as used in the Labour Force Survey includes all persons, who at any time during the reference week, did any work for pay, profit or family gain (as an employer, employee, own account worker or unpaid family worker). Persons who did not work during a vacation, labour dispute, or due to social or religious reasons, but who nonetheless had a job, a farm, or an enterprise to return to, are also considered to be employed. Those on temporary layoff with pay, but who would definitely be called back to work are also included in the employed category.

The term "unemployed" includes both actively and inactively unemployed persons. Actively unemployed includes all those persons who do not work during the reference week but are actively looking for work during the reference week. Inactively unemployed includes persons who are not looking for work because they believe no work is available, or if it is available, they are not qualified. It also includes those who would have looked for work if they had not been temporarily ill, or there had not been bad weather conditions, and those waiting on job applications prior to the reference week. Persons who are not included in the labour force are those classified as employed or unemployed as stated above, housewives, students, retired or disabled persons, and those not interested in seeking employment. There are difficulties and problems in determining trends in labour force participation due to differences in the concepts and measures employed by the Statistics Department for ascertaining employment rates for different parts of Malaysia. Limitations are also encountered in terms of the coverage and the representativeness of the sample in various labour force surveys. The discussion will therefore be limited to Peninsular Malaysia only.

Table 2 shows the labour force participation rates by age group and sex for the period 1970 to 1992. As we can see, less than 50 per cent female in each age group are in the workforce, whereas in the case of the males, it is more than 80 per cent. However, a significant increase in female labour force participation rates is noted after 1970. For example, for women in the age groups of 15-64 years, the rate increases from 36.3 per cent in 1970 to 46.6 per cent in 1992, which is sustained until recent times. The most notable increase is in the age group of 20-24 years, where the female participation rate increased from 41.9 in 1970 to 65.0 in 1992.

Table 3 shows the percentages of population in the labour force by sex and educational attainment covering the period 1980-1995. It is evident from the figures that for both males and females, there has been some reduction in the labour force participation rates of those with no formal education and an increase for those with lower secondary education. This is consistent with the finding that as more people are now educated and have better qualifications, their proportion in the labour force has also increased over time. It is

---

[1]   The discussion in this sub-section draws heavily from Yahya (1993).

Table 2. Labour force participation rate by gender and age group, Peninsular Malaysia, 1970-1992
(Percentages)

Age group	1970		1975		1980		1985		1990		1992	
	Male	Female	Male	Female	Male	Female	Male	Female	Male	Female	Male	Female
15 - 19	52.3	33.0	54.3	39.4	47.9	33.5	43.7	28.2	44.1	31.4	39.8	29.5
20 - 24	87.1	41.9	94.0	56.4	91.1	54.0	90.7	58.3	89.1	63.9	88.0	65.0
25 - 29	93.5	38.4	98.1	46.3	92.4	44.6	98.1	49.2	97.3	53.9	97.7	54.5
30 - 34	94.4	39.0	98.9	47.5	98.0	40.5	98.8	47.3	98.4	50.2	98.6	51.2
35 - 39	94.0	40.0	98.8	52.4	98.2	42.7	98.9	48.5	98.8	47.8	98.5	50.3
40 - 44	93.2	40.0	98.7	52.1	97.7	43.8	98.3	50.4	98.5	48.8	98.1	47.6
45 - 49	91.5	40.7	97.2	53.2	96.6	41.4	97.8	48.7	97.2	48.5	97.0	47.7
50 - 54	86.7	36.6	93.2	49.4	92.7	36.5	93.5	40.0	93.3	40.9	91.6	37.5
55 - 59	75.6	29.2	83.3	37.5	77.4	30.8	76.6	32.6	71.3	29.4	74.7	28.9
60 - 64	65.2	23.7	72.0	28.5	68.6	25.0	67.1	23.9	59.9	24.0	60.6	20.9
15 - 64	83.4	36.3	86.0	47.3	86.6	39.3	84.6	44.6	84.4	46.8	83.9	46.6

Source: Yahya Siti Rohani (1993).

Table 3. Labour force participation by gender and educational attainment, Peninsular Malaysia, 1980-1995

Educational attainment	Year and sex											
	1980		1985		1987		1989		1990		*1995	
	Male	Female	Male	Female	Male	Female	Male	Female	Male	Female	Male	Female
No formal education	88.1	44.1	87.7	43.2	85.6	43.7	84.6	41.4	83.3	40.2	81.6	33.8
Primary	95.1	42.4	94.2	41.9	93.3	42.9	92.7	41.6	91.9	42.4	91.2	38.2
Lower secondary	73.7	34.6	76.6	35.8	77.1	37.4	78.3	37.9	79.4	39.4	84.4	40.6
Upper secondary	77.1	55.0	77.3	54.8	80.0	55.3	81.6	54.7	81.4	57.2	77.1	50.4
Form six	67.4	51.3	66.6	50.8	73.7	56.2	73.0	56.2	73.0	56.2	71.5	62.1
College/University	93.0	87.6	91.8	83.4	87.7	79.2	88.0	80.1	88.6	80.4	82.3	69.7

Source: Yahya Siti Rohani (1993).

* Based on unpublished data from the Department of Statistics, Malaysia.

also evident from table 3 that except for college and university education, labour force participation rates for males are much higher than females (almost double) at all levels of education. The figures show that labour force participation for females increases significantly up to 80 per cent or more for highly educated women and becomes comparable to that for men. This implies that most of better educated women compete well with men and participate almost equally in the formal and wage sector of the economy.

(c) Employment structure of the economically active population[2]

As mentioned before, the structural transformation of the economy has resulted in changes in the distribution of the female labour force in different industrial sectors. Table 4 shows that almost 68 per cent of the economically active females were employed in

---

[2]   This sub-section draws heavily from Jamilah Ariffin (1994), Part one: Economic Sectors and Women.

Table 4. Percentage distribution of economically active population by gender and industry, Peninsular Malaysia, 1970-1990

Industry	Percentage distribution							
	1970		1980		1985		1990	
	Male	Female	Male	Female	Male	Female	Male	Female
Agriculture & fishing	49.6	67.9	37.5	49.3	28.6	33.7	28.9	28.2
Mining & quarrying	2.3	0.7	1.4	0.3	1.1	0.2	0.7	0.2
Manufacturing	9.3	8.1	11.8	16.3	13.0	18.9	15.2	24.3
Construction	3.1	0.5	6.4	1.0	10.7	1.2	8.7	0.7
Electricity, gas, water	1.0	0.1	0.2	0.1	0.8	0.5	0.9	0.1
Wholesale, transportation, storage and communication	5.0	0.5	6.9	2.3	9.7	5.2	9.9	5.4
Services	18.1	16.4	22.7	19.5	19.3	21.2	18.8	21.4
Total	**100.0**	**100.0**	**100.0**	**100.0**	**100.0**	**100.0**	**100.0**	**100.0**

Source: Malaysia, *Sixth Malaysia Plan, 1991-1995,* Kuala Lumpur, Government Printers, 1991.

the agricultural sector in 1970, which decreased to 28.2 per cent in 1990. On the other hand, the percentage of women in the manufacturing sector increased from 8 per cent in 1970 to 16 per cent in 1980 and about 24 per cent in 1990. Another distinctive increase in female labour force participation is observed in the service sector, where the percentage increased from 16 per cent in 1970 to 21 per cent in 1990. Males also exhibited a similar shift from agriculture to manufacturing sector, and showed increases in the construction and production workers as well.

Over the last two decades, wage employment in Malaysia has risen and the proportion of unpaid family workers and own account workers has declined. With the process of urbanization and industrialization, more women are now moving into wage employment and there is a visible shift in female labour force participation from the status of unpaid family workers and own account workers to the status of paid workers. However, it may be noted that in 1990, women were about 36 per cent of the total Malaysian work force, and about half of them were still working as unpaid family workers, mostly in rural areas. The percentage of male in the status of employer is always higher than that for females, and females always maintain a higher percentage of those classified as unpaid family workers.

2. Labour force participation in the informal sector

The Statistical Department of Malaysia does not have an operational definition of the informal sector and does not, therefore, collect data specific to that sector. However, the Labour Force Survey reports which give data on employment status[3] are one source of estimating the size of the informal sector, as the categories of own account worker and unpaid family worker reflect the number of workers in the informal sector.

Data obtained from Labour Force Survey report of 1987-1988, show that of the total persons employed, female constituted 35.2 per cent, and males around 64 per cent during the period 1985-1990 (the latest report for 1991-1992 is not available). If the own account workers and the unpaid family workers constitute the total women workforce in the informal sector, then the number of women within the informal sector comes to about

---

[3]   Data compiled from Labour Force Survey Reports, 1985-1986, 1987-1988, 1989-1990.

815,000 or 59 per cent of the total number of females employed in the Malaysian labour force during the period 1985-1990.

If we calculate the distribution of female employed persons by employment status, it is evident that the majority of females are employed as employees, i.e. 61.2 per cent. Women with the status of unpaid family workers are 21.8 per cent, and those categorized as own account worker are 16 per cent. The percentage of women with employer status is only 1 per cent.

As for the distribution of employed persons by occupation/industry, the data show that a significant proportion of these women (62 per cent), were in agriculture, forestry, hunting and fishing in 1985, and the proportion remained at 60 per cent in 1990. The second largest concentration of women within the informal sector is located in wholesale and retail trade, restaurants and hotels, where 23 per cent of women were categorized as either own account worker or unpaid family worker for the years 1986-1990. The smallest proportion of women in informal sector activities is within manufacturing, around 6 per cent. The other industries have averages of 3 per cent or less. It is reiterated that as gender-segregated data were not collected for each industry in detail, the precise rates of female participation in informal sector activities cannot be estimated. Given that the female component of the categories of own account worker and unpaid family worker constitutes 59 per cent of all women in the total labour force, it can reasonably be argued that the majority of workers in these two employment categories are females.

It is thus observed that the number of women in the informal sector is significant and likely to be on the increase with obvious repercussions for their overall employment position and economic status. Women's entry into the informal sector is usually based on limited options available elsewhere due to their limited education and skills. It is also observed that many of them work to supplement family income and to help lift the family out of poverty. Many women, especially those in the urban areas, first enter into formal sector employment, and then shift towards the informal sector activities after marriage. This is because of the incompatibility and conflict of two roles, working role and mothering role.

3. Trends in the shift of labour from the informal sector to the formal sector

Data compiled from the Labour Force Survey reports of 1987-1988 and 1989-1990 indicate that a majority of Malaysians workers in the employee category are in community, social and personal services, (about 29 per cent) and manufacturing (about 23 per cent). The participation of employees in community, social and personal services seems to show a decline over the years, while there is an apparent increase in the manufacturing sector. The most significant decrease is in the agriculture, forestry, hunting and fishing industry. There appears to be a shift from agriculture to manufacturing, thus indirectly showing a shift of labour from the informal sector to the formal sector.

As informal sector enterprises are small-scale with little capital, labour-intensive and with low technology, they are mainly concentrated in the subcontracting and service sectors. This is reflected by the high proportion of own account worker or unpaid family worker in selected occupations. For instance, in the agriculture, forestry, hunting and fishing industry, workers are most likely to be found in manual work of planting, harvesting and simple food processing such as drying fish, cleaning remains of captured animals etc. In the wholesale and retail trade, restaurant and hotel industry, the main informal activities are in food catering and from petty trading to hawking. In 1989, the ratio of hawkers to city/municipal population was estimated to be 1:35. As part of the process of economic expansion in Malaysia, most municipal and city councils were forced to provide more and more sites for petty traders and hawkers besides the usual morning and night markets in order to bring improvements in the health and cleanliness aspects of the mushrooming petty traders and hawkers sectors.

In the manufacturing sector, the informal sub-sector activities are mainly concentrated in subcontracting and the supply of components to the big manufacturers. These activities comprise of backyard unlicensed workshops producing component parts for cars and machinery and also for medium-sized factories in rubber glove manufacturing, who often subcontract their products for final inspection and quality check. In this instance, sub-contractors would collect the finished gloves and distribute them to their workers, who are mainly housewives, to inspect and check the gloves for holes.

E. Migration

Malaysia is primarily a migrant-receiving country when compared with its neighbouring countries such as Bangladesh, Indonesia, the Philippines and Thailand mainly because of its higher economic growth and development that has occurred during the past two decades. During the short period of economic recession in 1985-1986, some Malaysians were forced to go to other countries in search of higher incomes, and they were mostly men. The issue of migration in Malaysia, therefore, mainly pertains to internal migration.

1. Internal migration trends

Two types of internal migration trends are obvious in Malaysia:

(i) Intra-state migration

(ii) Inter-state migration

Intra-state migration refers to persons who have moved within the state (there are altogether 13 states in Malaysia). Inter-state migration is movement from one state to a destination in another state. On the basis of the cross-classification of data on migration by place of residence one year ago and place of residence at the time of the Malaysian-wide census, it is possible to classify the movement into four migration streams:

a) Rural-to-rural[4]

b) Rural-to-urban

c) Urban-to-urban

d) Urban-to-rural

Based on the analysis of census data in a study by Tan (1994), observation were made with regard to migration streams and their gender differentials:

(i) Overall, the general pattern is that men tend to migrate more than women, especially for longer distances.

(ii) Women tend to outnumber men in rural to urban intra-state movements as reflected by lower sex ratios (table 5). This lends support to Ware's (1981) observation that rural women are more likely than men to move to nearby towns. More recent data for 1990 also show that females predominate in intra-state migration streams for short distance, i.e. a ratio of 91 males per 100 females.

(iii) Among women there is greater tendency to move urban-to-urban inter-state than urban-to-urban intra-state. For example, the data for 1989 show that female urban-to-urban inter-state migrants constitute 23.8 per cent of migrants compared with 6.1 per cent of females moving urban-to-urban intra-state.

_____

[4] The definitions of rural and urban are strictly based on population cut-offs as of the 1980 Population Census. Areas with a population of 10,000 and above are designated urban and those below 10,000 population are referred to as rural.

52

Table 5. Sex ratio of migrants by migration type and stream, Peninsular Malaysia: 1982-1989

Type and stream	1982	1986	1989
Intra-state migration			
Rural-to-rural	102	101	106
Rural-to-urban	99	94	89
Urban-to-urban	111	117	94
Urban-to-rural	112	109	100
Inter-state migration			
Rural-to-rural	110	110	99
Rural-to-urban	106	100	89
Urban-to-urban	108	114	105
Urban-to-rural	139	115	113

Source: Tan Swee Heng (1994). Compiled from computer tabulations, Labour Force Migration Survey.

2. Age of internal migrants

The patterns of migration by sex are perhaps less striking than those by age. It is quite clear that young adults (15-34 years old) tend to dominate migration streams. The female migration stream is dominated by young women in the age group 15-34. It may be noted that the main ages for women migrants is the younger ages of 15-24 years while for men migrants it is 25-34 years (table 6).

3. Marital status

The association between marital status and migration is examined with respect to the age selectivity of female migration in Peninsular Malaysia. It should be noted here that the marital status of female migrants was recorded at the time of the survey and not at the time of migration. It is observed from table 7 that, in general male migrants include proportionately more of the never-married category. Among young women in the age group 15-24 years old, the proportion of migrant women in the married category is higher than non-migrant, implying that even for this largest group of female migrants, marriage migration appears to be an important factor. However, when we look at the trends for migrant women who are younger than 35 years of age, we find that between the years 1982 and 1989, the proportion of never-married female migrants has increased from 56.1 per cent to 63.0 in the 15-24 years of age, and from 14.8 per cent to 16.1 per cent for the 25-34 years age group. On the other hand, the proportion of married female migrants has decreased from 43.2 per cent to 36.3 per cent over the same period (table 7). This is indicative of a growing tendency among relatively younger and single women to migrate to other states.

4. Female migration and labour force participation

The overall trend of female migrants and labour force participation as shown in Tan (1994) indicate that never-married women have a higher labour force participation rate than the married or widowed (including the divorced and separated), as well as their non-migrant counterparts. This lends support to hypothesis that the migration of young and single women

Table 6. Proportion of migrants to total population by age group and sex, Peninsular Malaysia: 1982-1989

Age group	Female migrants			Male migrants		
	1982	1986	1989	1982	1986	1989
10-14	4.2	4.9	4.0	4.8	5.0	3.7
15-24	9.8	8.5	7.6	9.8	8.0	6.6
25-34	7.4	8.2	7.6	10.0	9.3	7.7
35-44	3.2	3.3	2.9	4.8	5.5	3.6
45-64	2.3	2.4	1.5	2.7	2.5	1.9
65 and over	2.2	2.4	1.6	1.5	1.5	0.9

Source: Tan Swee Heng (1994). Compiled from computer tabulations, Labour Force Migration Survey, 1989.

Table 7. Percentage distribution of female migrants (FM), non-migrant women (NM) and male migrants (MM) by marital status and age

Age and marital status	1982			1986			1989		
	Female migrants	Non-migrant women	Male migrants	Female migrants	Non-migrant women	Male migrants	Female migrants	Non-migrant women	Male migrants
Total (15-64 years)									
Never-married	35.9	32.5	49.9	32.1	33.0	46.6	37.4	33.0	50.2
Married	59.0	59.2	48.7	62.2	59.4	52.4	57.8	59.8	48.9
Widowed/divorced	5.1	8.3	1.4	5.7	7.6	1.0	4.8	7.2	0.9
15-24 years									
Never-married	56.1	76.3	86.4	57.4	79.1	86.8	63.0	81.2	88.2
Married	43.2	23.2	13.5	41.5	20.4	13.1	36.6	18.5	11.8
Widowed/divorced	0.7	0.5	0.1	1.1	0.5	0.1	0.4	0.3	–
25-34 years									
Never-married	14.8	16.5	23.3	12.8	18.3	24.9	16.1	19.2	29.8
Married	82.5	80.6	76.0	84.4	79.4	74.6	81.9	78.6	69.6
Widowed/divorced	2.7	1.9	0.8	2.8	2.3	0.5	2.0	2.1	0.6
35-44 years									
Never-married	5.1	4.6	6.2	4.9	5.7	4.8	8.0	6.5	8.9
Married	83.8	87.6	92.1	87.0	88.0	93.1	78.4	87.2	89.7
Widowed/divorced	11.1	7.8	1.7	8.1	6.3	2.1	13.6	6.3	1.4
45-64 years									
Never-married	2.6	1.7	3.2	1.7	1.7	0.2	1.7	2.3	5.6
Married	54.1	69.5	84.2	54.1	4.1	92.3	56.2	72.6	87.1
Widowed/divorced	43.3	28.8	12.6	44.2	44.2	5.7	42.0	25.2	6.4

Source: Tan Swee Heng (1994). Compiled from computer tabulations, Labour Force Migration Survey, 1989.

(especially in age group 15-24) is economically motivated. Likewise, the lower participation rates of married migrant women suggest that their migration is a consequence of family migration.

The trends in labour force participation rates of men and women migrant population are shown in table 8. It appears that the labour force participation of female migrants is higher among those with secondary and higher levels of education. However, no significant differentials exist in the labour force participation rates of migrant and non-migrant women, within the same level of education.

Essentially linked to the issue of the labour force participation is the migrants' occupation pattern which is important for obtaining an insight into their adaptation and contribution to the workforce in their respective destinations. Table 9 shows the distribution of female migrants and non-migrants by broad occupational categories.

The occupational data of the female migrants (aged 15-64 years) reveal that female migrants, on the whole, are more likely to be employed in service occupations and in production work. On the other hand, about a third of the non-migrant women are found in occupations related to agriculture. However, it may be noted that in 1989, the proportions of female migrant workers in the so-called white collar occupations including the professional and administrative and managerial and clerical, was about 30 per cent among female migrants compared with about 25 per cent of the

Table 8. Labour force participation rates of female migrants (FM), non-migrant women (NM) and male migrants (MM) by education and age group, Peninsular Malaysia, 1982-1989

Age group	1982			1986			1989		
	Female migrants	Non-migrant women	Male migrants	Female migrants	Non-migrant women	Male migrants	Female migrants	Non-migrant women	Male migrants
Primary level and lower									
15 - 24	45.7	49.9	96.0	45.8	50.5	96.4	44.1	50.7	91.2
25 - 34	34.0	41.9	98.8	33.0	40.0	98.0	38.9	40.4	97.9
35 - 44	42.7	49.3	97.3	34.2	47.8	97.7	45.9	45.5	96.3
45 - 64	29.4	39.4	81.5	23.3	38.3	81.1	34.0	37.4	77.6
Secondary level and higher									
15 - 24	49.1	41.4	77.9	46.3	41.5	77.0	61.1	41.8	80.7
25 - 34	55.1	58.8	98.2	53.1	59.7	98.9	50.9	57.8	97.1
35 - 44	48.8	58.3	97.5	39.2	55.5	98.8	44.4	56.8	99.0
45 - 64	54.2	35.3	85.0	25.2	41.7	82.2	15.8	45.2	81.6

Source: Tan Swee Heng (1994). Compiled from computer tabulations, Labour Force Migration Survey, 1989.

Table 9. Percentage distribution of employed female migrants (FM), non-migrant women (NM) and male migrants (MM) by occupation, Peninsular Malaysia: 1982-1989

Occupation	Year of survey								
	1982			1986			1989		
	Female migrants	Non-migrant women	Male migrants	Female migrants	Non-migrant women	Male migrants	Female migrants	Non-migrant women	Male migrants
Professional	14.4	7.9	10.4	15.7	9.7	10.7	15.1	9.7	12.2
Administrative	0.7	0.5	4.0	1.5	0.8	4.5	0.5	0.7	2.7
Clerical	21.0	12.8	10.9	19.2	14.6	9.4	14.0	15.1	8.0
Sales	6.1	9.2	7.4	7.6	11.3	9.2	7.2	12.0	8.6
Services	20.9	12.9	14.4	23.5	14.4	16.9	18.9	14.3	14.5
Agriculture	16.6	34.9	17.5	14.1	28.1	18.3	9.2	23.1	16.9
Production	20.3	21.8	35.4	18.4	21.1	31.0	35.0	25.2	37.1
Total	**100.0**	**100.0**	**100.0**	**100.0**	**100.0**	**100.0**	**100.0**	**100.0**	**100.0**

Source: Tan Swee Heng (1994). Compiled from computer tabulations, Labour Force Migration Survey, 1989.

non-migrant women. In case of male migrants, the highest proportion is employed in production occupations (37 per cent in 1989).

5. Summing up

Based mainly on the analysis of migration trends and patterns by Tan (1994), the yearly volume of internal migration in Peninsular Malaysia is estimated to involve 5 to 6 per cent of the total population. Migration is generally known to be selective of the males.

However, a declining sex ratio in the rural to urban and urban to urban migration, both within and between the states suggests an increasing trend of females in migratory movement within the country. The peak age of female migration is between 15-24 years.

Although there is evidence that the never married female migrants are more likely to move to urban destinations, their proportion is not significantly different from the non-migrant females within the same category of age and marital status. The data on education show that the younger female migrants have generally higher educational levels, especially those migrating in the age group of 25-34 years.

The majority of female migrants can be separated into two contrasting types. One group comprises relatively younger females (15-24 age group) with less education who have higher labour force participation in service and production-related occupations. The other group comprises older women 25-34 age group who are more educated and have found employment in professional and clerical occupations.

Reflecting on the overall comparison of female migrant and non-migrant women, it can be concluded that the occupational structure is in consonance with the findings on education differences among the migrants. This could imply that migrants are not greatly disadvantaged in the labour force situation at their respective destinations.

F. Economic and cultural issues

This section will discuss the economic and cultural issues of women in the context of two major aspects of Malaysian population. The first is the gender-segmented labour market and the second discusses inheritance laws affecting women.

1. The segmented labour market in Malaysia and related aspects

This section draws heavily from Jamilah Ariffin, Susan Horton and Guilherme Sedlacek's paper (1996). The structure of the Malaysian labour market has changed with the rapid growth of the Malaysian economy. The rise of export industries (often employing young and single women) has been an important component of the growth success. Prior to 1970, the labour market was characterized by extreme segmentation along ethnic lines. As part of New Economic Policy, the government has made rigorous attempts to change the employment structure of the economy. As such, women's employment has changed rapidly along with other changes in the Malaysian economy. There have been dramatic increases in the share of women workers in certain sectors, particularly in manufacturing and clerical occupations. Women's earnings have risen substantially relative to men's. However, child-care and child-rearing remain women's primary responsibility. Due to lack of appropriate day-care arrangements and other benefits, women in urban areas tend to leave the labour force permanently after having children and to leave temporarily in rural areas and return to work once the children are somewhat older. This, combined with the relatively high birth rate in Malaysia, limits women's possibility of pursuing a career or make further advancement in the labour force.

(a) Issues in the gender-segmented labour market

The findings from research conducted by Ariffin, Horton and Sedlacek (1996) show that unmarried women tend to participate more in the labour force than married women, and employment rates for married women increase with income (i.e. those married women who worked tended to have higher educational and social backgrounds). For unmarried women, employment rates are lower for Malay than for Chinese women and this is related to social norms prevalent among the predominantly Muslim Malays. Women have reported high rates of unemployment and underemployment. The unemployment rate for women is twice that of men, and women form three quarters of the passively unemployed labour force (discouraged workers). Malay working women face barriers to employment in certain sectors in urban areas: they are over-represented in clerical, professional and technical, but under-represented in other occupations.

The data cited in Ariffin et al. (1996) show that Malaysian women's participation rates on aggregate, are quite close to those in

Indonesia, the Philippines and the Republic of Korea, between 40 and 45 per cent for the working age population, with a slight upward trend in the 1980s. A further disaggregation of these data reveals some differences by urban/rural location, race and age. The main findings are that female participation rates have been increasing over time in urban areas and decreasing in rural areas. In urban areas, the stereotype is of young, single women working in export industries or sales, relatively dead-end jobs. There is also a smaller group of more educated and married women who combine work with household responsibilities and most of these women are in feminized occupations such as nursing, teaching, and clerical type of work.

There are also differences by race in women's age-participation profiles. Participation by Malay women has a relatively flatter age profile than that for Indian women, and the pattern is steepest for Chinese women. There are quite large differences in participation rates by race at some ages. For example, participation by Malay women in the 18-23 age group is 14 per cent lower than for Chinese women. This reflects traditional views among Malay Muslim groups which have in the past discouraged work among young single women. The situation, however, has changed somewhat over time with increased demand for young single women workers in export industries.

(b)   Differences in wages and earnings by gender

Despite the implementation of the equal pay for equal work policy in the public sector since 1969, wage discrimination against women still persists in the private sector. Differences in wages and earnings by gender continue to exist for certain production occupations, especially in the manufacturing sector and in the plantation estate although there is some indication of narrowing of these differentials. Gender discrimination against women occurs in a more disguised and subtle form in the public

sector, although in principle, there is no discrimination on the basis of sex, either in recruitment or remuneration. In the case of promotions, researchers and women officers have long known that, given a choice, superiors tend to choose men rather than women candidates (Rohana, 1992). However, there is also some positive discrimination towards women in certain situations, such that it is easier for women officers to obtain job transfers to join their husbands within Malaysia, whereas it is very difficult for working husbands to obtain a job transfer to join the family. In the case of following husbands who have gone abroad for further studies, women officers are not accorded any privilege and often have to take leave from their job without pay, and therefore lose out in terms of seniority, or have to resign from their jobs.

There are limited published data on earnings and wage rates in Malaysia, and usually no distinction is made between male and female earnings. However, in the public sector, because of the equal pay policy, there are no wage differentials in terms of gender. In the private sector, some differences exist in wages between men and women, but it is difficult to estimate its quantum as the data collected have been rather limited in scope.

(c)   The effect of socio-cultural institutions on women's labour force participation

The findings from studies conducted by Ariffin and others (1996), further indicate that Malaysian women workers do not quit work upon marriage, but many do because of motherhood as child-care facilities at the work place are lacking, and support of the extended family has been diminishing. Women in dead-end jobs are most likely to discontinue work, whereas those jobs that are perceived to offer a good chance for occupational mobility, women are more likely to continue working.

The labour market conditions which affect the bargaining power of married women workers and the type of technology utilized are important in determining women's continuation of work. For example, in the mid-1980s, when the technology in electronics factories was very labour-intensive and strenuous, most factory managers in the manufacturing sector were of the opinion that the productivity level of women production operators declined rapidly when they had young children. Industrial companies preferred to employ single women so as to avoid additional costs of maternity leave and maternity benefits.

In the early 1990s, with rapid economic growth and labour shortages, particularly in electronics, the situation has reversed. Employers currently cannot afford to lose their women workers, and now provide them with wage incentives as a motivation to stay in work despite marriage and motherhood. With the difficulties of child-care responsibilities and attending work at the same time, it is more likely that women would stay home for a short time after the birth of a child, and then go back to informal sector activities where they have flexible work-hours to adjust to their dual-role responsibilities.

There are, however, other institutional factors which effect women's labour market participation. In this context the role of protective legislation, minimum wage laws, equal-wage and equal opportunity legislation are discussed. It is useful to note at the outset that the Federal Constitution of Malaysia makes no reference to sex or gender. Thus, it is difficult to obtain redress for discrimination against women from the courts. Nor do the labour laws in Malaysia contain clauses with reference to gender or sex, and the implementation of these laws applies equally to both sexes. However, there are some provisions in the labour laws which apply exclusively to women workers, usually with the intent of protecting women workers. The Employment Act of 1955 (revised in 1981) is the law which regulates all labour relations, such as contracts of service, wages, rest days, hours of work, holidays, termination,

layoffs and retirement. Maternity leave is available. Both the government and private sectors provide 60 days' leave.

One omission in the labour laws is that there has been no legal recognition of the principle of 'equal pay for equal work'. In the public sector, the principle is by no means new, and has been implemented for at least three decades. Although the private sector accepts the concept in principle, in practice there are many instances in which women workers are subject to wage discrimination, for which there is no legal recourse. Nor has there been any equal opportunity legislation. And because of the overriding importance of redressing inequalities by ethnic background, the Malaysian Government was until 1996 reluctant to endorse formally the ratification of the 1988 Convention on Elimination of Discrimination Against Women (CEDAW).

Another segregating force in the labour market is that there is no prohibition on gender-specific job advertisements. In fact, job advertisements for female factory workers who are young, single and educated abound in local newspapers and on public posters.

To conclude, there have been enormous changes in Malaysian labour market institutions in the last twenty years in three important ways. First, labour laws that aimed at protecting women workers have been amended to adapt to the new industrial situation where the majority of factory labour is female. The type of industries promoted by export-oriented industrialization since the 1970s (in particular electronics, semi-conductors and the garment industry) mostly depend on women's labour.

Second, because of urbanization and the increased cost of living, many urban families in Malaysia depend on two incomes. Most husbands do not object to their wives working outside the home and bringing in a much-needed supplement to household income. Women's increased education, delayed marriage, reduced fertility, and the influence of

Westernization have also contributed to increased women's participation in paid employment. However, child-care arrangements have not yet developed to adapt to this situation.

Third, due to the rapid expansion of the Malaysian economy, acute labour shortages in manufacturing were experienced until recently. However, the lack of suitable child-care facilities, the reluctance of employers to adapt to the changing needs of women workers, and some cultural constraints have contributed to the under utilization of female labour force.

Given pronatalist policies and a relatively high birth rate in Malaysia in relation to its level of per capita income, this situation may in future hinder further increases in women's participation and advancement into more permanent careers, as well as limit further advance in women's relative earnings.

From the above discussion, it appears that the full potential of Malaysian women can be developed further. Prior to the recent economic downturn, the bargaining power of women workers was high due to the tight labour market situation and high demand for women workers, which could have been utilized to their advantage. Despite this, however, women still lag behind their male counterparts in terms of authority, and equality of pay. The present gender realities prevent women with high abilities and strong motivation from developing their full potential. They are not given the opportunity to hold powerful administrative and leadership positions in their work place and participate in the public decision making process.

The position of women factory workers in terms of gender issues is even worse. Even though the government has declared that all government departments should establish crèches, no substantial progress, has been achieved. The introduction of flexibility in working time was also agreed to by the government in principle, but is not yet widely practised. As a starting point, steps could be taken to individualize the working career by permitting employees to take leave for facilitating child-bearing and child-care responsibilities. A second step includes the option for early or gradual (phased) retirement. This latter point has already been implemented in the public sector in Malaysia.

2. Inheritance laws

Inheritance laws apply differently to Muslims and non-Muslims and have their effects on the status and position of women in the family. The Distribution Act applies to intestate succession among non-Muslims. It states that when a man dies, his property will be divided such that his wife will get one-third and the children will receive the remaining two-thirds. If the couple has no children, the wife will receive half, and remaining half will be for his parents, or brothers and sisters if the parents are not living. When the woman dies intestate, all her property will go to her husband whether or not the couple has children.

For Muslims, the rule is that women would get half the share of what men are entitled to. The justification for this lies in the menfolks' responsibility to support all members of their family.

Children of single non-married women, whether Muslim or non-Muslim, are not entitled to inherit from their biological father. An illegitimate Muslim child may inherit from his mother, whereas non-Muslim child may inherit from his mother's estate only if the mother has no other legitimate children. A non-Muslim child who is adopted under the Adoption Act may inherit from his adopted father. On the other hand, Muslim adopted child has no rights of inheritance from the adoptive family unless provision is made by will.

The practice of inheritance laws as provided in the dictates of religion is also rooted in the socio-cultural system and attitudes of individuals, and has its own repercussions on women's position in Malaysian society.

G. Conclusion

This paper has attempted to trace the path of Malaysian women's participation in the development process and to ascertain their status as a consequence of their participation.

It is clear from the discussion on educational attainment, labour force participation, and migration patterns as well as gender-related issues in terms of economic and cultural matters that the position of the present generation Malaysian women is better than in their mothers' generation. Owing to greater educational attainment and involvement in paid employment, women now have wider opportunities and career choices as well as greater freedom and mobility in terms of social economic and political participation.

With the rapid process of economic development since political independence in 1975, and the successful implementation of several development programmes, both Malaysian men and women have benefited. The question that who has benefited more brings forth the pertinent issue of gender equality and equity. Some relevant and related points in this context are outlined below.

Firstly, Malaysian development plans and programmes are gender neutral. If Malaysian women have benefited from them, it is not purposeful but merely incidental.

Secondly, due to religious and cultural dictates which have retained their strong influence on men's and women's views, the concept of gender equality is not fully acceptable to all sections of Malaysian society. It is only acceptable to feminists, a small group of educated and professional elite men and women. The majority of Malaysians are sceptical and prejudiced about the concept of gender equality. Some are fearful that it will cause a serious upheaval of long-standing revered Asian values. As such, even when women are highly educated and hold full-time jobs (a process engineered by sound economic-driven development policies of the government), the issue of dual-role burden of working mothers is still unresolved. The most popular step taken by the government to lighten this burden is to shift the household duties arena to domestic maids, as reflected by the policies encouraging the in-migration of female foreign workers. To resolve the situation of tight labour market, male migrant labour are also brought in to take over the dirty, dangerous and demanding jobs. The issue of gender equality within Malaysian context, therefore, is never confronted squarely or debated seriously.

Thirdly, because of the sudden economic downturn in 1998, Malaysia is now facing gloomy economic prospects and an uncertain future. This situation would have severe setbacks for the attainment of gender equality. It is only in times of prosperity that the government can be persuaded to listen to feminists lobbying for enhancing gender-based programmes to improve the position of women vis-à-vis men. In times of economic depression, the attention of government is focussed on specific survival issues, with no priority given to gender issues. Hence, feminists would need greater perseverance and efforts to convince government planners that it is precisely in times of economic downturn that poor women, particularly those from single female-headed households need all the social safety-net support available.

REFERENCES

ASEAN (1996). *The Advancement of Women in ASEAN: A Regional Report*. Jakarta: Secretariat Publications.

Fadzim Othman (1997). Women in the agriculture sector in Johor. Report submitted to the State Government of Johor. Unpublished.

Idris Nor Aini, Madeline Berma and Faridah Shahadan (1996). *Wanita Malaysia Dalam Era Pembangunan Industri*. Kuala Lumpur: Universiti Kebangsaan Malaysia Press.

Jamilah Ariffin (1992). *Women and Development in Malaysia*. Kuala Lumpur: Pelanduk Publications.

_____ (1993). *Reviewing the implementation of the Nairobi Forward-Looking Strategies for the Advancement of Women in Malaysia: Malaysia's country paper for the forthcoming World Women's Conference, 1995 in Beijing, China*. Unpublished.

_____ (1994). *Reviewing Malaysian Women's Status: Country Report in Preparation for the Fourth United Nations World Conference on Women*. Population Studies Unit Publication, University of Malaya, Kuala Lumpur.

_____ Susan Horton and Guilherme Sedlacek (1996). Women in the labour Market in Malaysia. In *Women and Industrialization in Asia*, Susan Horton, ed. Routledge: London and New York.

Malaysia (1981). *Fourth Malaysia Plan 1981-1985*, Kuala Lumpur: Government Printers.

_____ (1986). *Fifth Malaysia Plan 1986-1990*, Kuala Lumpur: Government Printers.

_____ (1991). *Sixth Malaysia Plan 1991-1995*, Kuala Lumpur: Government Printers.

_____ (1996). *Seventh Malaysia Plan 1996-2000*, Kuala Lumpur: Government Printers.

Malaysia Department of Statistics (1980). *Population and Housing Census Malaysia*, Kuala Lumpur: Government Printers.

_____ (1988). *Internal Migration in Peninsular Malaysia, 1986*, Kuala Lumpur: Department of Statistics.

_____ (1991). *General Report of the Population Census, Volume I*, Kuala Lumpur: Government Printers.

_____ (1992). *The Labour Force Survey Report: Malaysia, 1992-1993*. Kuala Lumpur: Government Printers.

Mansor, Norma (1990). The Development Process and Women's Participation in The Public Sector. Paper presented at the Colloquium on Women and Development: Implications for Planning and Population Dynamics. Population Studies Unit Publication, University of Malaya, Kuala Lumpur.

_____ and Nik Rosnah (1993). The development process and women participation in the government revisited. Paper submitted to HAWA under the Women and Development project. Unpublished.

Rohana Jani (1992). *Tanggapan kakitangan awam terhadap penglibatan kaum wanita dalam sektor awam*. Lapuran yang diserahkan kepada Unit Pengajian Kependudukan, Universiti Malaya. Unpublished.

Sim Ong Fon (1993). Women in business. Paper submitted to HAWA, under the Women and Development Project. Unpublished.

_____ (1997). Women and industrialization in Johor: A gender perspective and trend study. Report submitted to the State Government of Johor. Unpublished.

Tan Swee Heng (1994). Female migration in the context of national migration trends and patterns, Peninsular Malaysia 1981-1990. In *Readings on Women and Development*, Jamilah Ariffin, ed. Population Studies Unit Publication, University of Malaya, Kuala Lumpur.

Tey Nai Peng (1993). Demographic and health situation of Malaysian women in relation to men. Paper submitted to HAWA under the Women and Development Project. Unpublished.

_____ (1994). Demographic and health status in Johor – A gender perspective.

Report submitted to the State Government of Johor. Unpublished.

Ware, H. (1981). *Women, Demography and Development*. Canberra: The Australia National University Press.

Yahya Siti Rohani (1993). The development process and women's labour force participation – a macro level analysis of patterns and trends 1957-1990. In *Readings on Women and Development*, Jamilah Ariffin, ed. Population Studies Unit Publication, University of Malaya, Kuala Lumpur.

_____ (1994). Economic sectors and women: labour market. In *Reviewing Malaysian Women's Status: Country Report in Preparation for the Fourth United Nations World Conference on Women*, Jamilah Ariffin, ed. Population Studies Unit Publication, University of Malaya, Kuala Lumpur.

IV. WOMEN IN DEVELOPMENT: CURRENT SITUATION AND EMERGING POLICY CONCERNS IN THE PHILIPPINES

Aurora E. Perez*

Introduction

Any discussion on women and development necessarily impinges on women's productive and reproductive roles and how those affect their choices and behaviour in the demographic as well as in the social and economic realm. Generally speaking, a society is regulated by normative pressures that influence women's life options and their decisions to fulfill their expected roles. Understanding the prevailing gender relations system that defines roles of both women and men is important for sensitizing development planners towards gender-responsive development plans and goals. Gender sensitive development planning is considered to be instrumental in transforming women into active and equal partners of national development.

There is no debate that if economic growth is aimed at promoting social equity and effective participation of the population in the political and economic mainstream, women must be integrated in development activities. The major issue of concern is how to get women actively participating in development activities based on principles of gender equity and equality. Despite a development-oriented policy and planning process in the Philippines which promotes participation of women in all development activities, the role of women is generally emphasized more in terms of biological reproduction than in economic productive activities. This is reflected in most economic indicators which do not account for women's contribution to production. This problem is often attributed to data inadequacy and measurement problems in the informal sector of the economy where most women workers are involved.

The purpose of this paper is to present the circumstances of contemporary Filipino women in pursuing both their reproductive and productive roles. The size of the female population is estimated at 34 million in 1995, comprising close to one-half (49.6 per cent) of the country's human resources. The first part of this paper provides a descriptive analysis of a mix of survey and census data on four major spheres that shape the conditions for women's active participation in development and determine women's share in the benefits derived from development. In this regard, the modern Filipino women's situation is described in four fields for which recent indicators are available: demography, reproductive health, economic activity, and public life. The influence of education, as an indicator of women's social position, on fertility, reproductive health, economic activity, and public life is also examined using available data for the most recent time period. The second part of the paper discusses existing legislation that bears on the connection between women and development. More specifically, discussion is related to policies addressing issues of women empowerment and gender equity and how those affect women's roles in overall socio-economic development. On the whole, the paper should be treated as a first step in moving from the level of principles to a level of examination of evidence, which can provide policy directions in the midst of recently emerging views on women, population, and development.

---

* Director, University of the Philippines Population Institute, Quezon City.

A. Women's social position in society

Social heterogeneity is associated with widely varying patterns of social behaviour of women regarding age at marriage, childbearing, living arrangements, and labour force participation, among others. These behaviours define and reflect many aspects of women's lives, in particular their social position in society. [In the past, Filipino women have been portrayed as objects of change rather than agents of change, as often coping rather than initiating and as bystanders rather than participants. Today, however, with the objective of achieving gender equality and equality, the issue of integrating women into development is clear. It has now become indispensable to mainstream women into male-dominated scenes in public life or politics and industrial employment.]

The major problem is the relative lack of change in the situation of women, usually disadvantageous and discriminatory, because of their relatively inferior social position in the family, community, and the society at large. However, efforts to end the historical denial of equity to women are thought to be made easier by access to education that is open to both men and women without any cultural restrictions or impediments. But data on educational attainment and employment indicate unjust economic relations that affect women's reproductive role and health needs in ways which bear upon their ability to gain control over decisions significantly affecting their lives. Overcoming prejudices is, therefore, necessary for providing opportunities to women and transforming them into agents, not mere objects of development and social change. Despite some improvements made in closing the gender gap in socio-economic development indicators, it is observed that conditions of poverty in Philippines limit a substantial number of women's ability to contribute to and take full advantage of the benefits of social and economic development.

1. Filipino women's education

Of all social development investments that improve women's position in society, education appears the most powerful and instrumental factor in altering their situation of disadvantage. Education influences women's aspirations as it broadens their view of the world and enhances their knowledge that allow them to make independent decisions about their rights and entitlements. Clearly, as women's education increases, awareness of the self is most likely to increase and some measure of autonomy is gained.

Census data during the last twenty-five years show a narrowing of the gender gap in literacy. Between 1970 and 1990, the overall literacy rate increased by around 11 percentage points, with women's literacy rate rising by 12.3 percentage points as against 9.7 percentage points increase for males. In 1990, the literacy rate for women and men were about the same.

Data on the highest grade completed for the population 25 years and older show that although larger proportions of men finish four years of high school education there are more women completing at least four years of college education. For example, data from the recent 1995 census show that the proportion of females completing an academic college degree is 14.10 per cent compared with 11.62 per cent of males, a difference of almost 3 percentage points. At lower levels of education, however, there is little difference between males and females (table 1).

A more refined measure of the educational status of women relative to men is educational training and field of specialization. It sheds light on the content of education and the differentiation between men and women with respect to human capital formation and development. Data on college graduates by discipline and field of study show that women outnumber men in the education and health related professions. For example, in the year 1995-1996, the proportion of women

Table 1. Percentage distribution of household population aged 25 years and over by sex and highest level of education completed: 1995

Highest grade completed	Both sexes		Male		Female	
	Number	Per cent	Number	Per cent	Number	Per cent
Total	28 495 507	100.00	14 196 110	100.00	14 299 398	100.00
No grade completed	1 342 493	4.71	606 176	4.27	736 317	5.15
Pre-school	68 884	0.24	33 245	0.23	35 640	0.25
Elementary	11 857 833	41.61	5 843 155	41.16	6 014 678	42.06
1st-4th grade	4 075 642	14.30	2 109 844	14.86	1 965 797	13.75
5th-7th grade	7 781 398	27.31	3 733 016	26.30	4 048 383	28.31
High school	8 206 591	28.80	4 246 418	29.91	3 960 173	27.69
Undergraduate	3 011 302	10.57	1 517 212	10.69	1 494 090	10.45
Graduate	5 193 874	18.23	2 728 934	19.22	2 464 940	17.24
Post-secondary	891 986	3.13	497 016	3.50	394 970	2.76
Undergraduate	148 046	0.52	85 521	0.60	62 525	0.44
Graduate	743 891	2.61	411 429	2.90	332 462	2.33
College undergraduate	2 125 044	7.46	1 162 560	8.19	962 484	6.73
Academic degree holder	3 665 170	12.86	1 648 922	11.62	2 016 248	14.10
Post-baccalaureate	107 117	0.38	52 925	0.37	54 193	0.38
Not stated	233 067	0.82	108 059	0.76	125 008	0.87

Source: National Statistics Office, 1995.

completing a college degree in education and health sciences was about 79 per cent compared with only 20 per cent for men (table 2). On the other hand, men largely dominate the engineering and law professions. Such differentials are more obvious in urban than in rural areas.

In most Filipino households, men still complete fields of study that command high paying jobs, whereas women are mostly employed in low-wage jobs usually overburdened with work. This observative is borne out by data from the Department of Education, Culture, and Sports in 1993 which reveal that the ratio of female to male engineers is 1:15, and that the ratio of females to males in health related courses is 1:4. In 1996, there was 1 female for every 5 male engineers. By contrast, there was 1 male for every 3 female graduates in health related courses, which mainly pertained to nurses and midwives. Over time, there has not been substantial change in the content and fields of study of female education. The roots of socialization on the girl child's nurturing role in the family are deep and may take a long time to change.

B. Gender relations and women's reproductive role

The strength and significance of the relationship between women and population has been increasingly recognized in a number of research studies which clearly document that systematic discriminatory gender systems influence the timing of marriage, the levels of fertility, incidence of infant and child mortality, abuse and exploitation of women migrant workers on both domestic and global scenes, the incidence of unplanned pregnancies, the practice of clandestine abortion, and the incidence of deaths related to pregnancy. Frequently, policy implications of such studies centre around interrelated aspects of women's status and empowerment, levels and patterns of fertility and trends in population growth. The argument usually put forward is that higher levels of gender inequality provide greater incentives for both men and women to desire more children due to economic and social advantages they provide, and the fewer options women have in economic life. Where their relative position is low, women are also likely to experience high social, economic, and personal costs of

Table 2. Number of graduates by discipline group and sex, academic years 1992-1993 and 1995-1996

Discipline group	Total no. of college graduates	Male		Female	
		Number	Per cent	Number	Per cent
SY: 1992-1993					
Arts and Sciences	35 363	11 889	33.62	23 474	66.38
Education	47 335	9 844	20.80	37 491	79.20
Engineering	125 877	118 378	94.04	7 499	5.96
Health Related Courses	58 160	11 114	19.11	47 046	80.89
Business Education	69 045	20 391	29.53	48 654	70.47
Agriculture	11 016	5 343	48.50	5 673	51.50
Criminology and Law	7 423	5 942	80.05	1 481	19.95
Religion and Theology	1 259	1 224	97.22	35	2.78
Total	**355 478**	**184 125**	**51.80**	**171 353**	**48.20**
SY: 1995-1996					
Arts and Sciences	30 592	9 685	31.65	20 907	68.35
Education	45 545	9 361	20.55	36 184	79.45
Engineering	40 518	33 860	83.57	6 658	16.43
Health Related Courses	47 483	9 833	20.71	37 650	79.29
Business Education	96 736	21 533	22.26	75 203	77.74
Agriculture	15 633	7 241	46.32	8 392	53.68
Criminology and Law	2 206	1 339	60.70	867	39.30
Religion and Theology	1 266	1 199	94.70	67	5.30
Total	**279 979**	**94 051**	**33.59**	**185 928**	**66.41**

Source: Commission on Higher Education, 1994 and 1997.

adopting fertility control due to their limited knowledge of, and access to contraceptives. The succeeding discussion dwells on three particular aspects of women's status that are known to strongly influence childbearing: their educational level, their employment status, and their use of family planning services and other programmes.

Women's relative position to men in Philippine society and its relationship to fertility are complex. Empirical evidence has increasingly shown the multiplicity of women's domestic and public roles and the variety of dimensions in which women may or may not exercise power, including the social, economic, and reproductive arenas. Local literature reveals that a Filipina's role in keeping the purse does not necessarily correspond to her independence in household decision-making, particularly when there is spousal disagreement. A study by Casterline *et al.*, (1997) underscores the finding that one of the social forces behind

large unmet family planning needs among Philippines women is husband's disapproval of contraceptive use (Macro International and NSO, 1994; NSO, 1998).

1. Women's social position and childbearing

As suggested by several studies, gender roles in Filipino households depict childbearing and childbearing as being mostly within women's domain of influence, whereas major household expenditure decisions are less likely to be. The question then arises whether the objective of fertility control can be achieved without empowering women in other critical spheres of life. Although roles and responsibilities are gradually changing, the traditional custom of giving men priority in most decisions within the household and family continue to prevail in the Philippines, particularly in rural areas. In fact, the strong pro-natalist characteristic of Philippines social structure provides a justification for power imbalances in Filipino households. Using data from the Women in Development Survey of 1983, Alcantara (1994) shows that when the couple has no children, the balance of power is biased towards the husband; but once children are present in the family, the balance of power tilts in favour of the wife. Thus, the gender power relations system in the Filipino household raises a fundamental question whether educated women who have lower fertility tend to have greater freedom or equality in their domestic spheres than uneducated women.

(a)   Education and contraceptive use

While a National Family Planning Programme was launched since the mid-sixties, acceptance and use of contraceptive methods by Filipino couples has not reached the level that would ensure a significant drop in the family size. Despite the increase in contraceptive use from 15.4 per cent in the late 1960s to 40 per cent in the early 1990s and 46.1 per cent in the late 1990s, the average number of children born to a women is around four. In 1993, the National Demographic Survey (NDS) data revealed that 15.1 per cent of the contraceptive users relied on traditional methods, which have proved to be less effective in preventing unplanned and unwanted pregnancies. In 1998, the proportion of contraceptive users relying on traditional methods increased to 17.9 per cent.

Overall, of the total contraceptive users, only 10.8 per cent have primary or less education but 43.0 per cent have a high school education and 47.1 per cent are college educated. One of the consistent findings of research on contraceptive prevalence is that more educated women avail themselves of family planning services and use more effective methods, while the lowest level of use of any contraceptive method is among women with no education. Furthermore, it is noted that the contraceptive failure rate among women with primary education or less is almost twice as high as that of women with college education. Such differentials in contraceptive use and failure are attributed to differences in access to correct information about contraceptive methods among women with varying years of schooling (Perez and Tabije, 1996).

Despite high levels of education among Filipino women, obstacles to contraceptive use are posed by inadequate spousal communication and to gender power relations within the household, which have resulted in high proportions of women not wanting any more children but not using any contraceptive method. A recent study on unmet need for family planning in rural and urban settings of the Philippines reveals that pronatalist attitudes of husbands and their dominance in decision-making when spousal disagreements arise, emerge as important factors contributing to women's unmet need for family planning, and their inability to meet their reproductive goals and choices including contraceptive method choice, the number of children they want and the timing of their pregnancies (Casterline, *et al.*, 1997). In another study by Perez and Palmore (1994), less educated women and women not working were found to have higher unmet need for family planning.

(b)   Education and childbearing

There is wide acceptance of the argument that education promotes an ideology of independence and egalitarian marital relationships, resulting in women's control of fertility. The available data indicate no significant gender differentials in literacy rates and school enrolments, and that women are more likely to finish a college degree than men. In 1990, the proportion of academic degree holders among females (8.3 per cent) was over 2 percentage points higher than for males (6.0 per cent). A similar pattern was observed in 1995 with 18.17 per cent of the women and 13.0 per cent of men obtaining college degrees (NSO, 1995).

The effects of education are clearly rejected in fertility differentials. The National Demographic Survey (NDS) in 1993 showed that women with elementary education had a total fertility rate (TFR) of 5.5 as against only 2.8 for college-educated women. Hence, a Filipino woman with low or no education can be expected to have almost twice as many children as a better-educated woman. One argument given to explain this differential behaviour in fertility is that in very poor families, where women are likely to have little schooling, each new child represents an additional potential worker, and in the absence of social support and income security, the larger the pool of household labour force the better the chances of increasing household earnings. But educated women, who are more likely to educate their children, perceive greater benefits in having a few skilled and well educated children than having many unskilled and uneducated ones.

(c)   Education and age at marriage

Another theoretical route by which education tends to lower fertility is through its effects on age at marriage. Education empowers women to develop as individuals, not just as attachments to husbands or as low position members of extended families. It gives them self-confidence and the awareness to believe that marrying at a young age to obtain the support and protection of a husband is not their only option in life. Young women who are able to obtain work after they finish school are likely to find the prospects of earning their own money more attractive than the prospects of early marriage.

The age at which women marry has a major influence on childbearing patterns. Women who marry at an early age have greater exposure to the risk of childbearing and tend to have more children than women who delay marriage. In general, better educated women tend to marry late. Data from the 1993 NDS reveal that for the country as a whole,

the median age at marriage for women is 21.4 years. However, it is lower in areas where the proportion of women who ever attended high school or college is lower. Metro Manila, for example, with a relatively higher proportion of women who ever attended high school or college (85 per cent) has a median age at marriage of 24 years for women, four years later than that of Bicol with a much lower proportion of women ever attending either high school or college (55 per cent). In the Philippines, nearly one in 3 women reaches age 25 without marrying. Latest estimates using the 1995 Census data reveal an average age of marriage of 24 years for women and 26.5 years for men. This increase is presumably associated with longer duration of schooling among women and men as the proportions completing college degrees have also increased between 1990 and 1995.

(d)   Education and child mortality

Just as education is important in determining the number of children a woman bears, it also largely determines whether those children live or die. As one would expect, the more years of schooling a woman has, the less likely she is to experience the death of a child. Research evidence shows that with each additional year of schooling of a woman there is a 7-9 per cent decline in infant and child deaths. Several explanations are offered for this finding. One is that educated women are more likely to seek appropriate sources of medical care and attention and to persist in obtaining accurate diagnoses and treatment for the sick child. The other is that more educated women start childbearing at a later age, space their pregnancies with longer birth intervals and have fewer children. As such, they are at much lower risk of experiencing child deaths than less educated women. Others explain the differential in infant and child mortality by women's education in terms of the effect of education on women's own health conditions and the health of their children. The 1993 NDS data reveal the highest infant mortality rates were for mothers with no education (76 deaths per 1,000 live births) and lowest for mothers with college education (27 deaths per 1,000 live births). The same pattern is observed for child mortality rates which are highest at 81 deaths per 1,000 live births for mothers with no education and lowest at 8 per 1,000 for college-educated mothers.

2. Women's social position and reproductive health status

While there is general consensus that lower fertility is associated with women's social position and facilitates the achievement of economic development goals, there is yet to be agreement on how the narrow objective of fertility reduction can safeguard women's health and survival risks related to pregnancy and other reproductive health problems. In Philippines, like most developing countries, family planning has been singularly focused on achieving fertility reduction goals. Despite the progress in medical technology that has dramatically reduced infant mortality rates and increased life expectancies, services for major reproductive health problems such as infertility, sexually transmitted diseases or gender-based violence significantly affecting women's well-being, are extremely limited. Reproductive morbidity measures have only recently been integrated into data collection activities and are, therefore, too scant at present to make an assessment.

(a) Maternal mortality

There is an evidence of a decline in the maternal mortality ratio among Filipino women. However the estimates vary by source. Statistics from the Department of Health reveal a reduction of maternal mortality from 190 to 80 deaths per 100,000 live births during the period 1970-1990. The 1993 NDS survey data reveal that maternal mortality ratios declined from 213 during 1980-1986 to 209 deaths per 100,000 live births during the 1987-1993 period. In 1995, the Technical Working Group on Maternal and Child Mortality of the National Statistical Coordinating Board estimated further decline in regional and provincial maternal mortality levels. For the country as a whole, the maternal mortality ratio is estimated at 180 maternal deaths per 100,000 live births. However, it varies from a low of 116 per 100,000 live births in the province of Cavite in Southern Tagalog to a high of 333.7 per 100,000 live births in the province of Sulu in Mindanao. This disparity in maternal mortality conditions is partly explained by development differentials between the two provinces and differences in women's living conditions. For most women, particularly those in rural and remote areas, inadequate prenatal care and lack of information on complications associated with pregnancy account for much of the elevated risk of death during pregnancy and childbirth.

In addition, there are increased risks of deaths arising from complications of unsafe abortion practices among women who terminate unwanted pregnancies. An analysis of hospital – based admissions of women due to post-abortion complications reveals that about 400,000 induced abortions occurred in 1994 in the Philippines (Perez *et al.*, 1997). Service providers who are inadequately trained for safe abortion procedures undertake a large proportion of these pregnancy terminations in secret. The social taboos and the cultural pressure of keeping these matters secret among women make them internalize physical and emotional pain and experience discomfort arising from their reproductive and sexual roles such as those associated with forced sexual relations, unwanted pregnancies and induced abortions. This is particularly true of women of low socio-economic status who are not fully aware and confident enough to make independent choices and to determine when to have children. In fact, a large number of women have been socialized to endure physical malaise and suffering associated with their reproductive functions: in menstruation, sexual relations, pregnancy or childbirth. To them, these are the overriding symbols of womanhood.

(b) Tetanus toxoid injections

Some other reproductive health indicators that reflect women's access to, and utilization of, health care services are whether pregnant mothers have received tetanus toxoid injections, prenatal care and assistance from trained personnel at delivery. Tetanus toxoid injections are given during pregnancy to prevent neonatal tetanus. The 1998 National Demographic and Health Survey (NDHS) data show that of all births in the preceding five years prior to the survey, 69 per cent of mothers had at least one dose of tetanus toxoid, indicating an increase of 4 percentage points from the earlier proportion derived from the 1993 NDS. In both these surveys, the proportion of births where mothers had at least one dose of tetanus toxoid vary significantly between the less and the better-educated women. However, an improvement in coverage of pregnant women is observed between the two survey dates as the rural-urban differentials observed in 1993 that mostly favoured pregnant women in urban areas disappeared by the time of the 1998 survey.

(c) Prenatal care provider

Prenatal care and assistance at delivery can reduce health risks for both mothers and children. The 1998 NDHS data show that for births five years prior to the survey, 86 per cent of mothers had received prenatal care from doctors or nurses or midwives. This is not a substantial increase from the 83 per cent of such births estimated in the 1993 NDS. As overall existing health services have improved, trained prenatal care providers do not reach all pregnant women for services. In both the surveys, the data reveal that women in urban areas have greater chances of receiving prenatal care – especially from doctors – than women in rural areas. Access to trained prenatal care providers, in particular, to medical doctors, is likewise much greater among women with some college education than among those with lower education.

(d) Assistance in childbirth

Despite the advances in medical technology and education of women, levels of maternal death have not improved as much as have those of infant death. Improving women's overall heath or nutritional status does not simply avert most of the complications that cause maternal deaths. The substandard health services and the inadequate availability of medical supplies at the time of labour, delivery and immediately after birth are some of the factors contributing to high maternal death rates and need programme attention. Data on the proportion of medically assisted deliveries for births during the five years preceding the 1993 NDS and the 1998 NDHS show a slight increase from 53 per cent to 56 per cent. Preliminary results from the 1998 NDHS indicate that deliveries under the care of medical doctors are more common for highly educated women (63.5 per cent) than those with one to six years of schooling (10.7 per cent), and for those in urban areas (47.7 per cent) than in rural areas (16.8 per cent). Many women, especially those in remote rural areas, live far from sources of adequate obstetric care.

It may also be noted that in 1993 only 30 per cent of deliveries are reported to have occurred in medical facilities including health centres, hospitals, etc. It is likely that the same trend may have continued to the present time. Births at home may not be unsafe provided that the woman's family and the birth attendant are trained enough to provide effective services at the right time to avoid delivery complications. In the face of rising costs of health care, poor women and their families may not seek professional help in medical facilities even in cases of medical emergencies.

The evidence presented above suggests that socio-economic disadvantages of women and community characteristics of under-development, at least in part, affect women's reproductive health status differentials in the

Philippines. Improvements in social and economic position of women can counter the deleterious effects of social deprivation on women's reproductive health.

C. Gender relations and women's productive role

There is a Chinese adage that women "hold up half the sky", and yet even to this day women remain virtually invisible in the field of economic production. As early as the 1970s, Boserup (1970) pointed out that women often do not share in the benefits of development programmes and may, in fact, be negatively affected by them. The invisibility of the woman worker is mostly attributed to the fact that her work is performed mainly in subsistence farming in the countryside, or in the underground economy of urban places. More recently, however, there has been a surge of subcontract work and the beginning of the process of opening up domestic economies to a global economy under the auspices of trade liberalization. Literature on women's productive role and progress in their economic independence has grown substantially. As a concept, women's labour force participation is not unidimensional, but is quite complicated, particularly when measuring its demographic impact, as it can never be culture-free.

1. Women's employment status

In the Philippines, there are more women than men in the working age groups but the labour force participation rate has generally been much higher for males than females. In 1990, the male labour force participation rate of 79.8 was nearly 1.7 times higher than the female rate. In other words, more than half of women (about 53 per cent) in the working ages remained economically inactive. The lower participation of women may partly explain why the expected impact of women's employment on childbearing is not as visible. The evidence shows that despite the relative advantage in educational attainment over their male counterparts, Filipino women workers continue to remain disadvantaged with regard to their employment status, wages, and work conditions. For instance, the majority of female workers in the professional, technical and related categories of occupations are employed in low-paying jobs such as nurses and teachers which are considered to be of low status, and perhaps involve limited training requirements. Men dominate jobs and occupations which carry higher status and higher pay such as doctors and engineers. Data from the 1993 Annual Survey of Establishments reveal that women managers, executives, and supervisors are still far less in number and they are paid significantly lower than their male counterparts. Further, female unpaid family workers account for 22.7 per cent of the total employed females. On the other hand, the corresponding proportion of unpaid family workers among males is only at 10.5 per cent.

The picture did not change much until recent years. Data from the April 1998 Labour Force Survey reveal that of the total household population (10 years old and over) of 55.3 million, women comprise 27.7 million or 50.1 per cent. But only 38 per cent and 37 per cent of these women are in the labour force and employment, respectively. Thus, women account for only one in three of the labour force and two in five of unemployed persons. It may be noted that the unemployment rate for women has been estimated at 17.6 per cent as compared with 13.9 per cent for males in April 1998. An examination of the marital status of female workers underscores the magnitude of the multiple burdens borne by women workers. Data from the most recent Labour Force Survey of April, 1998 indicates that of the total employed females, about 60 per cent are married, 30.4 per cent single and the remaining are widowed and separated. This means that about three in five women workers are married and one in three is single. Married working women often face the consequences of interrupted labour force participation during pregnancies and child rearing. This tendency

71

among women often translates to a slower pace of career development and delayed work promotion when compared with single female workers and male workers.

Implicit in data from the April 1998 Labour Force Survey (LFS) is the reality of women's struggle to merge two separate roles and spheres of life into work and home responsibilities. One in three of employed females were self-employed and own-account earners, which allow more flexibility in adjusting to the demands of home and child care while earning. For the year 1998, the proportion of such workers is 41.9 per cent for women in the urban areas and 29.8 per cent in rural areas. These data suggest better opportunities for self-employment among women in urban than in rural areas. The reverse,

however, is observed for the year 1997 when 38.3 per cent of women in urban areas, but 73.3 per cent in rural areas were employed in this category (table 3). The explanation for these opposite findings is that the 1998 data reflect a differential in entrepreneurial skills and access to credit between rural and urban women and also differences in the coverage of economic activities in the two types of areas. Whatever the explanation, the fact remains that many women are faced with the dual burden of employment and housework and are constantly in search of practical solutions to the everyday challenge of balancing work and family life.

A further perusal of the April, 1998 LFS data on employment in different industrial groups by gender indicates that females dominate employment in wholesale and retail

Table 3. Employed persons aged 15 years and over by class of worker and urban-rural residence: 1997-1998

Class of worker	Total	Male		Female		Total	Male		Female	
	Number	Number	Per cent	Number	Per cent	Number	Number	Per cent	Number	Per cent
Total	**28 103**	**17 813**	**63.38**	**10 290**	**36.62**	**27 836**	**17 539**	**63.01**	**10 297**	**36.99**
Wage and salary	13 386	8 578	64.08	4 808	35.92	13 761	8 898	64.66	4 863	35.34
Worked for private	11 240	7 472	66.48	3 768	33.52	11 595	7 774	67.05	3 821	32.95
Worked for government	2 146	1 106	51.54	1 040	48.46	2 166	1 124	51.89	1 042	48.11
Own account	10 415	7 275	69.85	3 140	30.15	10 344	6 871	66.43	3 473	33.57
Self-employed	9 325	6 451	69.18	2 874	30.82	9 499	6 263	65.93	3 236	34.07
Employed	1 090	824	75.06	266	24.40	845	608	71.95	237	28.05
Unpaid family workers	4 302	1 960	45.56	2 342	54.44	3 731	1 770	47.44	1 961	52.56
Urban	**12 747**	**7 682**	**60.27**	**5 065**	**39.73**	**12 791**	**7 580**	**59.26**	**5 211**	**40.74**
Wage and salary	8 053	4 912	61.00	3 141	39.00	8 127	4 973	61.19	3 154	38.81
Worked for private	6 684	4 196	62.78	2 488	37.22	6 777	4 270	63.01	2 507	36.99
Worked for government	1 369	716	52.30	653	47.70	1 350	703	52.08	647	47.92
Own account	3 809	2 379	62.46	1 430	37.54	3 794	2 243	59.12	1 551	40.88
Self-employed	3 318	2 048	61.72	1 270	38.28	3 355	1 950	58.12	1 405	41.88
Employed	491	331	67.41	160	32.59	439	293	66.74	146	33.26
Unpaid family workers	885	391	44.18	494	55.82	870	364	41.84	506	58.16
Rural	**15 356**	**5 225**	**34.02**	**10 131**	**65.98**	**15 045**	**9 959**	**66.20**	**5 086**	**33.80**
Wage and salary	5 333	1 667	31.26	3 666	68.74	5 634	3 925	69.67	1 709	30.33
Worked for private	4 556	1 280	28.09	3 276	71.91	4 818	3 504	72.73	1 314	27.27
Worked for government	777	387	49.81	390	50.19	816	421	51.59	395	48.41
Own account	6 606	1 710	25.88	4 896	74.12	6 550	4 628	70.66	1 922	29.34
Self-employed	6 007	1 604	26.70	4 403	73.30	6 144	4 313	70.20	1 831	29.80
Employed	599	106	17.70	493	82.30	406	315	77.59	91	22.41
Unpaid family workers	3 417	1 848	54.08	1 569	45.92	2 861	1 406	49.14	1 455	50.86

Source: National Statistics Office, *Labour Force Survey, 1997 and April, 1998.*

trade, and in community, social and personal services, accounting for 64.5 per cent and 55.2 per cent of workers, respectively. On the other hand, males dominate the agriculture, construction and transport, and communication sectors (figure 1).

Figure 1. Number of employed persons by major industry group, April 1998
(in thousands)

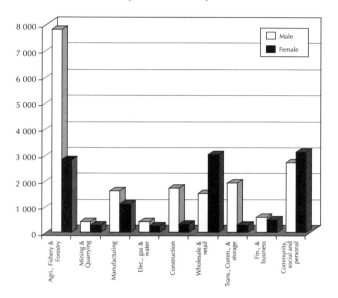

Figure 2. Number of employed persons aged 15 years and over by major occupation group, April 1998
(in thousands)

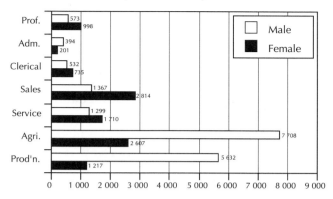

Source: National Statistics Office, *Labour Force Survey, Apirl 1998.*

Table 4. Comparative earnings (out of the one-peso wage pie) of employed males and females: 1994

	Male	Female
Industry group		
Agriculture, forestry and fishery	P 0.642	P 0.358
Mining and quarrying	0.659	0.341
Manufacturing	0.606	0.394
Electricity, gas and water	0.760	0.240
Construction	n.a.	n.a.
Wholesale and retail trade	0.629	0.371
Transportation, storage and communication	n.a.	n.a.
Financing, insurance, real estate and business services	0.552	0.448
Community, social and personal services	0.567	0.433
Occupation group		
Professional and technical workers	0.539	0.461
Administrative and managerial workers	0.538	0.462
Clerical workers	0.524	0.476
Sales workers	0.645	0.355
Service workers	0.659	0.341
Agricultural workers	0.644	0.356
Production and related workers	0.594	0.406

Source: National Statistics Office, *Labour Force Survey, 1994.*
n.a. (not available)

The number of employed persons in major occupation group shows that most females are working as sales workers (27.3 per cent), agricultural workers (25.3 per cent), service workers (16.6 per cent), and production workers (11.8 per cent), whereas men are mostly found in agricultural and production related occupations. Compared with male workers, females are predominant in sales and service occupations (figure 2). It is then not surprising that women have largely lower earnings than men. Evidence of this is reflected in the 1994 labour force survey data on comparative earnings which reveal that out of the one-peso-wage-pie, men always have higher shares compared with women, particularly in agricultural, and sales and service occupations where women predominate (table 4).

Thus, one may reinforce the argument that relatively low wages and dead-end jobs outside the formal sector for Filipino women motivate them to have a large number of children to ensure that there will be someone to take care of them in old age. Given the work situation and conditions of Filipino women workers, it is not surprising to note little differentials in the number of children between

73

working and non-working mothers. On the other hand, for better educated women high opportunity costs of having a large number and closely-spaced children may motivate them to use contraception and hence enhance their chances of retaining labour force participation with higher pay in the formal sector of the economy. An analysis of data in Cebu Province indeed substantiates the notion that women wage workers in white-collar jobs are more likely to adopt contraceptive use in the year following childbirth (Doan and Brewster, 1998). In a study on how family planning influences the lives of Western Visayas women, it is found that adoption of contraceptives enables women to increase their opportunities for economic improvement and allows them to manage the child care trap better.

2. Migration and employment

Migration has been viewed as a vehicle for improving an individual's social and economic status. The 1990 population census data underscore the extensive participation of women in migration for employment purposes, particularly in the younger age groups of 15-39 years. Female migrants tend to work as domestic helpers in cities and urban areas. In fact, half of female migrants with gainful occupations in the country's urban areas belong to the domestic helper category (Villamil, 1998).

Filipino women also figure prominently in international labour markets and have significantly contributed to the economies of the newly industrialized nations of East and South-East Asia. In the process of globalization and trade liberalization, there is an increasing concern that economic liberalization may lead to further increases in gender inequalities in wages and income. It is observed that women workers are more vulnerable to adverse consequences of global economic trends as they are likely to experience job losses in uncompetitive industries that will have to undergo corporate downsizing. As initial income inequalities between women and men

workers are already high, Filipino women are likely to continue to seek work abroad in service occupations. Available data show that the number of Filipino overseas workers almost doubled between 1990 and 1995, from 417,301 to 782,297, and the number of male overseas workers is 54.3 per cent of total overseas workers in 1995 (NSO, 1995). Moreover, it is noted that about 92 per cent of these Filipino overseas workers are in fact contract workers.

Data from the 1995 census on female overseas workers by age show that the highest proportion of women (23.9 per cent) are in the age group of 25-29 years compared with 17.9 per cent of men in the same age group (table 5). The table further shows that a majority of women overseas workers fall in the younger age groups of 20-39 years (72.6 per cent). In terms of educational levels of these overseas workers, 39.21 per cent of women are college graduates compared with 48.35 per cent of men. The proportion of women overseas workers who are high school graduates is

Table 5. Percentage distribution of overseas workers aged 10 years and over by sex, age group and educational attainment, 1995

Characteristics	Male		Female	
	Number	Per cent	Number	Per cent
Age group				
10 - 14	5 016	1.18	5 429	1.52
15 - 19	8 332	1.96	14 716	4.12
20 - 24	38 814	9.13	62 327	17.45
25 - 29	76 182	17.92	85 329	23.89
30 - 34	79 880	18.79	61 827	17.31
35 - 39	79 413	18.68	50 183	14.05
40 - 44	58 369	13.73	32 182	9.01
45 & over	79 115	18.61	45 183	12.65
Total	**425 121**	**100.00**	**357 176**	**100.00**
Education				
No grade completed	3 514	0.83	4 512	1.28
Elementary	41 218	9.76	50 144	14.17
High school graduate	115 654	27.38	128 390	36.28
Post secondary	56 093	13.28	30 829	8.71
College	204 187	48.35	138 742	39.21
Post baccalaureate	1 692	0.40	1 257	0.35
Total	**422 358**	**100.00**	**353 874**	**100.00**

Source: National Statistics Office, *Census of Population and Housing, 1995.*

Figure 3. Percentage distribution of overseas workers 10 years old and over by sex and educational attainment, Philippines, 1995

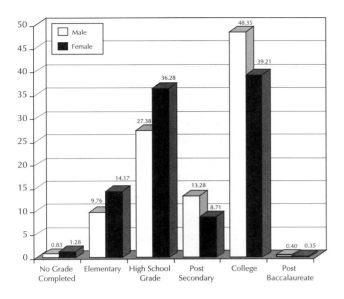

Source: National Statistical Office, *Census of Population and Housing, 1995.*

36.3 per cent compared with 27.4 for men (figure 3 and table 5). This means that more women than men with elementary and high school degrees are working overseas, whereas the reverse is true for post secondary and college graduates (see table 5). The differential in human capital leads to disparities in opportunities for higher-paying jobs abroad that mostly favour the better-educated male worker.

Data from the Philippine Overseas Employment Administration indicates the dominance of females in contractual work abroad. For example, in the year 1994, females constituted about 60 per cent of total overseas workers, mostly working as domestic helpers and entertainers in most east and south-east Asian countries (table 6). The predominance of female contract workers is maintained in the first six months of 1998, constituting 59.3 per cent of the total, showing the highest proportion in the service workers category (89.56 per cent), followed by professionals (73.97 per cent) and clerical workers (47.08 per cent). On the other hand, men outnumber women workers in managerial, administrative and production related jobs (table 6). What clearly emerges from these data is that gender disparities in employment status of Filipina workers still exist and the disadvantaged position of women in this

Table 6. Deployment of newly hired overseas foreign workers by skill category and sex, 1994 and January-July 1998

Skill category	Total Number	Male Number	Male Per cent	Female Number	Female Per cent
Jan. - Dec. 1994					
Professionals	77 018	15 510	20.14	61 508	79.86
Administrative and managerial	726	645	88.84	81	11.16
Clerical and related workers	3 837	2 612	68.07	1 225	31.93
Sales workers	2 376	1 505	63.34	871	36.66
Service workers	94 458	10 426	11.04	84 032	88.96
Agricultural workers	1 257	1 225	97.45	32	2.55
Production, transport, labourers	89 039	75 561	84.86	13 478	15.14
Total	**268 711**	**107 484**	**40.00**	**161 227**	**60.00**
Jan. - Jul. 1998					
Professionals	30 411	7 915	26.03	22 496	73.97
Administrative and managerial	218	172	78.90	46	21.10
Clerical and related workers	1 729	915	52.92	814	47.08
Sales workers	1 335	764	57.23	571	42.77
Service workers	42 813	4 468	10.44	38 345	89.56
Agricultural workers	209	203	97.13	6	2.87
Production, transport, labourers	42 691	34 145	79.99	8 546	20.01
Total	**119 406**	**48 582**	**40.69**	**70 824**	**59.31**

Source: Philippines Overseas Employment Agency, 1994 and 1998.

regard continue to prevail both in domestic and international markets.

Given this situation, it is expected that the current economic crisis will adversely affect many women who were formerly employed as paid workers in export-oriented companies such as the semiconductor and garments industries. For those who will be thrown out from the workplace and lose their jobs, this would mean sliding back to their former status as unpaid family workers and as self-employed workers, if not being pushed into prostitution. For those working abroad, it would most likely mean returning to the Philippines and being unemployed, revisiting the drudgery of poverty.

3. Employment and childbearing

The proportion of women in the labour force working for pay has been small until recently, and most women who produce goods for household consumption are not given monetary compensation for their efforts. However, with increasing urbanization, industrialization, and modernization, women are joining the ranks of the employed in increasing numbers. Although a woman with paid work may not always have complete control over the money she brings home, a woman with some earnings is no longer totally dependent for survival on her husband or children. Thus, through its potential of empowering women, work with pay is another aspect of women's status believed to have significant implications for the number of children they want and have, and their use of contraceptive methods. The 1993 NDS data reveal that in regions where the proportion of working women is higher, total fertility rate is much lower. For example in Metro Manila where more than one-half of women aged 15-49 years are working, women have 2.8 children on average, compared with Ilocos where only one-third of the women are working and have 4.8 children on average. Nevertheless, it is noted that despite the increasing participation of women in the labour force, the overall population growth rate of the country remains high when compared to other South-East Asian countries.

4. Employment and child mortality

It is argued that women's participation in the labour force, while improving women's status, may have negative effects on child health and nutritional status because of mothers' reduced time available for child care and being absent from home (Popkin, 1983; Garcia, 1990; Zablan, 1983). The empirical evidence from an analysis of the 1993 data, however, suggests trade-offs in child health and mortality and inadequate social capital among women. Indicators of infant and child mortality show that children of mothers in urban areas always have a survival advantage and that children whose mothers are well educated stand better chances of survival during the first five years of life. For example, the mortality rate for children under five whose mothers had no education was 151.8 deaths per 1,000 live births compared with only 35 deaths per 1,000 live births for mothers with college education.

D. Women in public life

While previous discussion has centred on educational attainment and labour force participation of women, their participation in decision-making outside the home is also important for depicting their role in development planning. This is perhaps the most neglected aspect in term of statistical evidence and articulation in policies and programmes for the advancement of women's participation in development. Participation of women in key decision-making roles in senior and high levels of policy-making bodies is necessary for representing women and formulating gender sensitive policies and programmes for the country's development.

Traditionally, Philippine society views politics as a male affair with the consequence of women being detached from political issues, political institutions and structures. Filipino women fought for political enfranchisement as early as 1937, and since then have progressed from being voters to being political candidates and leaders themselves. In the Philippines, as elsewhere, women pursuing political careers do not receive as much encouragement and support as do men. Nevertheless, there has been increasing visibility of women in elective political positions, even though they constitute a small proportion of the total number of candidates for elective posts. In 1995, only 6 women ran for the Senate as against 22 men candidates. Of the 12 senatorial slots, only 3 women candidates were elected. In the lower House, the participation of women candidates was even lower. Of the 190 proclaimed winners in 1995, only 20 were women, constituting 10.5 per cent of the total number of seats in the House of Representatives (table 7). The recent elections in May 1998 show that only 4 women senators were elected out of the total of 23, and 25 women out of the total 222 representatives. Today, under the party list system, there are 2 women representatives for the legislative branch of government for the advancement of women's well-being as a manifestation of mainstreaming Filipino women in political structures and policy development.

At the local level, however, women have made great strides in participation in local governance and politics between 1992 and 1998. The greatest increase in political participation was in the position of provincial governors whose number increased from 7 in 1992 to 13 in 1998, indicating a gain of 7 percentage points. This was followed by an increase in the proportion female of city mayors and city councillors (table 8). All these indicators are reflective of the advances made by women in actual involvement in decision-making and formulation of policies and programmes for development. Women's increasing participation in law-making involves them in nation-building and is considered an affirmation of the movement from rhetoric to action on women's empowerment for participatory nation-building.

Table 7. Number and percentage of women elected to the Senate and House of Representatives by election year, 1947-1995

Election year	Total no. of positions	Female	
		Number	Per cent
Senate			
1947	8	1	12.50
1955	8	1	12.50
1961	8	1	12.50
1963	8	1	12.50
1965	8	1	12.50
1967	8	2	25.00
1969	8	0	0.00
1971	8	1	12.50
1978	165	9 *	5.45
1984	181	10 **	5.52
1987	23	2	8.70
1992	24	4	16.67
1995	12	3	25.00
1998	25	4	16.00
House of Representatives			
1946	8	1	12.50
1949	100	1	1.00
1953	102	1	0.98
1957	102	1	0.98
1961	104	2	1.92
1965	104	6	5.77
1969	109	3	2.75
1987	202	19	9.41
1992	200 ***	22 ***	11.00
1995	190 ****	20	10.50
1998	222	25	10.36

Source: Commission on Elections, 1998.

Notes:
*	IBP member
**	Mambabatas Pambansa member
***	Includes sectoral representatives for women and elderly
****	Proclaimed winners as of July 1995

Last 12 Senators elected in 1992 served only for 3 years;

12 Senators were elected in 1995 to complete the 24-seats until 1998.

The gains that have been made in women's political emancipation indicate their increased participation in decision-making in government. This process promotes women's political empowerment and contribution to development policy formulation and legal reforms for women's advancement and well-being. Following the rationale of the

Table 8. Number and percentage of women elected to local government positions by election year: 1992 and 1998

Local government positions	Female		Total number of positions	Female		Total number of positions
	Number	Per cent		Number	Per cent	
Governors	7	10	73	13	17	78
Vice-Governors	5	7	73	6	8	78
Municipal/City Mayors	122	8	1 602	216	13	1 607
Municipal/City Vice-Mayors	141	9	1 602	164	10	1 607
Municipal/City Councillors	1 645	13	13 052	2 096	16	13 144

Source: Commission on Elections, 1998.

linkage between politics, economics, and national development in a democratic context, increased women's participation in politics is recognized as a sign of achievement of democracy when national development policies and legislation are decided jointly by women and men.

For the gains in women's participation in public life, credit needs to be given to women's advocacy work for the enactment of laws in compliance with international agreements and commitments of the Philippine Government to the Beijing Platform of Action that paved the way for improving women's status. These achievements are articulated in the Philippine Human Development Report 1997 which underscores a better performance in improving women's status than in poverty eradication indicators. For the years 1995 and 1996, the gender empowerment measure (GEM) among the ASEAN nations indicates the Philippines is the pace setter in enabling women to actively participate in the economic and political life of the country. In fact, Philippines is the first Asian country to pass a law against sexual harassment. Another landmark in mainstreaming women in development is the 1995 Philippine Gender-Responsive Development Plan. Yet, much remains to be done to achieve the objectives of gender equality and equity in all spheres of life.

E. Critique of selected legislation on women

Legal reform is thought to be an avenue through which empowerment of women and improvement in their relative position in society can be attained. Movements for legislative advocacy among women's groups have increased substantially as an off-shoot of the 1994 Cairo and 1995 Beijing Conferences where gender equality, equity and empowerment of women figured prominently as basic to the realization of women's full potentials and energies.

It is noteworthy that prior to these international conferences the equality between women and men was expressed as state policy in the 1987 Constitution of Philippine's. But this Constitutional mandate on gender equality does not necessarily mean cultural attitudes have changed. A brief critique of some aspects of selected legislation like the New Family Code aimed at empowering women will illustrate this point.

1. The new family code

The New Family Code was signed into law in 1987 with a view to eliminating discriminatory practices against Filipino women in the family, which were prominent in the Civil

Code of 1950. This is a fundamental step towards bringing women to the fore as central figures in Filipino families and has made provisions for the husband and wife to be jointly responsible for the support of the family and the management of the affairs of the household. However, there are still provisions on administration of conjugal properties that disadvantage women. It is stated that husband and wife jointly exercise the powers of administration, except that the law, in what is certainly discriminatory with respect to property relations, provides that the husband's decision shall prevail in cases of conflict with the wife.

Clearly, the above provision can have constraining effects on women's decisions about making choices in productive and reproductive matters. Advocacy for reform on this provision should be a lively action agenda of women's groups and advocates for gender equality as it affects decision points that determine patterns and levels of childbearing and the women choices about having a certain number of children. Spousal disagreements on contraceptive use, contraceptive method choice, and the timing of the birth of children are common areas of couple disagreement. What is appalling is that despite high levels of education of Filipino wives and mothers, in cases where husbands disagree, women advance negotiations rather than assert themselves, if not totally give in to what the husband desires, as a mode of conflict resolution. What this suggests is that the influence of culture and tradition restricts women's enjoyment of their fundamental rights and entitlements in different spheres of life.

2. Women in Development and Nation-building Act

This law was passed as Republic Act 7192 in 1992 to promote the integration of women as full and equal partners of men in development and nation building. Specific to women's employment concerns, the law provides that "married persons who devote full-time to managing the household and family

affairs, shall upon the working spouse's consent, be entitled to Pagtutulungan: Ikaw, Bangko, Industriya at Gobyrno (PAG-IBIG), Government Service Insurance System (GSIS), or Social Security System (SSS) coverage to the extent of one-half of the salary and compensation of the working spouse". Again, the noble intention of the law to safeguard women's well-being in terms of giving compensation to the unvalued work of a full-time housewife, largely depends on the consent of the working spouse. As such this does not truly endow housewives with economic empowerment.

In addition to the above provisions, its implementing rules and regulations state that the National Economic and Development Authority (NEDA) has a set allocation of official development assistance for gender-responsive projects: 5 per cent for the first year, and 10-30 per cent thereafter. After 6 years, there seems to be little compliance with this allocation despite the provision of guidelines and minimum requirement of information that should go into agency compliance reports.

3. The Migrant Workers and Overseas Filipinos Act

The salient features of this law are the codification and institutionalization of policies on overseas employment and the establishment of a higher standard of protection and welfare of migrant workers and their families, irrespective of whether the migrants are documented or undocumented. It is, indeed, a response to the needs of women migrant workers who are mostly concentrated in the service and entertainment occupations which are unprotected sectors of foreign labour markets.

This law, however, is riddled with conflicting policy statements. One outstanding inconsistency in the statement is the declaration that "the State does not promote overseas employment as a means to sustain economic growth and achieve national development", while simultaneously stating that the "deployment of Filipino overseas workers, whether land-based or sea-based, by local service contractors and manning agencies employing them shall be encouraged".

4. The Anti-sexual Harassment Act

This law is based on the premise of full respect for human rights and dignity of workers and employees as well as applicants for employment, students or those undergoing training, instruction or education. It explicitly states about the responsibility of the employer towards the prevention and resolution of sexual harassment cases as they are held liable for damages arising from the acts of sexual harassment. As the administrative implementation of this law is left to employers and to academic and training institutions, it has been noted that there is lack of response to the issue of "hostile environment" between peers or co-employees in certain places.

The few laws cited above render the perception that women are free from gender discrimination and that full integration of women in development is guaranteed. Nevertheless, the loopholes in the written laws and the deficiencies and gaps in their implementation still exist and need to be addressed. As gender-differentiated data become available, the weaknesses of the laws become even more visible. Inadequate resources of government pose constraints on effective monitoring of compliance of different agencies and institutions to these laws. Clearly and sadly, existence of laws with various provisions does not instantly mean complete elimination of social and cultural barriers that tend to marginalize women's role in national development.

F. Emerging policy issues and suggestions

The foregoing review of relevant literature on the interrelationships between gender relations, women's relative social position, health status and fertility via the effects of education and employment has identified several emerging policy issues and concerns areas of women and development.

The importance of sustained investment in education of girls and an increase in women's participation in fields of study that command better pay in the occupational structure is underscored. The process of educational expansion should carefully examine the content of schooling for women rather than only provision the of a minimum number of years of schooling. Emphasis should be given to enabling women to recognize the potential empowering effect of their education, both in the formal and non-formal education systems, in a culturally sensitive manner.

In areas of women's economic activities and participation in the labour force, there is a pressing need to modify and develop income-generating opportunities for women, as revealed by the disadvantaged position of women workers in the country's occupational and income structures. Specific measures could be taken to assist working mothers in meeting the demands of earning income and fulfilling family obligations of child care and household chores at the same time, particularly in households where husbands, by normative pressure, rarely assist in child care and household chores. In the workplace, women workers, in particular pregnant women, have to be protected from the health risks of exposure to hazardous elements in factories and industrial plants.

The fact that many Filipino women exceed their desired family size deserves steadfast attention. The existence of unmet family planning need is a matter of concern for family planning programme managers and provides the basis for broadening their activities and services not only for women but also for men by involving them in the programme. The new population bill, which emphasizes a gender-responsive population policy with a reproductive health perspective, should be given political support for its immediate execution. This bill provides an opportunity for the family planning programme managers to improve the effectiveness of contraception by taking into account women's situations with a gender-sensitive lens rather than limit it to recruiting new acceptors only with little sensitivity to gender relations systems and couple behaviour that influence either acceptance or rejection of family planning.

G. Conclusion

The analysis of the gender relations system in Philippine society and an examination of the underlying mechanisms through which such system affects women in both their productive and reproductive roles has revealed that much more work needs to be done. The process of empowerment that enables women to effectively participate in national development activities must begin at home where the confidence and enhanced self-worth gained by a woman in her own family should be sufficient enough to ensure protection against gender discrimination at the workplace and elsewhere in the public sphere. What is most essential is Filipino women's self-determination on matters of reproduction based on principles of gender equity and shared responsibility by males in the fulfilment of their productive and reproductive roles.

REFERENCES

Alcantara, Adelamar N. (1994). "Gender roles and the status of married Filipino men and women". *Philippine Sociological Review,* volume 42, Nos. 1-4. (January-December).

Battistella, Graziano (1995) "Data on international migration from the Philippines". *Asian and Pacific Migration Journal.* (Quezon City), volume 4, No. 4, pp. 589-612.

Bisgrove, Eilene Z. and Meera Viswanathan (1997). A framework for the analysis of the impact of family planning on women's work and income. *Family Health International.* No. WP97-01.

Boserup, Ester (1970). *Women's Role in Economic Development.* New York: St. Martin's.

Bureau of Women and Young Workers (1995). *Facts and figures on women: Philippines.* Bureau of Women and Young Workers-Department of Labour and Employment.

Buvinic, Mayra, Margaret A. Lycette and William P. McGreevey (eds.) (1983). *Women and Poverty in the Third World.*

Baltimore, Maryland: Johns Hopkins University Press.

Casterline, John B., Aurora E. Perez and Ann E. Biddlecom (1997). "Factors underlying unmet need for family planning in the Philippines". *Studies in Family Planning,* (New York), volume 28, No. 3, pp. 105.

Defo, Barthelemy Kuate (1993). Effects of socioeconomic disadvantage and women's status on reproductive health. CDE Working Paper 93-18, Madison: Center for Demography and Ecology.

Doan, Rebecca and Karin L. Brewster (1998). Type of employment, use of prenatal services and contraceptive practice in the Philippines. *Studies in Family Planning* (New York), volume 29, No. 1, pp. 69-78.

Feliciano, Myrna S. (1997). Legal development concerning women in the Philippines. (Unpublished). College of Law, University of the Philippines. Diliman, Quezon City.

Garcia, M. (1990). Resource allocation and household welfare: study of the impact of personal sources of income and food consumption, nutrition and health in the Philippines. Thesis submitted to the Institute of Social Studies, Netherlands.

National Commission on the Role of Women and Asian Development Bank (1995). *Filipino Women: Issues and Trends.* Manila.

National Commission on the Role of Filipino Women (1997). *Plan Framework of the Philippine Plan for Gender-Responsive Development 1995-2025.* Manila.

National Statistics Office (1994). *Functional Literacy and Mass Media Survey.* Manila.

_____ (1994). *National Demographic Survey 1993.* Calverton, Maryland: Macro International Inc.

_____ (1994). *National Safe Motherhood Survey 1993.* Calverton, Maryland: Macro International Inc.

_____ (1998). *National Demographic and Health Survey, 1998. Preliminary Report.* Calverton, Maryland: Macro International Inc.

Perez, Aurora E. (1997). "Making space for Filipino men in fertility management". *Women's Health Concerns Policy Brief,* Series 1997-1. Quezon City: Center For Women's Studies. University of the Philippines.

Perez, Aurora E. and T.L. Tabije. (1996). *Contraceptive Discontinuation, Failure, and Switching Behaviour in the Philippines.* DHS Working Papers No. 18. Calverton, Maryland: Macro International Inc.

Perez, Aurora E. and James Palmore (1997). "Reevaluating the unmet need for family planning in the Philippines". *Asia-Pacific Population Research Reports,* No. 10. Honolulu: East-West Center Programme on Population.

Philippine Legislators' Committee on Population and Development (March 6, 1998). The social and economic consequences of family planning use in southern Philippines, part 1. *Population Talkpoint.* Issue No. 1, Batasan Complex, Quezon City.

_____ (March 13, 1998). The social and economic consequences of family planning use in southern Philippines, part 2. *Population Talkpoint.* Issue No. 2, Batasan Complex, Quezon City.

_____ (March 27, 1998). How family planning influences the lives of Western Visayas women, part 2. *Population Talkpoint.* Issue No. 4, Batasan Complex, Quezon City.

_____ (April 3, 1998). How family planning influences the lives of Western Visayas women, part 3. *Population Talkpoint.* Issue No. 5, Batasan Complex, Quezon City.

_____ (April 10, 1998). How family planning influences the lives of Western Visayas women, part 4. *Population Talkpoint.* Issue No. 6, Batasan Complex, Quezon City.

Popkin, B.M. (1983). "Rural women, work, and child welfare in the Philippines". In *Women and Poverty in the Third World,* Mayra Buvinic, Margaret A. Lycette and William P. McGreevey, eds. Baltimore, Maryland: Johns Hopkins University Press.

Population Information Programme, Center For Communications Programmes, Johns Hopkins School of Public Health. *Empowerment of Women.* Selected references from POPLINE, The Bibliographic Population Database. Maryland, U.S.A.

Simmons, Ozzie G. (1988). *Perspective on Development and Population Growth in the Third World.* New York: Plenum Press.

The Cairo-Copenhagen-Beijing Interface Steering Committee (1995). *Paving the Road to Beijing.* Advocacy Papers for the Fourth World Conference on Women. Philippines.

─────── (1993). *Population Change, Development and Women's Role and Status in the Philippines.* New York: Economic and Social Commission For Asia and the Pacific.

─────── (1995). *Population and Development.* Programme of Action adopted at the International Conference on Population and Development. Cairo, 5-13 September 1994. Volume 1. ST/ESA/SER.A/149. New York: United Nations.

─────── (1995). *Review and Appraisal of the World Population Plan of Action, 1994 Report.* New York: Department For Economic and Social Information and Policy Analysis Population Division.

United Nations (1996). *The Beijing Declaration and the Platform for Action.* Fourth World Conference on Women, Beijing, China, 4-15 September 1995. New York.

Villamil, Winfred M. Female migration, wage differentials and rural risk: The case of Bicol migrant. (Ph.D. Dissertation). University of the Philippines. Diliman, Quezon City.

Zablan, Z. (1983). "Trends and differentials in mortality". In *Population of the Philippines: Current Perspectives and Future Prospects*, Manila: Mercedes B. Conception, ed. PDPR, National Economic and Development Authority.

V. WOMEN IN DEVELOPMENT IN SINGAPORE

Stella Quah*

Introduction

The term "Women in Development" has become fashionable over the past decade in the mass media and among journalists, writers, researchers, policy makers and the public around the world. As the meaning of the term is muddled, the parameters of this discussion must be defined clearly before proceeding.

The life conditions, aspirations and values of women vary significantly across countries and need to be analyzed from a wide range of perspectives. This paper will address the theme of women in development in Singapore from the sociological perspective of stress generated by conflicting role expectations. More specifically, it will discuss the problems faced by Singaporean women in their striving to attain a coherent social life whereby the joys and benefits of marriage and motherhood may be successfully combined with their developing as intelligent, efficient, hard-working, and thriving income earners. The focus is on contemporary Singapore where the striving for coherence is a relatively new phenomenon as it may be traced back about three decades and it has increased in intensity owing to the mounting social pressures on women to succeed on both fronts, their homes and their jobs. For those who are familiar with recent social science research, this problem of opposite demands on women is not new and it is not unique to Singapore. What, then, will be the contribution of this discussion? The paper will identify and discuss the interesting and perhaps uniquely Singaporean combination of three factors – or contradictory signals – and the way in which women try to organize their lives around them. These three factors are: the traditional values on the role of women, the exigencies of an industrial

economy that encourages and rewards female participation in the labour force, and the modern values of gender equality. This paper is divided into four sections. A brief background on relevant socio-economic and demographic features of Singapore is provided in the first section. The main factors or contradictory signals of women's role in development are described and discussed in the second section, followed by the analysis of the struggle and striving for coherence in the third section. The fourth or concluding section summarizes the main findings.

A. Relevant background features

The discussion of women in development must be conducted in the context of the specific society where they live. Accordingly, the most relevant socio-economic features of Singapore are presented in tables 1 to 7. The figures in table 1 give the main demographic and socio-economic indicators for the years 1986 and 1996 to indicate the general direction of change during a period of ten years. As table 1 shows, the population of Singapore has increased from 2.52 million in 1986 to 3.04 million in 1996, and the overall ethnic distribution of the population into Chinese, Malay and Indian communities remains relatively stable. A large majority of the population is Chinese (77.3 per cent in 1996), whereas Malays and Indians form the two numerically small but socio-politically significant minorities. The average age of population increased from 27.8 years in 1986 to 32.2 years in 1996 indicating a relatively young population. However, as indicated by the Index of Ageing, the proportion of elderly people is increasing, primarily due to the improvement in the standard of living and the resulting increase in life expectancy. Singapore shares the global feature of longer life expectancy among women

* Associate Professor, Department of Sociology, National University of Singapore.

as indicated by the elderly sex ratio. The level of economic development in Singapore is high as reflected by high GNP per capita, low unemployment rate and high proportion of savings (table 1).

Considering that Singapore is basically an urban metropolis, the important sectors of the economy are manufacturing, construction and services. Agriculture plays a negligible role in the economy. Consequently, the types of jobs in the labour market, educational facilities, modes of communication and transport, entertainment options, leisure activities, and all other aspects of living in Singapore are reflective of the life style in large cities. This is a feature that distinguishes Singapore from its neighbouring south-east Asian countries where the agricultural sector is an important contributor to the national income and a large proportion of the total population lives in rural areas.

Based on data from the five major population censuses of Singapore from 1947 to 1990, the marital status of women by age cohort is presented in table 2 in a historical sequence. The historical changes in the patterns of singlehood, marriage and divorce are evident from the table. Although the proportion of single women in all age cohorts has increased substantially from 1947 to 1990, the tendency towards being married remains strong as also explained elsewhere (Quah, 1998).

Table 1. Selected demographic and socio-economic indicators, Singapore, 1986 and 1996

Indicators	1986	1996
Resident population[1]	2 518 600	3 044 300
Ethnic composition[2] (Percentage of population in each ethnic group)		
Chinese	77.9	77.3
Malays	14.2	14.2
Indians	6.8	7.3
Others	1.0	1.3
Population density (persons per square kilometre)[1]	4 051	4 702
Median age (in years)[1]	27.8	32.2
Aging Index[1] (Residents aged below 15 divided by residents aged 15-59)	34.1	43.9
Sex ratio (males per 1,000 females)[1]	1 028	1 012
Crude birth rate (per 1,000 population)[1]	14.8	15.4
Crude death rate[1]	4.6	4.7
Total fertility rate (per 1,000 females aged 15-44)[1]	1 433	1 702
Gross reproduction rate (per 1,000 females aged 15-44)[1]	688	818
Elderly sex ratio[1] (Males per 1,000 females among residents aged 60 & over)	874	861
Mean age of females at first marriage[1]	25.1	26.5
Proportion of single females aged 30-39[1]	15.9	18.2
Female literacy rate (resident females aged 15 and over)[1]	78.9	87.8
Gross National Product (per capita in Singapore $)[3] (in US$ at US$1 = S$1.65)	14 712 (8 916)	36 851 (22 334)
Average unemployment rate (years 1980 and 1996)[4]	3.5	2.0
Gross National Saving as per cent of GNP[4]	34.2	50.1

Sources: [1]   Department of Statistics, Singapore (1997a), various pages.
         [2]   Department of Statistics, Singapore (1997b), various pages.
         [3]   Department of Statistics, (1997a:4) for 1986; and Ministry of Trade and Industry (1998:viii) for 1996.
         [4]   Ministry of Trade and Industry, (1998:viii). Figures refer to 1980 and 1996.

Table 2. Percentage distribution of female population aged 15 and over by marital status and age group, census years 1947 to 1990

Age group and marital status	1947[a]	1957[b]	1970[c]	1980[d]	1990[e]
Below 20 years					
Single	71.4	80.0	95.1	97.7	99.3
Married	27.7	19.7	4.8	2.3	0.7
Widowed	0.5	0.1	*	*	–
Divorced	0.4	0.2	*	*	–
Total	100.0	100.0	100.0	100.0	100.0
Number	41 198	65 542	120 059	139 184	202 474
20-24 years					
Single	50.5	33.0	64.6	73.8	78.5
Married	46.9	66.0	35.0	25.8	21.2
Widowed	2.1	0.5	0.2	0.1	–
Divorced	0.5	0.5	0.2	0.3	0.3
Total	100.0	100.0	100.0	100.0	100.0
Number	34 918	58 012	100 554	143 360	113 877
25-29 years					
Single	8.6	9.2	22.6	34.0	39.2
Married	87.0	88.6	76.2	64.8	58.9
Widowed	4.0	1.6	0.6	0.3	0.7
Divorced	0.4	0.6	0.6	0.9	1.2
Total	100.0	100.0	100.0	100.0	100.0
Number	31 882	51 950	66 095	124 124	140 049
30-34 years					
Single	6.8	4.4	9.6	16.7	20.9
Married	85.0	91.5	87.8	80.6	76.2
Widowed	7.6	3.3	1.5	1.0	0.9
Divorced	0.6	0.7	1.1	1.7	2.0
Total	100.0	100.0	100.0	100.0	100.0
Number	31 555	39 777	67 919	103 672	143 677
35 and older					
Single	6.6	4.8	4.6	5.3	8.5
Married	58.4	62.0	68.2	69.8	70.4
Widowed	34.6	32.8	26.2	22.9	18.7
Divorced	0.4	0.4	1.0	2.0	2.4
Total	100.0	100.0	100.0	100.0	100.0
Number	120 600	168 391	266 388	356 196	528 664

Sources: [a] Calculated from the 1947 Census report by Del Tufo (1949:207-255).
  [b] Calculated from the 1957 Census report by Chua (1964:124).
  [c] Calculated from the 1970 Census report by Arumainathan (1973:II-2).
  [d] Calculated from the 1980 Census report by Khoo (1981a:64).
  [e] Calculated from the 1990 Census figures in Lau (1992a:39).

Note: * Less than 0.01 per cent.

Table 3. Percentage distribution of women by economic activity status by marital status, census years 1957 to 1990
(percentages)

Marital status and activity status	1957[a]	1970[b]	1980[c]	1990[d]
Single				
Economically active	24.8	35.6	53.0	69.0
Economically inactive	75.2	64.4	47.0	31.0
Total	100.0	100.0	100.0	100.0
Number	151 168	353 026	434 542	407 000
Married				
Economically active	14.0	14.7	29.7	43.2
Economically inactive	86.0	85.3	70.3	56.8
Total	100.0	100.0	100.0	100.0
Number	238 078	332 784	453 001	636 600
Widowed				
Economically active	25.8	15.5	16.1	16.5
Economically inactive	74.2	84.5	83.9	83.5
Total	100.0	100.0	100.0	100.0
Number	57 729	71 258	83 006	97 500
Divorced				
Economically active	46.5	47.6	61.6	67.0
Economically inactive	53.5	52.4	38.4	33.0
Total	100.0	100.0	100.0	100.0
Number	1 665	4 288	10 686	16 700

Sources: [a] Calculated from the 1957 Census report by Chua (1964:192). The figures refer to the population aged 10 years and over. The 1947 figures are not included because the 1947 census did not include data on the economic activity status of men and women according to their marital status.

[b] Calculated from the 1970 Census report by Arumainathan (1973:II-63). The figures refer to the population aged 10 years and over.

[c] Calculated from the 1980 Census report by Khoo (1981b:35). Figures refer to the population aged 10 years and over.

[d] Calculated from the 1990 Census figures by Department of Statistics (1991b:51), which are based on a 10% sample. The figures refer to the population aged 15 years and over.

Note: Economically inactive includes students, homemakers and others.

Table 4. Average age of divorcees and average duration of marriage, 1980 to 1995

Divorces	1980	1985	1990	1995
Under the women's chapter				
Male divorcee's average age (years)	36.6	37.2	37.0	39.7
Female divorcee's average age (years)	32.8	33.5	33.5	36.2
Average years of marriage	11.6	11.6	12.0	13.0
Under the Syariah court				
Male divorcee's average age (years)	35.0	36.0	35.9	38.3
Female divorcee's average age (years)	29.9	31.4	32.2	35.1
Average years of marriage	9.0	8.6	8.8	9.8

Sources: Department of Statistics (1988a:81-82 & 96-97); Department of Statistics (1991a:43, 46) and (1996b:25, 27).

87

Table 5. Average number of children born alive per married woman by ethnic group and education, census years 1970 to 1990

Ethnic group and education	1970[a]	1980[b]	1990[c]
All married women	4.0	3.4	2.9
Ethnic group			
Chinese	3.9	3.4	2.9
Malays	4.8	3.9	3.4
Indians	4.0	3.4	2.8
Others	2.7	2.8	2.4
Educational level			
No formal education	4.8	4.3	4.6
Primary	3.4	2.3	2.4
Secondary	2.2	1.6	1.6
Tertiary	1.9	1.6	1.4

Sources: [a]   Figures taken from Arumainathan (1973:I-68-69; 74-75).

[b]   Figures on ethnic groups taken from Department of Statistics (1991b:10). Data on educational level compiled in Quah (1990b:266).

[c]   Figures taken from Lau (1992a). Data are census figures on resident ever-married females.

The trends in women's participation in the labour force as shown in table 3 offer a general view of the changes in women's economic activity rates according to their marital status. The period covered is from 1957 to 1990. The most striking change over this historical period is the significant (almost three fold) increase in the proportion of economically active women, both single and married.

The patterns of marital dissolution by age and average duration of marriage are shown in table 4. The figures cover a period of fifteen years from 1980 to 1995 and indicate separately the situation following the two legal systems in operation in Singapore. The Women's Charter as we will see later, has jurisdiction over family matters such as marriage and divorce among non-Muslim Singaporeans, whereas the Syariah court has such jurisdiction for Muslim Singaporeans. In general, the obvious trend is that Muslim marriages ending in divorce last less longer than non-Muslim marriages with an average of 9.8 years for Muslims compared with 13.0 for the non-Muslims in the year 1995. Table 4 also shows that the average age of divorce has increased among women. This pattern is most likely to be a direct outcome of the trend towards later marriages as observed in table 2.

Procreation and motherhood are affected by life circumstances and characteristics such as ethnicity and level of education (table 5). Of the three main ethnic groups, Malay women are most likely to have large families. However, observing the changes over time from 1970 to 1990, one discerns clearly the impact of education on family size. The more educated a woman is, the more likely she is to have a small number of children or none at all (cf. Quah, 1990). This aspect is shown in table 6 where the number of children born decreases as the educational level of ever-married women increases (see also Quah, 1994; 1998). For example, in 1990, 75.5 per cent of women with no formal education had three or more children compared with 22.8 per cent with secondary school and only 16.7 per cent with a post-secondary level of education (table 6).

Table 7 compares the living arrangements of women and men by age group. Irrespective of age, the overwhelming majority of the population live in nuclei family, and the proportion of women in nuclear family is greater than men (92.3 per cent vs. 84.3 per cent).

This overview of the main characteristics of Singapore, presented in a set of seven tables, provides the background needed to proceed with the discussion of the conflicting role expectations faced by Singaporean women. The following discussion is based on my analysis of the situation of women in Singapore over the past three decades (cf. Quah, 1990; Quah, 1994: 177-217).

Table 6. Percentage distribution of ever-married women by number of children born alive and formal education, census years 1970 to 1990

Number of children and level of formal education	1970[a]	1980[b]	1990[c]
All ever-married women			
No children	5.2	9.2	11.5
One child	13.7	16.0	16.2
Two children	15.5	20.8	27.2
Three or more children	63.6	54.2	45.2
Total	100.0	100.0	100.0
Number	40 317	545 069	708 240
No formal education			
No children	4.7	4.2	3.8
One child	10.6	9.5	7.0
Two children	12.6	14.6	13.6
Three or more children	72.1	71.7	75.6
Total	100.0	100.0	100.0
Number	25 860	304 989	200 528
Primary school education			
No children	9.0	12.5	8.2
One child	16.1	22.7	13.5
Two children	18.6	27.6	29.0
Three or more children	56.2	37.2	49.3
Total	100.0	100.0	100.0
Number	8 483	172 132	211 452
Secondary school education			
No children	15.2	21.4	17.6
One child	23.8	28.9	24.0
Two children	23.7	30.8	35.6
Three or more children	36.9	18.8	22.8
Total	100.0	100.0	100.0
Number	5 833	59 234	240 374
Post-secondary school education[d]			
No children	–	20.9	25.0
One child	–	27.1	25.1
Two children	–	33.7	33.1
Three or more children	–	18.3	16.7
Total	–	100.0	100.0
Number	–	8 679	55 886

Sources: [a] Data from the 1970 census report by Arumainathan (1973:II-502). The data refer to a sample of ever-married females.

[b] Data from the 1980 census report by Khoo (1981c:65-66).

[c] Data from Lau (1992a:118-120) on resident females aged 10 years and over.

[d] The highest level of education included in the 1970 census report was "Secondary and above".

Table 7. Percentage distribution of persons by living arrangements, by gender and age, 1990

Living arrangements	Age				
	>15	15-29	30-59	60+	All
Women					
Family nucleus	99.9	83.4	95.1	94.0	92.3
Non-family nucleus	0.1	16.6	4.9	6.0	7.7
Total	100.0	100.0	100.0	100.0	100.0
Number	30 115	46 957	59 035	13 624	149 731
Men					
Family nucleus	99.8	71.1	86.5	89.3	84.3
Non-family nucleus	0.2	28.9	13.5	10.7	15.7
Total	100.0	100.0	100.0	100.0	100.0
Number	32 296	53 104	63 686	11 695	160 781

Source: Data from Department of Statistics (1991c) based on a 10 per cent sample of persons living in private households.

B. The main contradictory signals

Three trends that affect the social definition of gender roles may be identified in Singapore, namely: a revival of traditional values, the exigencies of a modern economy leading to the state's intervention in encouraging female participation in the labour force, and the concept of gender equality promoted through universal education and modernization. These issues may be analyzed in the context of a specific question, are these trends heading towards a collision course? The search for an answer requires us to look into each of these trends individually.

1. Traditional values

More than ever before, Singaporeans are experiencing today stronger exhortations from their political leaders on the importance of cultural traditions. The message that one must never forget one's roots (Tay, 1982; Lee, 1982b, 1984; *Straits Times,* 1990a; Lee, 1996) is underscored for all Singaporeans, whether their cultural tradition is Malay, Indian, Chinese or any other. Nevertheless, in a country where the majority of the population is Chinese (77 per cent) with two main minorities as Malays (14 per cent) and Indians (7 per cent), the message for the strengthening of traditional values is a call that unites and separates the

communities at the same time. On the one hand, there are some universal values that form part of the cultural tradition of communities all the world over. The importance of forming a family and being part of it is one of those values commonly found in comparative and cross-national studies. There are also value dimensions that are common to Singaporeans from any ethnic background, among which filial piety and parenthood are prominent as a life goal (Quah, 1990). On the other hand, the plea for tradition may be divisible if one accentuates the values from his/her cultural or religious tradition that are different from those of other ethnic communities (Zainul and Arun, 1990; 87-88; Quah, 1990; 97-98). Thus, even within the context of cultural traditions, one finds discrepancy concerning the importance of being one nation and the imperative of distinguishing one's culture from the cultures of fellow countrymen.

How would this discrepancy affect the social meaning of gender roles? Cultural traditions involve certain beliefs and values on what is right and wrong including the prescription for correct or proper behaviour of individuals as men and women in the community, as well as their obligations and rights in their association with one another. Among the influences that shape the social meaning of gender roles in Singapore, these cultural beliefs and values are important and surprisingly similar. As indicated elsewhere (Quah, 1990) and as will be elaborated later, women, whether Chinese, Malay or Indian, are inclined to see marriage and motherhood as two of the crucial goals in their lives. However, the present official encouragement to Singaporean Chinese to strengthen their own traditions has introduced a contentious dimension to the already controversial social definition of women's roles. That dimension is the legacy of Confucius.

In February 1982, the government announced that "Confucianism will be added as a sixth option in the Religious Knowledge Programme" introduced in the secondary school curriculum (*Straits Times*, 1982). This event marked the onset of the government's efforts to lead the Chinese Singaporeans towards the path of a re-encounter with their ancient traditions. An elaborate process of public education on the thought of Confucius was undertaken. Its main features were the numerous talks, public forums and discussions led by a group of international Confucius scholars. They were especially invited by the government to lead the way in the quest for the best possible approach to the application of Confucius' thought to modern life among Singaporean Chinese.

The presence of the invited Confucius scholars and their contributions to the debate were amply displayed in the press and other mass media during 1982 and 1983. The Religious Knowledge Programme ran its course and was terminated in 1989. But the idea of going back to Confucian roots has not relented. On the contrary, it is promoted through the annual "Speak Mandarin" campaign which in 1990 adopted an assertive slogan: "If you are Chinese, make a statement...in Mandarin". The crucial idea behind the campaign, according to its promoters, is to emphasize the importance of Mandarin as the best vehicle for the transmission of Chinese cultural traditions to the new generations of Singaporeans of Chinese descent. Mandarin, they argue, is the only

access to the Chinese classics, primarily to the teachings of Confucius.

It is beyond the scope of this discussion to dwell on the cosmology of Chinese thought. But, it is relevant to identify the definition of the social roles of men and women in the writings of Confucius for two main reasons, as indicated earlier. Briefly restated, one reason is the emphasis given by some political and community leaders to the need for Singaporeans to revive and maintain their cultural roots (*Straits Times*, 1990a). The other reason is that Confucius is presented as the key exponent of the cultural legacy among the Chinese more than the Taoist or any other Chinese tradition.

In the search for the Confucian position on the status and roles of men and women in society, one finds that a predominant part of his teachings was addressed primarily or almost exclusively to men. Three decades ago, in his comparative analysis of Socrates, Buddha, Confucius and Jesus, the "paradigmatic individuals" in history, philosopher Karl Jaspers (1957:47) protested:

> One is struck by Confucius' indifference towards women. He has nothing to say of conduct in matrimony, speaks disparagingly of women...and frequently remarks that nothing is so hard to handle as a woman. The atmosphere around him is distinctly masculine.

Jaspers' point is readily verified by a review of English translations of Confucius' texts (for example, Waley, 1938; Doeblin, 1940; Ware, 1955). This explains why the same comment is found in many other analyses of Confucian thought (see Creel, 1949, 1962; Fung, 1948; Chan, 1963; Chai and Chai, 1973; Lu, 1983; Fry *et al.*, 1984; Tu, 1984; Lincoln, 1985; Chung, 1989). For example, in their comparative study of Asian religions, George Fry and his colleagues (1984:106-7) conclude that "Confucius taught a philosophy of male domination. While the husband was to be 'righteous' to his wife, she was to be 'obedient'

91

to her husband". These authors also point out that "while Confucius speaks of the father-son relationship, he has nothing to say about the function of the mother"; they note that overall, "female figures are notoriously absent from the Confucianist tradition".

Confucius made some references to women, for example in the Analects, Book I.13, Book III.22, Book IV.18, Book IV.19, and Book V.1. Yet, as Black (1986:169) points out, "when women are casually mentioned in these texts, it is generally in terms of kinship or marriage ties", I agree with Black that "if there is anything on which Confucian texts are clear, it is that the male should be dominant" (1986:170).

While most analysts agree on this central feature of Confucius' teachings, there is no clear consensus on the explanations given for the Confucian directive on the subjugated role of women. Black (1986:170) feels that Confucius neglected this aspect as his "reasons for female submission to male are frequently unstated". Others differ. It is possible to assume that no explicit explanations were considered necessary by Confucius if he was referring to the prevalent values of his time. Indeed, some argue that Confucius' teachings are simply a forceful reminder of fundamental values in Chinese society. Jaspers (1957:43-44) argues that Confucius, as any other philosopher, "does not advance his ideas as his own" but rather, brings forth ideas from a superior source; Confucius was "the voice of antiquity" advocating "not imitation of the past but repetition of the eternally true".

Following the same line of explanation, Creel (1949:125-27) states that, as far as family relations are concerned, "Confucius seems to have added little that was new", considering that the value of subordination to authority was already evident in the works of earlier writers. In the same vein, Chung (1989:153) suggests that subordination was crucial and required manifestation of loyalty and obedience, which

Confucianism deemed as "virtues central to all human relations". These virtues were expressed in the "subordination of the son to the father, the wife to the husband, and the subjects to the rulers". Chung feels that this emphasis on subordination is expected given that the fundamental aspect of Confucianist doctrine "was to maintain the immutable harmony – and equilibrium underlying both the universe and human society".

Furthermore, as the strong voice of cultural tradition, Confucius has personified Chineseness across time. His philosophy dominated the schools of China for almost twenty-five hundred years. Fry and his colleagues (1984:88) added that "in one sense, Confucius was China, China was Confucius". It is precisely this aspect of Confucianism that is most relevant in the context of the present discussion about the impact of traditional values on the social roles of women in Singapore. The teachings of Confucius, as I indicated earlier, are promoted by some Chinese community leaders in Singapore as embodying the quintessence of traditional Chinese culture and, thus, as the traditional values that all Chinese should follow. For the majority of Singaporeans who are of Chinese descent, this message is one of the contradictory social signals they receive, as will become apparent as this discussion proceeds.

Naturally, traditional values also shape the roles of men and women among the other two main ethnic minorities in Singapore, the Malay and the Indian communities. Among the Malay community, the religion of Islam is the main driving force in defining roles of men and women. In Singapore, Islamic law principles apply to regulations on marriage, marital relations and divorce, among other family aspects. Some of these regulations vary slightly from those applied in other Muslim countries. In fact, variations in Islamic family law are also found among the states in the Federation of Malaysia. Under the Muslim Law Act in Singapore, Islamic principles on the equality between women and men are manifested in matters such as the consent of the bride as a requirement for the legal registration of the marriage (Ahmad, 1984:198); the wife's right to retain her own property after marriage (1984:218-19) and her right to maintain a suit in her own name and to be sued as if she was unmarried (1984:215).

While gender equality is upheld by the above regulations, Muslim law contains some other provisions that reflect a differential perception of the status of men and women. The two most common examples of this differential treatment are found in the regulations on the capacity to marry and on divorce. Concerning the capacity to marry, Muslim law stipulates that "a woman who is already married is not allowed to marry again while the marriage is subsisting" but it is possible for a man "to marry more than one woman up to a maximum of four, provided he is able to treat his wives with equity" (Ahmad, 1984:206). As Ahmad clarifies, this flexibility for men has been restricted in Singapore by requiring that the Kathi (Registrar of Muslim marriages) holds an inquiry to satisfy himself that there is no lawful obstacle to the marriage according to Muslim Law and the Administration of Muslim Law Act (1984:206).

This principle of greater options to men in marriage is found in divorce legislation as well. International research findings indicate that, in general, divorce has a connotation of failure, either in the minds of the couple involved, in the public sphere, or both. This connotation tends to persist regardless of ethnic or religious differences (Wallerstein and Kelly, 1980; Wong and Kuo, 1983; O'Leary, 1987; Steinmetz, 1988; Wallerstein and Blakeslee, 1990). It is thus not surprising that among the Muslim community, although divorce is permitted, it is not encouraged and, in religious theory, it is frowned upon (Ahmad, 1984:220). Nevertheless, the husband may divorce his wife by pronouncing a *talak* or repudiation against her (1984:220). But a wife wishing to divorce her husband needs to follow a more complicated

process. She could apply for divorce on grounds of: (a) failure of condition or *carai taalik* (husband's failure to maintain her for more than three months or husband's assaulting her) but she has to present evidence to prove the charges; or (b) annulment of marriage or *fasakh*; or (c) by *kholo'*, that is by obtaining the husband's agreement upon payment of compensation to him. More importantly, Ahmad indicates that "While the *talak* can be the unilateral act of the husband, it is necessary for the woman to apply to a Kathi or a court for a degree of *carai taalik*, *kholo'* or *fasakh*" (Ahmad, 1984:221; Sharifah, 1986:186-7). Considering the above manifestations of gender equality and gender differentiation in the pronouncements of Muslim law, it is evident that two fundamental events in family life, marriage and divorce, are more affected by segregatory regulations than by those regulations enforcing equality.

In the case of the Indian community in Singapore, its internal diversity prevents easy generalizations. There are numerous ethnic subdivisions and religious groups in the Indian community (Ryan, 1971; Mani, 1979; Ling, 1989; Sandhu and Mani, 1993). This feature justifies the assumption that the Indian community is guided by both secular and religious traditions. One interesting example of the secular Indian traditions is The Laws of Manu. It deals with custom and convention and is a work of the Epic period of Indian philosophy originating around the sixth Century, B.C. While the section on the "Status and Duties of Women" contains numerous verses honouring women, there are explicit precepts on the behaviour of men and women. The following verses are the most relevant:

[2] Day and night women must be kept in dependence by the males of their families, and, if they attach themselves to sensual enjoyments, they must be kept under one's control... [3] Her father protects her in childhood, her husband protects her in youth, and her sons protect

her in old age; a woman is never fit for independence... [147] By a girl, by a young woman, or even by an aged one, nothing must be done independently, even in her own house... [154] Though destitute of virtue, or seeking pleasure elsewhere, or devoid of good qualities, yet a husband must be constantly worshiped as a god by a faithful wife. (Radhakrishnan and Moore, 1957: 190-191).

A common principle across the long history of ancient Indian philosophy (Radhakrishnan and Moore, 1957) is the subjugation of women and the dominance of men. The Laws of Manu represent the most explicit but by no means the only work stressing female subjugation. Discussing the contemporary situation of marriage and caste rules among Singaporeans of Indian descent, Mani (1979) suggested that Indians were becoming more flexible in expressing their dissenting views on traditional rules of marriage, but they still adhere to them in practice (Sandhu and Mani, 1993).

Gender segregation among the Singaporean Chinese is mostly dictated by a secular tradition, Confucianism (if one agrees that it is a philosophy, not a religion).[1] In contrast, the most influential tradition dictating gender segregation among Singaporean Malays is religious rather than secular; 99 per cent of the Malays in Singapore are Muslims according to the 1990 Population Census. However, in the case of Singapore Indians, both secular and religious influences are found. Indeed, in addition to the Indian secular traditions mentioned above, Singaporean Indians may also be influenced by their religious beliefs (Hindu, Muslim, Christian, Sikh or any other religion as the case may be)[2] when defining their beliefs on the appropriate roles of men and women in their community.

Nevertheless, the influence of traditional precepts, whether religious or secular, upon one's everyday life, is neither dominant nor constant. It is normal for people of all religious faiths and cultural traditions to interpret, adapt and transform their religion's precepts in their daily lives just as they adapt their cultural traditions and borrow from other cultures in their attempt to maintain control over their own lives. This latter process of pragmatic acculturation (Quah, 1989:5-8), combined with the inclination to adapt and interpret religious canons represents one of the methods used by women in their striving for coherence, shall be discussed later.

2. The exigencies of a modern economy

In addition to the influence of traditional values, the second main trend affecting the social definition of gender roles in Singapore is represented in the exigencies of a modern economy. Singapore is one of the four new industrialized economies or NIEs (together with Hong Kong, China; Taiwan Province of China; and the Republic of Korea) that surprised the global community by springing from obscurity to prominence within a relatively short span of two decades. These four little dragons distinguished themselves in the Third World by their fast pace of economic development and their sustained efforts to compete successfully in international markets. In the process, Singapore, like the other three NIEs, has had to make adjustments and changes of various kinds

---

[1] According to the *1995 General Household Survey* (Department of Statistics, 1996c), 14.3 per cent of the Singaporean Chinese were Christians; 17.9 per cent did not identify themselves with any religion; and 67.2 per cent were Buddhists or Taoist. The latter two are religious groups who basically accept that canons of behaviour taught by Confucius concerning the roles of men and women.

[2] The *1995 General Household Survey* (Department of Statistics, 1996c) indicate that Singaporean Indians have a wider variety of religions than their Chinese or Malay counterparts. The three largest religious groups among Indians are Hindus (52.6 per cent), Muslims (27.2 per cent) and Christians (13.6).

in the traditional ways of thinking and doing things.

Singapore, in particular, recognized at the outset, the need for a change in the traditional prescriptions defining the role of women if economic development plans were to be effectively implemented. Accordingly, two steps were taken by the government in the early 1960s concerning family and labour. On the aspect of family, the Women's Charter 1961 established the equality of women in marriage, divorce, and rights and duties regarding property and financial matters (Quah, 1981:36-37). This legislation represents the State's attempt to release women from their traditionally sanctioned subordination to men in so far as it was needed to encourage women to participate in the labour force.

Consequently, the following year, a significant change took place concerning the aspect of equality in the labour force. In the words of a Senior Minister of State, "a milestone was achieved when equal pay was accorded to female civil servants in 1962. Prior to this, women officers on monthly salaries were paid 80 per cent of their male counterparts' salaries". Other improvements in the conditions of employment for female civil servants made in the same year were to allow them to remain in the permanent establishment and to be entitled to pension rights even after they were married (Rahim, 1979:73). Notwithstanding the positive significance of this early government move towards gender equality, it is interesting to note that the principle of equal wages for equal work has not yet been incorporated into labour legislation. That is to say, this principle is not obligatory for the private sector. The government's position on this point has been to take the lead and hope that private sector employers will follow. Apparently that has happened in many cases (Rahim, 1979:73).

These early reforms have been followed by improvements in labour legislation over the past years. Two examples of the State's commitment in this direction are the special provisions of the Employment Act [Cap 122, Part IX, Articles 76 and 81] entitling female workers to eight weeks' maternity leave (to be taken four weeks before and four weeks after childbirth) and prohibiting their dismissal during maternity leave (Republic of Singapore, 1981:42; Ministry of Labour, 1987:36-39; Chua and Theyvendram, 1990:44-49; NTUC, 1996:22-23). Based on the idea of setting the example of taking the lead in labour equality, the latest government scheme for female civil servants includes some important improvements. These are: a maximum of 56 days' maternity leave for the first and second child; child care leave of absence without pay/salary for a maximum of four years from the birth of the child; the option of taking half-pay, two thirds, or three quarters of pay with proportionally reduced hours of work; and a maximum of five days a year of their unrecorded full-pay leave to attend to young children who fall ill (Seet, 1989:94).

In the context of Singapore, these are significant changes. However, Singapore is still far behind other nations mostly because this new scheme is not mandatory for the private sector as it only applies to women in the civil service. If the maternity leave for the civil service, which has doubled from eight to sixteen weeks with the full salary benefits, were to be mandatory for all women workers in Singapore, the scheme would put Singapore ahead of England and Germany and comparable to France (*Straits Times*, 1990b), but still behind Sweden (Ditch, Barnes, and Bradshaw, 1996). Sweden has a distinguished record of legislation in this regard with maternity benefits sanctioned by the Swedish Parliament in 1937. More significantly, in Singapore, parental leave after the birth of the child for both father and mother was passed in 1974 and extended to 270 days in 1978 (Quah, 1990:14-16). The move from *maternity* leave to *parental* leave for all workers is a fundamental step towards gender equality not only in the area of employment but also in the family. It represents the institutionalized recognition of the privilege and obligation of both parents to look after their children. Thus, even when improvements are made, the State is still sending mixed signals by not making the improvements mandatory for the private sector and by still seeing women as the care givers and discounting the role of men as fathers.

Besides enacting legislation, political leaders since the early 1960s, have periodically explained to the population the close link they perceived between Singapore's economic development and women's equality. An analysis of the pronouncements of political leaders over the past 30 years reveals a transition from the "one role" ideology to the "two role" ideology, as put forward by Bernard (1972).

The one role ideology assigns the traditional roles of childbearing, child rearing and housekeeping services (Bernard, 1972:236) exclusively to women. The two role ideology stresses the importance of devising adjustments that would make it easier for women to combine motherhood and the care of a home with outside activities that is with a job (1972:236-7). Bernard also presents the concept of the "shared role" ideology whereby the two important roles of child rearing and socialization should not be entrusted to one sex alone; both parents should participate and both should have the option of part-time participation in the labour force (1972:243). Bernard found the first formal manifestation of the two role ideology in a report from the Royal Commission on Population in the United Kingdom in 1949, and then in the establishment of the Commission on the Status of Women by President J.F. Kennedy in the United States in 1961. In both instances, the central argument was that women's participation in the labour force was an essential requirement for the nation's economic development and defence (1972:237).

This ideological change in the perception of gender roles, from one role to the two role ideology, took place in industrialized countries around the 1950s. Some optimistic observers believe that the two role ideology is now geared to move towards the shared role ideology, but no fundamental change in this regard has been observed in Western nations. In Singapore, as mentioned above, there has been a transition from the one role ideology to the two role ideology. Accordingly, two features distinguish the case of Singapore from that of industrialized nations. One feature is the manner in which the change in role ideologies took place. The other feature is the current emphasis on the two role ideology.

Regarding the manner in which the Singaporeans' transition from the one role to the two role ideology occurred, it was planned and implemented from the top by a predominantly male political leadership instead of being the outcome of the women's movement. The rationale comprises of these premises: the economic success of Singapore necessitates the full participation of women in the labour force; to attain full labour force participation, women must be freed from the traditional domestic role of wife and mother; and women be assisted in consolidating the two roles they are expected to fulfill, the domestic role and the role of income earner.

Some illustrations of this process will suffice. In a 1975 speech to trade union members on the role of women in industrial society, the then Prime Minister of Singapore, Lee Kuan Yew, summarized the basic principles of government intervention. His views, as narrated by Josey (1980:261-2) were:

> "Industrialization required women workers. This has led to the education of women – the key was education – . There have been no vociferous women liberation movement in Singapore. It had been government policy to encourage the education of women to their fullest ability and their employment commensurate with their abilities...What had not yet taken place in traditional male-dominant

Asian societies was the helping in household work by husbands...This change in social attitudes could not come by legislation."

The same principles and arrangements have been repeated consistently in the speeches of other government leaders over the past three decades. Most of them pointed out that educated females are needed because for Singapore to move up the technological ladder, it had to make maximum use of the available human resources (Rahim Ishak, 1979:73). In 1981, the then Minister for Trade and Industry said that the shortage of skilled, technical and professional manpower could be alleviated by encouraging women not to leave their jobs after marriage or childbirth and that child care facilities should be improved in this regard. It was also suggested that employers should offer better terms and conditions of employment (Tan, 1981:55). Other leaders had already affirmed this message (Ahmad, 1980) and repeated it (Wong, 1981; Chua, 1982; Seet, 1989; Wee, 1990). In fact, the government's efforts in helping women in the fulfillment of their dual role obligations – embedded in the two role ideology – have been said to be successful. Indeed, the two role ideology has been internalized, becoming part of the cultural landscape. A female government leader explained some years ago that: "in today's age women can complete their work more quickly and have more time in their hands to pursue careers and contribute to the economy". More importantly, the government's schemes of child care and encouraging foreign maids have also made it easier for women to go to work (Seet, 1989:94).

Another manifestation of the two role ideology may be detected in the reasons put forward for the lack of progress towards a more equitable sharing of roles between the genders. As indicated earlier, the former Prime Minister lamented in 1975 that the traditional Asian attitude of male domination could not be changed by legislation (Josey, 1980:262).

Echoing his feelings a few years later, Rahim Ishak indicated that "deep-rooted prejudices against women cannot be removed overnight by speeches or curbed by law". In his opinion, part of the solution was in the hands of women as he added that "respect has to be earned and I am confident that our Singapore women will respond to the challenge with a little help from their male counterparts" (1979:74).

A decade later, Mr Lee Kuan Yew provided another example of this way of thinking while responding to a question on what was the biggest failure of his [Lee's] tenure as Prime Minister (Smith, 1988:159). Lee replied:

"I underestimated the Chinese mother – We have had equal education for men and women here – And that produced a problem I did not foresee. The Chinese mother is a great force for education. She will make sure each child has a desk. She will nag about homework and keep the television off. But the Chinese mother also tells her *son* that he must be the master of his own house. Then he grows up and doesn't want a wife who has a Master's or a Ph.D. because he might not be the ruler of his own house – I underestimated the Chinese mother." (Smith, 1988:159-60).

These remarks are significant in two respects. On the one hand, the views of Lee Kuan Yew are highly influential in the shaping of Singaporeans' attitudes (a good example among others is the value of meritocracy and the corresponding rejection of nepotism as principles guiding the administration of public affairs). His views on the Chinese mother, however, would have a negative influence on attitudes towards gender equality because, at a first glance, Lee appears to be blaming the victim. He implies that the seeds of male dominance are sown by women. Yet, on the other hand, Lee's views about the situation may not be completely distorted as one finds discrepancies in gender values among women themselves. Hence, the need to discuss the women's struggle for coherence arises at this point. Before dealing with the women's efforts to reconcile with contradictory trends, the third trend of the promotion of the value of gender equality is discussed below.

3. The value of gender equality

It has been shown how two of the contradictory trends operate. On the one hand, traditional values define the social roles of men and women in terms of dominance and subordination. On the other hand, the practical necessity of utilizing all available human resources to attain higher economic development motivates the political leadership to promote some aspects of equality to help and encourage women to participate actively in the labour force in addition to looking after their families. The third factor in this equation is the value of gender equality.

Gender equality is the situation whereby women and men are considered equal in all spheres of life, that is, in terms of their rights and obligations as citizens of a nation, as individuals in a democratic society, as members of the labour force, and as partners in marriage and parenthood. It is clear from the preceding pages that the value of equality between men and women is not indigenous to Singapore society. It may be more appropriate to say that the idea of gender equality has been imported from other cultures, particularly from Europe and the United States.

The situation in Singapore shows some similarities and some differences with the processes of gender equality in Europe and the United States. In terms of similarities, one may observe that the pace and degree of changes that have occurred in Singapore's transition from an entrepot economy to an industrial economy have affected people's values and attitudes in terms of raising their awareness of the importance of universal education, the need for a skilled labour force and the need to tap all available talent, both male and female, to boost economic development.

Yet, as discussed earlier, Singapore has shown a significantly different implementation of those new perspectives. Notwithstanding the work of a handful of local female activists in the 1950s (Wong, 1990), it was the political establishment, spearheaded by its male political leaders, who began promoting some basic principles of gender equality in Singapore and created the space for women's participation in the political process. The gender equality principles promoted by the government since independence have been limited because the aim is not to make radical changes in the social definitions of male and female roles but, rather, to create the basic necessary conditions to bring women into the labour force without altering their traditional roles of wife and mother.

Some details on political participation of women are instructive at this juncture. The introduction of automatic registration of voters, including women, in 1955 increased the proportion of women voters from a mere 8 per cent to 50 per cent (Wang and Teo, 1993:286). Since then, women have participated in political activities to the extent that their votes in the electoral process represent their position. However, the historical trends on female participation as political and public candidates suggest a reverse pattern in Singapore when compared with Western nations. Two women activists commented candidly that "the women who joined the PAP (People's Action Party) since 1961 were moderate and, perhaps, somewhat passive when compared with the old firebrands" (Wang and Teo, 1993:290). The first two general elections held in Singapore in 1959 and 1963 involved the largest number of women candidates (9 and 11, respectively) in two decades. In 1959, the number of elected female Members of Parliament (MPs) was the largest when five women from two political parties won in the election. There were no female MPs from 1972 to 1984. Three women won in the election in 1984; four in 1988, and two in 1991 (Wang and Teo, 1993:288-289). Four women won seats in Parliament in the 1997 General Elections, two of them retaining their seats since 1984. The overall picture shows a decline in the proportion of female MPs from 9.8 per cent in 1959, to nil in the period 1972-1984, and a very slow and jagged upward trend to 4.5 per cent in 1997.

The question that needs to be asked at this point is: Is the Singapore establishment unique in not responding to the need for a more comprehensive gender equality? Perhaps not. The case of Japan, the most economically advanced Asian nation, suggests that the weight of tradition in Asia may successfully counteract or delay the pull towards equality of gender roles, that is, towards the shared role ideology.

In sum, a brief look at the three main contradictory signals received by Singapore women indicates the presence of a conflicting situation. Traditional values praise the dominant position of men and the virtue of female subordination. The exigencies of a modern economy have led the political leadership to promote the need for women to join the labour force and, as an incentive, to legislate the equality of women in some aspects of family and working life in order to facilitate their managing of two roles. But the value of gender equality has not been pursued with vigour at the top level despite the fact that the Singapore political leadership has demonstrated their capacity to promote successfully most of the goals they set out to attain.

It may be unrealistic to expect that the drive for comprehensive gender equality should be promoted by the government. Is this goal taken up by a women's movement in Singapore? No, or, at least, not as yet. During the past three decades, Singaporeans have been less than enthusiastic about mass movements generated at the grass root level. The nature of their political system, the rising standard of living attained by Singaporeans and their inclination towards social discipline (Quah,

1983) are among the most important reasons for the absence of social movements among women.

Nevertheless, a small group of the most educated women have worked, sometimes jointly, sometimes individually, for the organization of female groups to represent and voice the needs and aspirations of women. These women are found in associations such as the Singapore Council of Women's Organizations, the Singapore Women's Association, the Singapore Association of Women Lawyers, and the Singapore Business and Professional Women's Association. The only women's organization that most closely resembles a women's pressure group in Singapore is the Association of Women for Action and Research (AWARE). AWARE is the most recent of the women's groups and was registered in December, 1985. The three general objectives of the Association as stated in its Constitution are "to promote the awareness and participation of women in all areas; to promote the attainment of full equality; and to promote equal opportunities for women" (AWARE, 1985:3). AWARE has been active in organizing and promoting group discussions on gender issues and gender equality. It is also doing some intervention work with a local newspaper by setting up a hotline and providing telephone counseling for women in distress. The Singapore Association of Women Lawyers (SAWL) has also worked on providing legal aid and educating the public on aspects of gender equality (Singapore Association of Women Lawyers, 1986).

Nevertheless, the existence of AWARE and SAWL and their activities cannot be mistaken as a women's movement. AWARE, SAWL and the other women's organizations remain groups led and followed mostly by a minority among the highly educated women. The Women's Sub-Committee of the National Trade Union Congress (NTUC) and the Women's Wing of the People's Action Party (Wong, 1990) have a much wider constituency of female workers and female PAP members, respectively. Thus, their members come from a wider spectrum of social classes. But even these more pluralistic organizations do not seem to instill the high degree of enthusiasm and commitment required to mobilize the female population into a mass movement of gender equality concerns in Singapore.

In addition to the presence of women's organizations, the idea of gender equality in any society may be promoted or discouraged by the formal educational system at the primary and secondary levels. Higher education, on the contrary, is one of the most effective vehicles for the transmission of gender equality values (Kelly and Elliot, 1982; Bloom, 1987:106-107). While the textbooks and curriculum at the primary school level in Singapore had serious gender biases (Quah, 1980) that the system has tried to overcome, it may be stated that the values of gender equality are implemented in the educational system in the sense that it offers equal opportunities of entry and treatment to male and female students (with the exception of a smaller quota for female students who wish to study medicine). In 1995, females made up 47.8 per cent of all primary school pupils; 47.8 per cent of secondary school pupils; and 45.5 per cent of students at the National University of Singapore and the Nanyang Technological University (Department of Statistics, 1996a:226). This indicates that the female population of Singapore is, in general, well educated as compared with female populations in other Third World countries. Table 8 shows that although the number of female graduates from institutions of higher learning is still lower than the corresponding number of male graduates, the number of women graduates has increased steadily from about 1 in 10,000 female population in 1950 to 68.5 per 10,000 female population in 1996.

Why, then, with the presence of women's organizations and a well educated female population, are there no clear signs of a collective female will to gain comprehensive

Table 8. Graduates from institutions of higher learning, 1950-1996

Year	Males		Females	
	Total	Rates per 10,000 male population	Total	Rates per 10,000 female population
1950	90	1.7	53	1.2
1960	1 115	13.0	649	8.2
1970	2 216	20.9	1 485	14.7
1982	3 736	31.3	2 783	23.9
1986	5 827	45.6	4 591	37.0
1989	7 406	55.2	5 409	41.4
1992	8 704	61.1	7 595	54.5
1995	10 683	71.1	9 920	66.9
1996	11 469	74.9	10 359	68.5

Source: Rates calculated from population figures provided in Department of Statistics (1983:240-243); Department of Statistics (1992:29, 310, 312); Department of Statistics (1996a:23, 238); Department of Statistics (1997b:240).

gender equality in Singapore? As indicated above, the socio-political and economic environment of Singapore does not provide the motivation for mass movements. It appears that another important reason is that women exposed to the idea of gender equality find themselves struggling for congruity among three contradictory ideologies: the shared role ideology implied by the idea of equality; the one role ideology promoted by traditional values on female subordination; and the two role ideology justified by the exigencies of economic development.

C. Struggling for coherence

How are Singaporean women responding to the unenviable challenge of reconciling these opposing social expectations? There is no simple answer to this, but it appears that compartmentalizing different spheres of activity and separating attitudes from behaviour may be two of the most common approaches towards a pragmatic solution to the conflict. Moreover, these trends are discernible when examined with some specific data.

Compartmentalizing one's spheres of activity, that is, separating one's role obligations in terms of time, space, or both, helps to minimize the strain caused when those roles are incompatible (Burr, 1973:133; Burr, Leigh, Day and Constantine, 1979:82-84). It appears that the majority of Singaporean women opt for compartmentalization of two seemingly incompatible roles, the role of wife/mother and the role of worker, by engaging in each, one at a time. Table 9 shows that in 1996, about one out of every two women aged 15 years and above, participated in the labour force, a significant change from only three women out of every ten in 1970. More importantly, the labour force participation rate of females varies with age and with the main roles socially assigned to them. For example, in 1996 eight out of every ten Singaporean women aged 25 to 29 were working. This is the age cohort with the highest labour force participation rates. From age 30, women begin withdrawing from the labour force. In 1970, the tendency to withdraw from the labour force was evident

after age 25. What happened to women around the age of 25? This was the time in her life cycle when the average Singaporean woman married (Quah, 1990:252-253) and the time she believed was ideal for her to become a mother (Quah, 1988:4). As the actual and ideal age for marriage and parenthood has moved upward, so has the age of withdrawal from the labour force. As we can see from table 9, that in 1996, this trend was obvious among women aged 30 and older.

Comparing the trends in female labour force participation across time, another interesting feature in table 9 is that, while a substantial proportion of women withdraw from labour force, a small but steadily increasing number of women continue working after the age of 30. In other words, more women are taking up the stressful challenge of combining the responsibilities of home and job, for example, for women in the age group of 30-34,

Table 9. Labour force participation rates by age group, 1970, 1981, 1996

Age cohort	Gender	1970	1981	1996
Total population	Total	46.6	63.0	64.6
15 years and over	Males	67.6	81.1	78.7
	Females	24.6	44.8	51.5
15-19 years old	Total	49.5	45.1	20.1
	Males	55.7	44.1	21.7
	Females	43.0	46.1	18.5
20-24 years old	Total	73.5	85.9	76.1
	Males	92.9	92.5	74.3
	Females	53.6	79.0	77.6
25-29 years old	Total	64.5	79.4	88.1
	Males	98.0	97.8	96.4
	Females	30.8	60.3	81.4
30-34 years old	Total	60.0	73.0	82.1
	Males	98.3	98.4	98.2
	Females	22.7	46.7	68.0
40-44 years old	Total	60.8	66.5	77.4
	Males	98.1	98.2	98.2
	Females	17.8	37.0	56.9
50-54 years old	Total	55.0	55.8	67.5
	Males	88.1	89.9	91.4
	Females	17.8	22.3	43.7

Sources: Ministry of Finance (1979); Ministry of Trade and Industry (1982); Ministry of Labour (1997:4).

labour force participation rates increased from 22.7 in 1970 to 68.0 in 1996, and for age group of 40-44 years, from 17.8 in 1970 to 56.9 in 1996, indicating a tendency among women to adopt a two role ideology behaviour in recent years. Another illustration of the move towards two role ideology during the decade of 1986-1996 is shown in table 10. The proportion of married women in all occupations except 'other workers' category has increased substantially, particularly in blue-collar jobs such as production and machine operation and

in clerical jobs. The two largest proportions of married women are still found in administrative, managerial or executive positions (67.1 per cent in 1996) and in service and sales jobs (58.9 per cent in 1996).

While the increasing participation of women in the labour force is a sign of their moving away from the sole role of homemakers, the types of occupations they hold in the labour market reflect the extent to which women have advanced in traditionally male-dominated

Table 10. Number and percentage distribution of employed persons aged 15 years and over by occupation, marital status and sex, 1986 and 1996

Occupation	Sex and marital status	1986	1996
Professional, technical and related workers	Total number[2]	126 430	436 085
	% males	61.1	58.7
	% females	38.9	41.3
	% married women	46.3	51.9
	(all female workers)	(49 138)	(179 948)
Administrative, managerial and executive workers	Total number	68 116	215 341
	% males	78.8	79.9
	% females	21.2	20.1
	% married women	55.3	67.1
	(all female workers)	(14 466)	(43 329)
Clerical and related workers	Total number	180 632	263 290
	% males	30.3	23.3
	% females	69.7	76.7
	% married women	34.8	53.7
	(all female workers)	(125 828)	(201 855)
Service and sales workers	Total number	292 069	230 244
	% males	56.1	56.6
	% females	43.9	43.4
	% married women	49.0	58.9
	(all female workers)	(128 335)	(100 033)
Production, transport, operators and assemblers[1]	Total number	411 028	384 634
	% males	73.6	74.5
	% females	26.4	25.5
	% married women	43.3	62.4
	(all female workers)	(108 429)	(97 872)
Other workers	Total number	70 748	218 546
	% males	94.5	53.6
	% females	5.5	46.4
	% married women	66.2	46.0
	(all female workers)	(3 861)	(101 486)

Sources: Calculated from figures in Ministry of Labour (1987:62); and Ministry of Labour (1997:81).

[1] "Labourers" are included in 1986 but classified as part of "Other" in the 1996 Report.

[2] Total employed persons or 100 per cent.

occupations. The overall distribution of workers in the labour force has changed since 1970 due to Singapore's advancement in economic development. The highest concentration of female labour in 1970 was in the category of factory production workers or operators. With the upgrading and diversification of skills and improvement in the overall education of women, significant changes are observed in pattern and type of employment. To illustrate, the proportion of employed women in blue-collar jobs (production, machine or vehicle operation) decreased from 25.2 per cent in 1986 to 13.5 per cent in 1996; while the proportion of women in professional and technical occupations increased from 11.4 per cent in 1986 to 24.8 in 1996. There was also a modest yet meaningful increase from 3.4 per cent to 6.0 per cent of women in the administrative, managerial and executive positions from 1986 to 1996. There is still a tendency towards taking up lower-level clerical positions as the highest proportion of women are employed in these type of jobs (29.3 per cent in 1986 and 27.9 per cent in 1996, compared with only 7.6 per cent and 6.0 per cent for men in 1986 and 1996, respectively). Most of these occupations are stereotypical female jobs such as secretaries and clerks. However, there has been a robust drive towards computerization and the upgrading of this type of workers' skills in recent years.

The analysis, thus far, has shown that women are participating in larger numbers in the nation's economy, but they have not made inroads into the labour force significant enough to attain a similar distribution of male and female workers along the full spectrum of occupations. A related and relevant feature of the actual situation of women in the labour force is their income. Briefly stated, female workers are likely to earn less than their male counterparts. Table 11 shows the female average basic monthly wages as a percentage of male average basic monthly wages for selected occupations for 1990 and 1996. The three important features to be noted in table 11 are:

Table 11. Female average basic monthly wages as percentage of male average basic monthly wages, 1990 and 1995 selected occupations

Occupation	1990	1995
Professionals		
Accountant	75.8	84.6
Building architect	85.3	92.6
Chemical engineer	64.7	73.3
Computer programmer	88.4	93.5
General physician	82.2	94.2
Lawyer	81.8	87.6
Managers		
Marketing manager	80.7	75.9
Research & development manager	86.2	79.2
Clerical & sales workers		
Bank teller	82.5	84.9
Cashier	85.2	95.2
Typist	80.8	86.9
Trade salesman/saleswomen	85.8	94.8
Service workers		
Cook	66.5	61.6
Hotel housekeeper	107.1	115.3
Production, transport, operators		
Machine fitter	71.6	68.5
Welder	77.0	70.8

Sources: Calculated from figures provided in Ministry of Labour (1991:44-78); and Ministry of Labour (1996:50-67).

first, irrespective of the prestige of an occupation, most jobs are better paid when performed by men than by women. This differential earning power has existed for many decades and is by no means peculiar to Singapore. As mentioned earlier, analysts point to the same problem in industrialized countries (Ehrenreich, 1990; Ditch, Barnes and Bradshaw, 1996:58). Second, as the table compares wages for the same occupation, which in the context of Singapore's meritocratic ideology, implies that both male and female workers on those jobs have the same required qualifications. Consequently, the workers' gender becomes a significant explanatory factor for the wage difference, in addition to length of service and performance level. Third, to note a positive point, with the exception of managers, the wage discrepancy between male and female workers has diminished for most of the jobs during the past decade as women receive 85 to 95 per cent of male wages. The Singapore data on wages may not be directly comparable to data from other countries, and it cannot reach 100 per cent gender equity because of the national service increment, a unique Singaporean phenomenon.[3]

In sum, taking into consideration all other economic and social arrangements that might explain gender differences in wages, the relatively lower wages of women may still be interpreted as an indication of the prevalence of the two role ideology. Men's jobs in general, and husbands' jobs in particular, are considered to be more important than the jobs of women, or of working wives, given the social perception of men and husbands as the family's principal economic providers (Gronseth, 1973).

The figures in tables 1 to 11 provide information on social and economic behaviour of female population, that is, where female workers are found and what they earn. As women become more educated, they are more inclined to take up a job rather than to limit themselves to the domestic role. Despite the fact that women, on average, receive lower incomes than their male colleagues, and that the traditional values stress the virtue of full dedication to marriage and motherhood, it does not appear that women are deterred from seeking and holding a job. While most working women compartmentalize these roles by working only before marriage or motherhood, there is a growing trend towards the holding of both roles concurrently.

In addition to women's socio-economic situation and behaviour, the realm of attitudes and opinions also needs to be explored to identify the extent to which a separation of attitudes and behaviour is used by women in their struggle for coherence. That is, women may find it possible to reconcile with conflicting social pressures when they think liberal but act conservative. Table 12 compares the attitudes of a representative sample of Singaporean men and women to illustrate possible gender differences in the way people assess some important social situations. Attitudes towards five areas of life are presented namely, social relations, community involvement, a sense of control over one's life, education, and perceived standard of living. In the context of this discussion, the important message conveyed by the figures in table 12 is that there is a persistently high degree of similarity in the attitudes of men and women on all social matters. Among the three aspects of social relations, only one shows a statistically significant difference between the sexes. The majority of men and women feel that one must be careful in dealing with people (82.3 per cent in the case of men and 87.6 per cent in the case of women). A relatively smaller proportion of men and women believe that most people are helpful (35.9 vs. 44.1). But women are more inclined than men to believe that people try to be fair.

An interesting finding emerges from table 12 concerning community involvement, an aspect that is traditionally seen as the realm of men, particularly in Confucius' teachings. There are no gender differences in the way Singaporeans see the chances of poor and rich people in community involvement, but significantly more men (22.1 per cent) than women (16.9 per cent) say they are active in community affairs.

The conversations with this representative sample of Singaporeans revealed that there are no differences between men and women in terms of their sense of control over their own lives. Whether male or female, about one out of every two persons tend to believe that, in general, what happens to them may be "a matter of good or bad fortune". Nevertheless, when it comes to attaining success, the majority of both men and women (78.2 per cent men and

---

[3] The national service increment represents the social contract with all able-bodied males aged 18 to 40 whereby they are compensated for the two years that they must spend in compulsory full-time military training (NTUC, 1996:103-105).

Table 12. Attitudes of men and women towards five areas of life

Percentage of respondents agreeing with the statements below	Men	Women
Total	100.0	100.0
(N)	(751)	(870)
On social relations		
One needs to be careful in dealing with people[1]	82.3	87.6
Most of the time people try to be helpful[1]	35.9	44.1
Most of the time people try to be fair[2]	48.0	56.1
On community involvement		
Poor people have very slim chances of being heard in matters that affect the community[1]	62.6	60.0
Rich people can get away with almost anything because of their money[1]	52.8	53.6
I am an active person in the community[3]	22.1	16.9
On a sense of control		
It is not always wise to plan too far ahead because many things turn out to be a matter of good or bad fortune anyway[1]	51.5	46.7
Becoming a success is a matter of hard work. Luck has little or nothing to do with it[1]	78.2	80.1
On education		
People can learn more through working than going to school[1]	56.9	55.7
Education enables us to make the best possible use of our lives[1]	94.0	93.2
The least amount of schooling a young woman needs to get along well in Singapore is:		
Primary school	7.3	5.9
Complete 'O' levels	45.3	46.5
Complete 'A' levels	27.6	27.4
Tertiary education[1]	18.7	20.1
On standard of living		
Comparing myself with my father when he was my age in terms of my present standard of living, I am better off[1]	66.7	69.8
Comparing myself with my mother when she was my age in terms of my present standard of living, I am better off[1]	*	73.5
Comparing myself with my children when they reach my age in terms of my present standard of living, they will be better off[1]	75.7	78.8

Source: These are original data from a study on social class. For details on how the study was conducted see Quah, Chiew, Ko, and Lee (1991).

Notes:
[1] No statistically significant differences found.
[2] p <.004
[3] p <.02
* Question asked to female respondents only.

80.1 per cent of women, or about eight out of every ten persons), consider that it is hard work rather than luck that determines one's success in life. It is noteworthy that Singaporean women believe in the positive effect of hard work as much as their male counterparts. Hard work refers, among other things, to the attaining of appropriate skills. Indeed, the same trend is evident when the respondents express their views on education: nine out of every ten male and female Singaporeans agree that education enables them "to make the best possible use of their lives". As for the question on how much education a young woman needs to get along well in Singapore, no difference in opinion was found between men and women. The most common response from both men and women about schooling is that a young woman would only need to complete her 'O' levels or secondary school certificate (46 per cent). A relatively smaller but equal proportions of men and women think that a young woman should obtain her 'A' levels or Junior College certificate (27 per cent) or proceed to tertiary education (19.4 per cent). In sum, there is no evidence that women differ from men in their views on the importance of hard work and education and on how much education women should receive. Yet, as shown in table 13, people from all the three major ethnic communities are inclined to believe that men need to be better educated than women to get along well in Singapore.

The same pattern of affinity between men's and women's perceptions is found on standard of living changes across generations. Table 12 shows that the majority of men and women report that they are better off than their fathers in terms of standard of living. Following an optimistic view of the future, most men and women foresee that their own children will enjoy an even better standard of living. More importantly, seven out of every ten women say that they are better off now than their mothers were at the same age.

Taken together, the most significant findings in tables 12 and 13 are: first, that women do not differ from men in their attitudes towards the control they have over their own lives, the importance of hard work and education in attaining success, and the improvement they enjoy in the standard of living compared with their parents' generation; second, that most women do not perceive any serious obstacles that are impeding their attainment of success in life; and, in the opinion of both men and women, the perceived social requirements for male success stipulate that men should attain higher education than women (table 13).

If it is a prevalent belief that women need less education than men to get along well in Singapore, perhaps people also hold different views on what constitutes success for men and women. There are some indirect indications on this issue from two studies on attitudes towards family life in Singapore (Ministry of Community Development, 1987; Quah, 1988). As explained elsewhere (Quah, 1994), while the majority (64.5 per cent) of a sample of young educated women believe that marriage "is what gives meaning to a woman's life", an even higher proportion (71.1 per cent) do not seem to see marriage as the symbol of female success and assert that a woman "does not have to get married to live a happy life". Suggesting a liberal or modern view on life style options open to women, only a minority of women in the same study see marriage as "an obstacle for a woman's career" (28.2 per cent) and believe that women lose their independence when they get married (35.1 per cent). In fact, as illustrated in table 14, educated women tend to

Table 13. Percentage distribution of views on lowest education needed by men and women to succeed in Singapore by ethnicity

Lowest educational level needed	Chinese		Malay		Indian	
	Men	Women	Men	Women	Men	Women
'O' Levels[a]	45.5	54.8	38.6	47.6	45.7	54.6
'A' Levels	36.3	33.1	26.2	21.5	39.9	35.4
Tertiary	18.2	12.1	35.2	30.9	14.5	10.9
Total	100.0	100.0	100.0	100.0	100.0	100.0
(Number)	(413)	(414)	(233)	(233)	(173)	(174)

Source: Original data from same study referred to in table 12.

Note: [a] Includes a very small group of respondents who feel that primary school education is sufficient: only 5.8 per cent of them say that for girls, and 3.4 per cent for boys.

Table 14. Attitudes of men and women towards family life

Percentage of respondents agreeing with the statements below	Men	Women
On family relations[1]		
Total	100.0	100.0
(Number)	(378)	(380)
Have children to look after me in my old age[a]	57.7	61.8
Have children to carry on family line[a]	70.4	65.0
Have children to please family elders[a]	50.8	49.5
Prefer to live in a nuclear household (husband, wife and children only)[b]	42.5	52.9
Communication, care and concern are the most important factors for family happiness[a]	44.4	47.4
Most important principle of marriage[2]		
Total	*	100.0
(Number)	*	(233)
Being an understanding companion	*	75.1
Loving my husband	*	54.9
Managing the home	*	38.2
Having children	*	18.9
Obeying my husband	*	12.9

Sources: [1] Figures taken from Ministry of Community Development's (1987) study of a random sample of 758 persons with children below 21 years of age.

[2] Figures taken from Quah (1988:27), a study based on the total number of married women aged 28 or older who had postponed the birth of their first child for at least two years for reasons other than infertility of either spouse.

Notes: [a] No statistically significant difference between men and women.

[b] $p < .004$

* The Study covered women only.

define companionship (75.1 per cent) and love (54.9 per cent) as the most important principles of marriage in contrast to traditional marriage goals such as home management (38.2 per cent), procreation (18.9 per cent) or female subordination (12.9 per cent). Notwithstanding these liberal female attitudes, women do not differ from men on the aspects of family relations. Both men and women give traditional reasons for having children and show a similar ranking of communication, care and concern as

the most important factors for family happiness. Men and women differ, however, on the aspect of living arrangements. Women tend to favour a nuclear household where they would live with their husbands and children only, while men would prefer including their parents.

The substance of these findings corroborates the main points of tables 12 and 13. Singaporean women are inclined towards liberal or modern attitudes concerning hard work, education, life style options other than marriage, a non-traditional definition of marriage as companionship, and the feasibility of preserving a certain level of independence after marriage and of combining both career and family.

Yet, being influenced by both traditional and modern values, the Singaporean married woman faces contradictions in her everyday life. Two of the most serious contradictions are a pervasive feeling of inadequacy as a mother and the strain of shouldering the burden of home management in addition to her job responsibilities. This sense of inadequacy among working mothers has been present for some time as suggested by the married women's responses to an earlier survey on their role in the family (Ministry of Social Affairs, 1984). This study covered a representative sample of 3,000 married women aged 15 to 64 years. The women were asked if they agreed that "a non-working mother is a better mother than the one who works". A large majority of the women (71 per cent) responded that a full-time housewife is a better mother than a working mother. The most common reason given by the women who believed housewives to be better mothers was that non-working mothers can dedicate more time to their children. The negative perception of working mothers as care givers was held by women from all walks of life as there was agreement on this point among working and non-working women, women of different educational qualifications and women in different income groups (1984:52-54).

Another aspect of the burden of the two role ideology has also been documented which relates to the division of domestic labour, or rather, the lack of a meaningful division of domestic labour between husband and wife. There are two studies on the problem. The Report on the Family Survey (Ministry of Community Development, 1987) indicates that the wife, whether she is working or not, is the principal person responsible for housework. The majority of wives are responsible for indispensable tasks such as marketing and shopping for daily goods (65 per cent); cooking (77 per cent); doing the laundry (71 per cent); washing dishes (62 per cent); and cleaning the house (57 per cent). Conversely, only 5 per cent of the respondents reported that the husband is mainly responsible for marketing; and just 1 per cent indicated that the husband is responsible for the other four tasks. Attempts at sharing responsibility for household chores are rather modest. The proportion of couples reporting sharing responsibility was, in descending order: marketing, 22 per cent; cleaning the house, 17 per cent; washing dishes, 13 per cent; cooking, 9 per cent; and doing the laundry, 7 per cent (1987:25). Women from lower income families are less likely to be helped by the husband or by anyone else with the household chores. Indeed, another study on married women living in public housing apartments shows that between 86 to 99 per cent of all married women reported as being solely responsible for marketing, cooking, dish washing and house cleaning (Singapore Council of Women's Organizations, 1989:5).

In accordance with the two role ideology, husbands are more likely to be solely responsible for what is traditionally defined as male responsibilities such as paying for family expenses (60 per cent); earning a living (59 per cent) (Ministry of Community Development, 1987:25); and repairing things around the house (70 per cent) (Singapore Council of Women's Organizations, 1989:5).

D. The future: more of the same?

My argument in this analysis is, simply, that women in Singapore are confronted with a conflicting situation to which they feel they have to adapt. The conflict is created by the presence of three contradictory social trends namely, traditional social values, the exigencies of a modern economy, and the value of gender equality. As women see it, despite the limitations and deficiencies in each of these forces, they have some positive aspects. Traditional values promote family stability and a sense of social order; the need to maintain a fast pace in economic development and to provide the best for their families requires the women's contribution as much as the men's; and the principle of gender equality fits well with the value of meritocracy and the respect for hard work and educational qualifications. The Singaporean woman accepts these separate positive postulates but has to face the inevitable conflict that they produce. Her solution is, in my view, not satisfactory but it is a way of surviving.

Discussing women's struggle for coherence, I have referred in the preceding pages to research findings on both attitudes and behaviour of both men and women. The emerging picture confirms that women attempt to reconcile opposite demands and expectations of their roles in two ways. One approach used by most women is to compartmentalize, or separate, their two roles by allocating different segments of their life cycle to each one: they join the labour force only when they are single or childless. This solution is not good for women on a career track or women working due to financial necessity. The other approach is to separate attitudes from behaviour by opting for being liberal in thought but traditional in action. The most clear indications of this separation are the following contrasts: women put their hard-earned occupational skills to good use when they join the labour force and start a career, but they quit on the belief that good mothers must stay at home; women believe in hard work and education to attain success but they do not demand, as a collectivity, equality of treatment in the labour force; women believe in a marriage based on companionship and love rather than subordination, but they accept the traditional duty of housekeeper in addition to their job obligations as a corollary of the perceived unsuitability of men for these chores.

Looking into the future is always risky, particularly if one does not have solid bases for forecasting. Cautiously, then, I suggest that the three contradictory social trends are likely to continue during the next decade and bring us into the twenty-first century with the same anxieties of the twentieth century. There is a high probability that we will see more of the same struggle for coherence among women for as long as the Singapore Government continues fostering tradition in people's values; meritocracy and productivity continue as the force of economic development; the educational system continues providing wider horizons for human potential; and high technology continues improving Singaporeans' ability to keep in touch with the rest of the world.

The main challenge for sociologists studying gender roles is to identify through further research the best possible avenues for both men and women to be able to attain their life goals at minimum cost to themselves and to their families. The shared roles ideology may be one of several possibilities. But there are many important questions that still remain unanswered and need to be explored further. For example, can the shared roles ideology take root in different cultural soils? Would gender equality produce some side-effects more undesirable than the problems it is meant to solve? On the other hand, can a modern society avoid the implementation of gender equality altogether? Can any society become enlightened when half of its members regard the other half as inferior?

REFERENCES

Ahmad bin M. Ibrahim (1984). *Family Law in Malaysia and Singapore.* Malayan Law Journal, Singapore.

Ahmad Mattar (1980). Social change and women in Singapore. *Speeches*, vol. 3, No. 10, 58-61.

Arumainathan, P. (1973). *Report on the Census of Population 1970, Singapore,* vol's I and II. Singapore: Department of Statistics.

AWARE (1985). *Declaration and Constitution.* Singapore: AWARE (mimeo).

Bernard, J. (1972). Changing Family Life Styles: One Role, Two Roles, Shared Roles. In *The Future of the Family.* L.K. Howe, eds., New York: Simon & Schuster, pp. 235-246.

Black, A.H. (1986). Gender and Cosmology in Chinese Correlative Thinking. In *Gender and Religion: On the Complexity of Symbols.* C.W. Bynum et.al., eds., Boston: Beacon Press, pp. 166-195.

Bloom, A. (1987). *The Closing of the American Mind.* New York: Simon & Schuster.

Burr, W.R. (1973). *Theory Construction and the Sociology of the Family.* New York: John Wiley & Sons.

Burr, W.R., G.K. Leigh; R.D. Day; and J. Constantine (1979). Symbolic Interaction and the Family. In *Contemporary Theories About the family.* W.R. Burr, R. Hill, F.I. Nye, and I.L. Reiss, eds., vol. 2 General Theories/Theoretical Orientations. New York: The Free Press, 42-111.

Chai, C. and W. Chai (1973). *Confucianism.* New York: Barron's.

Chan, W.T. (1963). A *Source Book in Chinese Philosophy.* Princeton, N.J.: Princeton University Press.

Chua, M. and R. Theyvendran (1990). *The Singapore Employment Act and Guide.* Singapore: Aequitas.

Chua, S.C. (1964). *Report of the Census of Population 1957.* State of Singapore. Singapore: Government Printers.

_____ (1982). Women's increasing role in society, *Speeches,* vol. 6, No. 5, pp. 9-12.

Chung, Y. (1989). The impact of Chinese culture on Korea's economic development. In *Confucianism and Economic Development. An Oriental Alternative?* H.C. Tai, ed. Washington: The Washington Institute Press.

Creel, H.G. (1949). *Confucius and the Chinese Way.* New York: Harper & Row.

_____ (1962). *Chinese Thought from Confucius to Mao Tse-Tung.* London: Methuen.

Del Tufo, M.V. (1949). *A Report on the 1947 Census of Population, Malaya Comprising the Federation of Malaya and the Colony of Singapore.* London: The Crown Agents for the Colonies.

Department of Statistics (1983). *Economic and Social Statistics Singapore, 1960-1982.* Singapore: Department of Statistics.

_____ (1988a). *Statistics on Marriages and Divorces, 1987.* Singapore: Department of Statistics.

_____ (1991a). *Yearbook of Statistics Singapore, 1990.* Singapore: Department of Statistics.

_____ (1991b). *Census of Population 1990. Advance Data Release.* Singapore: Department of Statistics.

_____ (1991c). *Advance Data Release of 10 per cent sample from 1990 Census.* Singapore: Department of Statistics.

_____ (1992). *Yearbook of Statistics Singapore, 1991*. Singapore: Department of Statistics.

_____ (1996a). *Yearbook of Statistics 1995*, Singapore: Department of Statistics.

_____ (1996b). *Statistics on Marriages and Divorces, 1995*. Singapore: Department of Statistics.

_____ (1997a). *Singapore 1996 Statistical Highlights*. Singapore: Department of Statistics.

_____ (1997b). *Yearbook of Statistics Singapore, 1996*. Singapore: Department of Statistics.

Ditch, J., H. Barnes; and J. Bradshaw, eds. (1996). *Developments in National Family Policies in 1995*. York: University of York, European Observatory on National Family Policies.

Doeblin, A. (1940). *The Living Thoughts of Confucius*. New York: David McKay.

Ehrenreich, B. (1990). Sorry, sisters, this is not the revolution, *Times*, Fall, 15.

Fry, C.G. and others (1984). *Great Asian Religions*. Grand rapids, Michigan: Baker Book House.

Fung, Y.L. (1948). *A Short History of Chinese Philosophy*. New York: Free Press.

Gronseth, E. (1973). The Breadwinner Trap. In *The Future of the Family*. L.K. Howe, ed. New York: Simon & Schuster: 175-191.

Jaspers, K. (1957). *Socrates, Buddha, Confucius, Jesus. The Paradigmatic Individuals*. New York: Harvest Press.

Josey, A. (1980). *Lee Kuan Yew*. Singapore: Times Books International.

Kelly, G.P. and C.M. Elliot, eds. (1982). *Women's Education in the Third World:*

Comparative Perspectives. Albany, N.Y. State University of New York Press.

Khoo, C.K. (1981a). *Census of Population 1980 Singapore. Release No. 2. Demographic Characteristics*. Singapore: Department of Statistics.

_____ (1981b). *Census of Population 1980 Singapore. Release No. 4. Economic Characteristics*. Singapore: Department of Statistics.

Khoo, C.K. (1981c). *Census of Population 1980 Singapore. Release No. 9. Religion and Fertility*. Singapore: Department of Statistics.

Lau, K.E. (1992a). *Singapore Census of Population 1990. Statistical release 1, Demographic Characteristics*. Singapore: Department of Statistics.

Lee, H.L. (1996). What if Singapore were run along racial and non-meritocratic lines? *Straits Times*, 28 August. p. 28.

Lee, K.Y. (1982b). Why the three-generation family must be encouraged. *Speeches*, vol. 5, No. 9, pp. 8-13.

_____ (1984). Chinese culture can be preserved despite social changes, *Speeches,* vol. 8, No. 1, 8-15.

Lincoln, B. ed. (1985). *Religion, Rebellion, Revolution*. London: Macmillan.

Ling, T. (1989). Religion. In *Management of Success. The Molding of Modern Singapore*. K.S. Sandhu and P. Wheatly, eds. Singapore: Institute of Southeast Asian Studies, pp. 692-709.

Lu, M. (1983). *Confucianism. Its Relevance to Modern Society*. Singapore: Federal Publications.

Mani, A. (1979). Caste and marriage among the Singapore Indians. In *The Contemporary*

Family in Singapore, E. Kuo and A.K. Wong, ed. Singapore: Singapore University Press, pp. 189-207.

Ministry of Community Development (1987). *Survey on Family Life*. Singapore: MCD [Unpublished report].

Ministry of Finance (1979). *Economic Survey of Singapore 1978*. Singapore: SNP.

Ministry of Labour (1987). *Guide to the Employment Act*. Singapore: MOL.

_____ (1991). *Report on Wages in Singapore 1990*. Singapore: MOL.

_____ (1996). *Report on Wages in Singapore 1995*. Singapore: MOL.

_____ (1997). *Report on the Labour Force Survey of Singapore, 1996*. Singapore: MOL.

Ministry of Trade and Industry (1998). *Economic Survey of Singapore 1997*. Singapore: Ministry of Trade and Industry.

National Trade Unions Congress (1996). *A Guide to Labour Legislation in Singapore*. Singapore: NTUC Legal Service Department.

O'Leary, K.D. ed. (1987). *Assessment of Marital Discord*. Hilldale, N.J. Lawrence Erlbaum Associates.

Quah, J.S.T., ed. (1990). *In Search of Singapore National Values*. Singapore: Institute of Policy Studies.

Quah, S.R. (1980). Sex-role socialization in a transitional society, *International Journal of Sociology of the Family*, vol 10, pp. 213-132.

_____ (1981). The impact of policy on the family: can the family be strengthened by legislation? *Southeast Asian Journal of Social Science*, vol. 9, No. 1, pp. 33-53.

_____ (1983). Social discipline in Singapore: an alternative for the resolution of social problems, *Journal of Southeast Asian Studies*, vol. 14, No. 2, pp. 266-289.

_____ (1988). *Between Two Worlds: Modern Wives in a Traditional Setting*. Singapore: Institute of Southeast Asian Studies.

_____ (1989). *The Triumph of Practicality*. Singapore: Institute of Southeast Asian Studies.

_____ (1990). *Family as an Asset. An International Perspective on Marriage, Parenthood and Social Policy*. Singapore: Times Academic Press.

_____ (1994). *Family in Singapore. Sociological Perspectives*. Singapore: Times Academic Press.

_____ (1998). *Family in Singapore. Sociological Perspectives. Second Edition Revised and Expanded*. Singapore: Times Academic Press.

Quah, S.R.; S.K. Chiew; Y.C. Ko; and M.C. Lee (1991). *Social Class in Singapore*. Singapore: Times Academic Press.

Radhakrishnan, S. and C.A. Moore (1957). *A Source Book in Indian Philosophy*. Princeton, N.J.: Princeton University Press.

Rahim Ishak (1979) Role of women. *Speeches*, vol. 3, No. 4, pp. 72-74.

Republic of Singapore (1981). *The Employment Act* (Chapter 122 of Rev. Ed.). Singapore: Attorney-General's Chambers.

Ryan, N.J. (1971). *The Cultural Heritage of Malaya*. Kuala Lumpur: Longman Malaysia.

Sandhu, K.S. and A. Mani, eds. (1993). *Indian Communities in Southeast Asia*. Singapore: Times Academic Press.

Seet, A.M. (1989). Women: maximize your potential. *Speeches*, vol. 13, No. 5, pp. 92-96.

Sharifah Z.S. (1986). Women, divorce and Islam. *Sojourn*, vol. 1, No. 2, pp. 183-198.

Singapore Council of Women's Organizations (1989). *Report on the Survey of Married Women in Public Housing.* Singapore: The Straits Times Press.

Smith, A. (1988). *The Roaring '80s.* New York: Penguin.

Steinmetz, S.K., ed. (1988). *Family and Support Systems Across the Life Span.* New York: Plenum Press.

Straits Times (1982). Story of Moral education. 26 October, p. 14.

_____ (1990a). Ethnic groups asserting their identity a healthy trend. 17 November, p. 25.

_____ (1990b). EC women may get 14 weeks' maternity leave. 7 December, p. 10.

Tan, T.K.Y. (1981). The economy of Singapore: past development and future prospects. In *Issues Facing Singapore in the Eighties,* Ministry of Culture, compiler. Singapore: Information Division, Ministry of Culture, pp. 49-70.

Tay, E.S. (1982). Moral education is important. *Speeches*, vol. 5, No. 9, pp. 56-58.

Tu, W.M. (1984). *Confucian Ethics Today. The Singapore Challenge.* Singapore: CDI.

Waley, A. (1938). *The Analects of Confucius.* New York: Macmillan.

Wallerstein, J. and S. Blakeslee, (1990). *Second Chances. Men, Women and Children a Decade After Divorce.* New York: Ticknor & Fields.

Wallerstein, J. and J.B. Kelly, (1980). *Surviving the Breakup.* New York: Basic Books.

Wang, L.F. and N. Teo, (1993). Public Life and Leadership. In *Singapore Women. Three Decades of Change.* A.K. Wong and W.K. Leong, eds. Singapore: Times Academic Press, pp. 284-317.

Ware, J.R. (1955). *The Sayings of Confucius.* New York: Mentor.

Wee, K.W. (1990). Girl Guides and Girls Scouts: Role in nation-building, *Speeches*, vol. 14, No. 4, pp. 3-5.

Wong, A.K. (1981). Planned development, social stratification and the sexual division of labour in Singapore. *Signs*, vol. 7, No. 2.

_____ (1990). Women's role in politics. *Petir* (August), pp. 80-84.

Wong, A.K. and Kuo, E. (1983). *Divorce in Singapore.* Singapore: Graham Brash.

Zainul A. bin Rasheed and Arun Mahizhnan (1990). The new environment, the young Singaporeans and national values. In *Search of Singapore National Values.* J.S.T. Quah, ed. Singapore: Institute of Policy Studies, pp. 80-90.

VI. WOMEN IN DEVELOPMENT IN THAILAND

*Bhassorn Limanonda**

A. Importance of women in development: International concerns

For many decades, the international community has shown concern about issues of gender inequality. Several international meetings related to these issues were held where obstacles to the improvement of the role and status of women in relation to development were widely discussed. A brief description of the sequence of those meetings follows:

In 1946, the United Nations Commission on the Status of Women was formed to monitor the situation of women and promote women's rights around the world.

In 1952, the Commission initiated a Convention on the Political Rights of Women, which was the first global mandate for granting women equal political rights under the law – the right to vote, to hold public office and to exercise public functions.

In 1957 and 1962, conventions were initiated on equality of married women, guaranteeing them equal rights in marriage and in dissolving marriage.

In 1967, there was a Declaration on the Elimination of Discrimination Against Women.

The year 1975 was declared International Women's Year when the First World Conference on the Status of Women was held at Mexico City. It proclaimed 1976-1985 as the United Nations Decade for Women: Equality, Development, Peace. The Plan of Action adopted by the Conference stressed equality in politics, education and employment and included demands for child-care facilities and sharing of household duties between men and women (Leo and Burton, 1980). In addition, national and international agencies were requested for the first time to collect thorough statistical information on women.

In 1979, the United Nations General Assembly adopted the Convention on the Elimination of All Forms of Discrimination Against Women (CEDAW).

In 1980, the Second World Conference on Women was held at Copenhagen. The Comprehensive Programme of Action adopted by 147 countries attending the Conference called upon the governments to implement specific policies and programmes during the second half of the Decade for Women (1980-1985). This Programme of Action covered important new areas of concern, such as greater representation of women in policy-making positions and more attention to be given to the needs of migrant and refugee women, the elderly, and women living in extreme poverty. In the coverage of reproductive rights and women's health issues, the Programme of Action included new areas such as family planning, education in schools, better demographic data collection and elimination of female circumcision.

In 1985, the World Conference held at Nairobi, Kenya reviewed the progress during the Decade for Women. The assessment revealed that while more countries promised equality, the number of illiterate women in the world was still growing, they still worked longer hours for less pay than men and remained the world's largest group of poor people. The Conference agreed on such resolutions as equating prostitution with slavery and urging governments to include the value of housework in their gross national product. The Conference adopted the Nairobi Plan of Action on Forward-

---

* Associate professor, Institute of Population Studies, Chulalongkorn University, Bangkok.

looking Strategies for the Advancement of Women towards the Year 2000.

In 1994, the International Conference on Population and Development (ICPD) was held in Cairo, Egypt. Its Programme of Action stated that "Advancing gender equality and equity and the empowerment of women, and the elimination of all kinds of violence against women, and ensuring women's ability to control their own fertility, are cornerstones of population and development-related programmes. The human rights of women and the girl-child are an inalienable, integral and indivisible part of universal human rights. The full and equal participation of women in civil, cultural, economic, political and social life, at the national, regional and international levels, and the eradication of all forms of discrimination on grounds of sex, are priority objectives of the international community" (principle 4: UNFPA, nd).

In 1995, the Fourth World Conference on Women: Action for Equality, Development and Peace and the NGO Forum on Women were held in Beijing and Huairou, People's Republic of China. The Beijing Declaration stated that: "Women's rights are human rights.... The full realization of all human rights and fundamental freedoms of all women is essential for the empowerment of women" (UNFPA, nd). The governments participating in the Conference were determined to advance the goals of equality, development and peace for all women. The participating countries reaffirmed their commitment to the equal rights and inherent human dignity of women and men and other purposes and principles enshrined in the Charter of the United Nations, in the Universal Declaration of Human Rights and other international human rights instruments (United Nations, 1998).

At the regional level, the Bali Declaration on Population and Sustainable Development was adopted by the Fourth Asian and Pacific Population Conference in 1992, and the issue of

women's development was included in the Conference agenda. It was recognized that women's status affects such demographic behaviour as age at marriage, fertility, and infant, child and maternal mortality. These, in turn, have an impact on the improvement of women's status and their participation in the development process. The Declaration stated that "For the achievement of sustainable development, the full participation of women is essential, especially in the formulation and implementation of population policies and programmes. Given that women play an important role as managers of resources and in maintaining environmental quality, they must be involved in all decision-making relating to population and sustainable development" (United Nations, ESCAP, 1992). In recognition of the importance of women's contribution to development and the need to improve the status and role of women, many countries in the region have begun to formulate policies and implement programmes. Yet, achievement of these programmes still needs to be assessed.

B. Demographic, socio-economic and cultural profile of Thai women

The status or position of a woman in a society generally determines roles that she can take and kind of activities she can participate in. A better understanding of women's situation in terms of their socio-demographic and economic position would be helpful to identify problems and issues that have hindered the integration of women into the national development processes.

In this section, detailed information will be provided on various aspects of Thai women's life in general, and their status and roles in Thai society, in particular. These aspects will cover their demographic profile, including fertility, mortality, family formation, marriage and family planning; their socio-economic condition such as migration, education, participation in the labour force and politics; and the cultural conditions regulating the status and roles of women in society. In each aspect, a comparison between men and women will be made wherever possible. This analysis will reflect the relatively lower status and the disadvantaged position of women in each area. Once the problem areas are identified, appropriate strategies and further actions can be suggested for improvement of women's situation.

1. Demographic profile

In Thailand, from 1970 to 1995, the concern about population issues primarily focused on the control of population size. The reduction of fertility was carried out through the voluntary family planning programme in order to bring down population growth to a desirable level. After the International Conference on Population and Development (ICPD) in 1994, the population programme and service activities have been extended to cover areas of women's reproductive health and reproductive rights, and to promote male responsibility in family planning matters in accordance with the ICPD Programme of Action. In addition, the Eighth National Economic and Social Development Plan (1997-2001) has changed its direction slightly to focus on the improved quality of life of population, and accelerate the process of social and economic development. Thai women are recognized to play significant roles in demographic change and process of development.

(a)   Size of population and sex ratio

After the declaration of the National Population Policy in March 1970, the population growth rate in Thailand declined substantially from a little over 3 per cent per annum in the 1950s to 1.2 per cent in 1996. Further reduction in population growth is expected in the Eighth National Development Plan (1997-2001). This continuous decline has brought drastic change in the country's age structure. In 1960, the proportion of children under 15 years of age constituted about 43 per cent of the total population; this declined to 28.8 per cent in 1990, and is expected to decline

further to about 25 per cent in the year 2000. In contrast, there has been an increase in the size and proportion of population in the labour force ages from 52 per cent in 1960 to about 64 per cent in 1990. In the old age group of 65 years and above, the proportion increased from about 5 per cent in 1980 to 7 per cent in 1990 (National Economic and Social Development Board, 1994).

Regarding the population sex ratio, the 1960 census recorded a population of 26.2 million with a sex ratio of 100.4, the 1970 census counted 34.4 million with a sex ratio of 99.1, and the latest census taken in 1990 enumerated 54.5 million with a sex ratio of 98.3 (National Statistical Office, 1990). The declining trend in sex ratio at birth is considered to be attributable to problems of undercounting or underreporting of population during the censuses. On the other hand, records based on vital statistics, and data obtained through the Survey of Population Change (SPC), conducted periodically by the National Statistical Office, indicate a smoother and more stable trend of sex ratios from 1957 to 1993, ranging from 103-106 males per 100 females (Prachuabmoh Ruffolo et al., 1996). This statistical evidence is reflective of a more balanced sex ratio and lesser sex-biased values toward boys than girls in Thailand.

(b)   Fertility trends

In relation to declining population growth, the total fertility rate (TFR) fell from 6.3 births per woman during the early 1960s to 5.1 during the early 1970s, and to 3.5 children in 1984. A recent report of the Survey of Population Change (SPC) in 1991 indicated that the TFR dropped from 2.41 in 1989 to 2.17 in 1991 (Bennett et al., 1990; NESDB, 1994). According to the latest SPC of 1995-1996, the Thai TFR was as low as 2.02. The evidence from the Contraceptive Prevalence Survey (CPS) of 1996 indicated that the TFR was 1.98 during 1994-1995, with urban TFR estimated at 1.70, and rural TFR at 2.08.

The 1990 Census showed the regional differentials in fertility decline. Estimates indicate that the southern and the north-eastern regions still maintained the highest TFR (2.98 and 2.67, respectively), while the northern region and Bangkok Metropolis had the lowest TFR (below replacement level). The results from the CPS 1996 also showed similar regional variations in TFR. For example, the Bangkok TFR was 1.68; the northern was 1.78; the central was 1.92; the southern was 2.09; and the north-eastern was 2.11. It is expected that the decline in Thailand's TFR will continue but the pace will be much slower than that in the 1970s and the 1980s. These differentials in fertility, in many ways, reflect the differences in level of regional socio-economic development (NESDB, 1994; Chamratrithirong *et al.*, 1997).

(c)   Mortality pattern

Death rates in Thailand remained fairly high at about 30 per thousand population until the 1950s. Due to improved health care services and socio-economic development in the country, the crude death rate has declined to a level of about 5-6 per thousand population.

The rapid reduction of mortality has resulted in a rise in life expectancy of both the male and female population. The increase is more obvious among females. For instance, the results of the Survey of Population Change (SPC) in 1995-1996 indicated that the expectation of life at birth for men was 69.9 years and for women 74.9 years, showing a difference of five years. It is projected that expectation of life at birth will further increase and the rise will be more evident for women. This demographic change has significant implications for policy planning in terms of setting up appropriate programmes for health and caring of a large number of female elderly.

The infant mortality rate (IMR) has also shown a declining trend because of improvements in public health care services and socio-economic development. The IMR declined from about 84 per thousand live births in 1964-1965 to 45 in 1983, and to about 35 in 1991 and then to 30 per thousand live births in 1998 (NESDB, 1994; United Nations, ESCAP, 1998).

In recent years, non-infectious diseases such as cancer and heart disease and accidents have increasingly become important causes of death among the Thai population. In addition, the acquired immunodeficiency syndrome (AIDS) epidemic has become a serious public health problem in Thailand and is expected to contribute to a rise in the mortality rate in the 21st Century. It is projected that the cumulative number of AIDS-infected persons will exceed one million in 1999 at the national level. Data from the Ministry of Public Health (MOPH) civil registry, collected during 1986-1996 at the national level and for six selected provinces (three in the north and three in the south), indicated that owing to AIDS, mortality rates among females are generally lower than males. On the provincial level, the AIDS-related mortality rates are much higher in the north than the south for both males than females. For example, the highest increase in mortality rate was found among young females in the two selected provinces in the north (Chiang Rai and Phayao). Among 25-29 year-old females, mortality due to AIDS increased more than tenfold from 0.83 to 8.46 per thousand between 1990 and 1996. Among 25-39 year-old males in Phayao, mortality rates are three times higher than those of the national level and six times higher than in the southern provinces. The demographic impact of this differential loss of persons in the labour force and in the reproductive age groups will have its own implications in the northern provinces (van Griensven and Surasiengsunk, 1998).

(d)   Marriage and family formation

Several anthropological and sociological research studies conducted in the past have confirmed the fact that marriage timing of the Thai population is normally determined by cultural practices which do not encourage men and women to marry at very young ages. These cultural practices are reinforced by the forces of modernization, urbanization and socio-economic development which on balance improve the status and role of women (Limanonda, 1992).

Data available from the 1947-1990 population censuses have indicated moderate changes in marriage patterns among the Thai population. Percentage single at marriageable age groups, the singulate age at marriage and the proportion of permanent celibacy have increased, while the percentage currently married has decreased. Data from the last four censuses reveal that the singulate mean age at first marriage of females increased from 21.6 in 1960 to 22.0 in 1970, 22.8 in 1980 and 23.5 in 1990. Such changes are greater for the population residing in Bangkok and other urban areas.

The trend towards increasing proportion single for all age groups is also noted with some differences between rural and urban areas. For instance, in 1990, at ages 20-24 and 25-29 years, 41.9 per cent and 19.8 per cent of females in rural areas were still single, compared with 69.2 per cent and 43.4 per cent, respectively, in urban areas. Although age at marriage, on average, is relatively high, only a small percentage of Thai men and women remain single by age 50. For instance, in 1990, at ages 50-54, 4.2 per cent of males and 8.2 per cent of females in urban areas remained single compared with only 2.2 per cent of males and 3.4 per cent of females in rural areas. (Limanonda, 1992; National Statistical Office, 1960; 1970; 1980; 1990; 1996).

Owing to the fact that only a small proportion of married couples officially register their marriage, it is difficult to examine the trend towards increasing marriage dissolution. However, evidence from various research studies suggests that marriage dissolution, particularly separation and divorce, is quite common in Thai society. The limited evidence available from marriage registration also indicates an increasing trend in divorce rates in every region, especially in Bangkok.

(e)   Family system and role of women as head of household

The predominant type of household in Thailand is nuclear. The 1990 Census results indicated that the total number of households increased from 8.4 million in 1980 to 12.3 million in 1990. Of these, nearly 68 per cent (8.3 million) were nuclear family households. The number of female-headed households has also increased over time. According to the 1994 Household Survey, out of the total 15.8 million households, 3.2 million households (about 20.1 per cent) were headed by women, with an average number of 3.2 persons. Because of the high rate of marriage dissolution, 28.8 per cent of female household heads resided with single children, and 42.4 per cent lived with married children and other relatives. Approximately 66 per cent of these female heads had primary education but only 5.2 per cent had a university level of education (National Statistical Office, 1997b). As the majority of female heads have very low levels of education, its impact in terms of providing economic support and sustenance to the family members could be serious and warrant attention.

(f)   Reproductive behaviour

The first national demographic sample survey conducted in 1969-1970 (known as the LS Survey) indicated large differences in the reproductive attitudes and behaviour of rural and urban women. As regards the desired number of children, rural women preferred to have the highest number (3.94), followed by those in provincial urban areas (3.83), and in the capital city (3.57). However, the finding of the survey indicated that the actual family size of women aged 45-49 was higher than the desired size. For rural women, 6.7 was the average number of children ever born, with 5.1 living children. The provincial urban women had

118

5.7 children ever born and 5.0 living children, whereas women in Bangkok had 5.3 children ever born and 4.6 living children (Prachuabmoh Ruffolo *et al.*, 1972:69-70 as cited in Limanonda, 1996). This was the situation of fertility levels and reproductive behaviour of Thai married women in 1970 before the declaration of the national population policy aimed at promoting family planning practices.

With the onset of a strong campaign for family planning and a two-child family, significant change was observed in the reproductive behaviour of Thai women. According to a fertility survey in 1996, a majority of women in the reproductive ages expressed an ideal family size of approximately two children, with slight variations among regions. Moreover, women in younger age groups have smaller ideal family size than older women. For instance, the results of the survey on Social Attitudes towards children indicated that the ideal number of children of currently married women aged 15-29 was 2.65 as against 3.45 for women aged 45-49 (Wongboonsin and Prachuabmoh Ruffolo, 1995). The survey on Status of Women and Fertility in Thailand (1993) indicated no obvious difference between the average ideal number of children and the number of living children for women aged 15-44 years (2.1 and 1.9 children, respectively). A narrowing of the gap between the ideal and actual number of children in recent years reflects the changed reproductive behaviour of Thai women in different age cohorts (Chayovan, Wongsith and Prachuabmoh Ruffolo, 1995).

(g)   Family planning and fertility regulation

Since the declaration of the national population policy in March 1970, it is apparent that women's attitudes towards fertility and family size have substantially changed. This has directly affected the fertility regulation behaviour of Thai women. The percentage of women currently using contraceptive methods (CPR) has dramatically increased from about 8 per cent in the late 1950s to 15 per cent in

1970, and to 72 per cent in 1996-1997 (Bennett *et al.*, 1990; NESDB, 1994; Chamratrithirong *et al.*, 1997).

The success of the programme is mainly due to two factors: firstly, strong commitment of the government and the effective programme management and its implementation and, secondly, the active role played by Thai women as service providers and recipients. Approximately 90 per cent of family planning acceptors in Thailand are women. National Family Planning Programme (NFPP), statistics indicated that during the Seventh National Development Plan (1992-1996), there were large regional differences in contraceptive use. For example, the CPR was 84 per cent in the north and central regions, 77 per cent in the north-east, 75 per cent in Bangkok and 60 per cent in the south. These regional differences indicate that greater efforts are needed to improve the performance of the programme in specific areas, such as in the south, where religious beliefs promoting a large family size are prevalent, and among particular groups of population including rural poor, slum dwellers, adolescents and minority groups (NESDB, 1994).

Regarding the distribution of the methods used, the percentage of married women using the pill increased from less than 4 per cent in 1970 to over 15 per cent in 1975. The results of the Contraceptive Prevalence Surveys (CPS) of 1978 and 1981 indicated that the increase in contraceptive prevalence rate resulted largely from female sterilization and, to a lesser extent, from increased use of injectable contraceptives. The oral pill has remained the most commonly used method as more than one third of all women were pill users in 1981. In CPS3, 1984, the results indicated that female sterilization had become the most widely used method (36.5 per cent). The CPS of 1996 recorded an increase in the proportion of women using the pill (23 per cent) and injectables and a decrease in the proportion of female sterilization (22 per cent).

(h) Women as family planning providers

The role of Thai women in the family planning programme has been significant. As Tanothai, Teandum, and Na Pattalung (1982: 211-220) have stated: "apart from the strong commitment on family planning programme by the government, Thai women have played two significant roles which contributed greatly to the success of the national family planning programme: as family planning acceptor and as family planning provider".

At an early stage of the National Family Planning Programme, nearly all service providers were male physicians, particularly in areas outside Bangkok. After the encouraging results from the 1971 pilot project which allowed midwives in rural areas to distribute oral contraceptives, the Ministry of Public Health expanded the programme throughout the country. Since then, women have played an active role in recruiting new acceptors into the programme. In later years, trained nurses were recruited as service providers for IUD insertion and the injectable contraceptive programme at the local health centre at the village level. This made it more convenient for rural women to get services for different methods. In addition, trained nurses at the district hospital were allowed to perform sterilizations. The family planning and health care programmes have been strengthened by setting up the Primary Health Care Project under which local volunteers are recruited as village health communicators for providing health care information and certain types of contraceptives to women in rural areas. Among those volunteers, more females than males are registered as service providers (Tanothai, Teandum and Na Pattalung, 1982).

2. Social and economic conditions

(a) Educational attainment

In Thailand, the first major attempt to achieve universal education for boys and girls was made in 1921 when school attendance became compulsory for all children aged 7-14 years. A minimum level of public education of 4 years was included in the 1932 Constitution.

The statistics indicate that between 1937 and 1990, illiteracy rates have been consistently higher among females than males. For instance, in 1937, 85 per cent of females, compared with 56 per cent of males, were illiterate, and in 1990 this percentage had declined to 9 per cent for women and 5 per cent for men (Bavornsiri, 1982; National Statistical Office, 1997a). Based on census data from 1970 to 1990, more females than males are reported to have no education at all. However, it has been found that women residing in either provincial urban areas or Bangkok are more educated than rural males (Prachuabmoh Ruffolo et al., 1997, cited in Limanonda, 1996).

Since the 1960s, Thailand has experienced a tremendous increase in enrolment at all levels of education. At present, there is nearly universal primary education, and almost all children under age 12 are enroled. However, the proportion of both girls and boys who have left school after age 12 increases rapidly with age. The statistics show that nearly 66 per cent of all Thai youth had left school by age 15, and almost 90 per cent by age 20 (National Commission on Women's Affairs, 1994). For those who finished primary school, the proportions are nearly the same for boys and girls (between 65 and 70 per cent). However, the number completing secondary school are much lower in magnitude, particularly among the female population. For instance, in 1970, only 3.6 per cent of females and 6.3 per cent of males had attained secondary education, and in 1990, 11.5 per cent of females and 16.1 per cent of males had completed this level. At the university level, the proportion of the population that graduates is very small, both for males and females (National Statistical Office, 1997a).

There is evidence that parents are supportive of providing educational opportunities to a daughter as much as to a son. Girls are well supported by the family for attaining higher or advanced education if the family could afford it economically and/or a girl herself is capable enough to continue for higher education. Chayovan, Wongsith and Prachuabmoh Ruffolo (1995), in their analysis of data from 2,613 currently married women who were asked about the reasons for supporting education of sons or daughters, found that about 54 per cent of respondents approved of supporting both sons and daughters for higher education. The major reasons cited were that they wanted to be fair or show equal love for their children. About 31 per cent of women said that they supported more education for sons. The major reason was that they were worried for the safety of their daughters when travelling far away from home (47 per cent). The other remaining reasons cited were: a man should be a leader, a son is smarter than a daughter, a son should be well educated, and they expect support from a son in future. The 14 per cent of respondents who wanted daughters to be more educated than sons gave the major reasons as: a daughter is more well-behaved than a son, can find a good job, and can support the family in future. However, it is observed that parents' desire and expectations in this regard are not materialized to a great degree.

More recent data on the number of students in various educational levels has indicated that almost equal opportunities are provided to men and women for higher education. There are, however, some differences in field of study chosen by males and females at the university level. For instance, women mostly choose subjects associated with traditionally identified supportive roles, such as fine arts, humanities, teaching and home economics. On the other hand, men concentrate more in sciences, engineering, industrial mechanics, etc. (National Commission on Women's Affairs, 1994; National Statistical Office, 1997a).

(b)   Female labour force participation

Data on the economically active population in Thailand are not strictly comparable due to variations in definition over time. However, data from the past censuses and surveys provide useful information about labour force participation of the Thai population, especially women and their roles in economic development.

The National Economic and Social Development Plans indicate that Thailand's economic structure has shifted from concentrating on productivity in the agricultural sector to more modern industry and service sectors. The share of those engaged in the agricultural sector recorded a decline for both males and females between 1960 and 1990 (National Statistical Office, 1960; 1970; 1980; 1990).

In the past, when agriculture was a predominant occupation among Thais, a large number of rural women were an integral part of the agricultural labour force. Those women played an important role in farm and marketing activities and contributed significantly to family and national incomes, and controlled the family finances at the same time (Chayovan, Wongsith and Prachuabmoh Ruffolo, 1995).

Labour force participation rates among Thai women have been consistently high compared with other countries in the region. According to 1980 census data, 44.4 per cent of females aged 11 years and over were economically active. In 1990, 68 per cent of females aged 13 years and over were in the labour force. The corresponding proportion for males was about 81 per cent. It is argued that a high rate of female work participation is due partially to a liberal definition used for labour force which includes a large number of females working as unpaid family workers. The statistics from 1970 to 1996 on employed population classified by work status revealed that the proportion of women classified as unpaid family workers is almost twice that of males. In contrast, the proportion of males classified as employer, government and private employees and own account worker are much

121

higher than those of females (National Statistical Office, 1997a).

Women's work participation classified by type of occupation indicates that more than 50 per cent of females reported as employed were engaged in the agricultural sector, followed by trade, services and professions. These statistics are reflective of women working in low-status occupations and the limited opportunities available for them in the wage sector. In addition, women not only constitute a lower proportion of total paid employees, their average income remains lower than that of men. Despite the law ensuring equal pay for women, they usually receive, on average, lower pay than men for the same type of work. Moreover, when wages are classified into low and high categories, it is evident that larger proportions of female workers fall into the lower and lowest levels of salaries or wages (National Statistical Office, 1997a).

Recently, however, due to rapid socio-economic development and expansion in employment opportunities, larger proportions of women have started participating in male-dominated occupations and industry. A relatively greater economic independence of women in modern economic sectors has contributed to improving their status. Nevertheless, the number and proportion of these women is still small.

(c)   Female migration and spatial movement

Only limited information is available on female migration, their status in places of destination, and their roles in the development process in relation to their spatial movement. The evidence shows that the country has exhibited an increasing rate of female migration at both national and international levels. Women tend to move to places where job opportunities are available or are better. According to the 1988 Labour Force Survey, among those who worked as labourers, the proportion who were migrants was 85 per cent among females and 74 per cent among males.

During the period of rapid economic expansion in the past two decades, many industries were in great need of females who could work more effectively in certain kinds of production such as textiles, sorting transistors, assembling pocket calculators, computer chips, etc. As a result, a substantial number of women were recruited as labourers in factories. As such, a large number of female migrants have moved to the big cities for getting employment that requires little basic skill or training (National Economic and Social Development Board, 1994). According to population projections for 1980-2010, it is expected that in 4 out of the 7 defined regions, net migration of females will be consistently much higher than that of males.

The 1988 and 1989 Labour Force Surveys (Round 3) revealed that in both municipal and non-municipal areas the unemployment rate of female migrants was the highest, followed by that of male migrants and then the non-migrant population (National Statistical Office, 1990b; 1991). The 1989 Survey of Migration in three big cities in the north, north-east, and the south confirmed the finding that more male in-migrants got jobs and participated in the labour force than females, and this pattern was evident in each age group of 11-60 years old (National Statistical Office, 1992).

As for the age and sex selectivity of migrants, females were concentrated more in the age groups of 15-19 and 70 years and over, whereas males were concentrated more in the age group 20-54 years. Among the migrants, the stream to Bangkok Metropolis was dominated by women, being the major area of industrial and service sector employment.

Among the reasons for moving from rural to urban areas, 47 per cent of female migrants stated economic motivation as the most important reason to move. For males, pursuit of education was more important than for females. For those who moved within rural areas, the majority of males and females cited "moving to accompany family members" as the major reason, followed by economic motivation (National Statistical Office, 1995).

Regarding international migration, Thailand is both a sending and receiving country for migrants. As one of the country's policies, overseas employment is executed through exporting labour to other countries. Since the 1970s, Thailand has exported large numbers of unskilled and semi-skilled workers from the rural north-east to the middle-east. In the 1980s, due to the Gulf crisis, the export of labour migrants shifted to east and south-east Asian countries where economies were expanding. It has been estimated that in 1989, Thailand sent about 125,000 migrant workers abroad. In Malaysia, Thai migrants were primarily employed in the construction industry. In Brunei Darussalam and Singapore, Thai male workers dominated the construction and shipbuilding industries while female workers were employed in factories.

Some studies have indicated that a substantial number of Thai women have travelled to such areas as Brunei Darussalam; Hong Kong, China; Japan; Malaysia; Taiwan, Province of China; the United States of America and Europe in search of employment and have engaged in the entertainment business, including providing sex services. This has given rise to the problem of racism against foreigners in some countries of destination.

(d) *STDs/HIV/AIDS and other health problems*

As described earlier, mortality rates in Thailand have dropped to very low levels, and life expectancy of women has dramatically increased over the past few decades. However, Thai women still face several types of health risk which deserve attention for policy formulation.

Although the maternal death rate has been reduced, it is still a problem for many women, particularly in rural areas. It is found that the highest incidence of maternal deaths is caused by direct obstetric causes such as hemorrhage and other pregnancy related problems. Incidence of anemia is high among pregnant women in every region in Thailand, ranging from 18 per cent in the north-east to 23 per cent in the south. In addition, all forms of malignant neoplasm is the second most frequent cause of death for women (National Commission on Women's Affairs, 1994).

However, the evidence shows that incidence of classic sexually transmitted diseases (STD), gonorrhoea, syphilis, hemophilus ducreyi, non-gonococcal urethritis and lymphogra nuloma venereum, has decreased over the past few years probably because of increased condom use during commercial sex and decreased participation of men in such activities. It has been estimated that condom distribution by the Ministry of Public Health increased from 5-10 million pieces annually to 60 million in 1993, and another 50-60 million condoms were sold through commercial channels (NESDB, 1994). Although the decline in STDs is a sign for optimism, very little attention is given to the newly emerging STD, chlamydia trachomatis among young adults in recent years. The STDs among women have caused infections of the reproductive tract which have led to infertility, adverse pregnancy outcome and cancer. In addition, STDs are implicated as an important co-factor in the spread of human immunodeficiency virus (HIV).

By the mid-1990s, the AIDS epidemic had increased rapidly in the country. The official figures released by the Ministry of Public Health indicated that from September 1984 to July 1993, the cumulative number of AIDS patients was 43,186. Of these, 16 per cent were women and a large majority of them (76 per cent) were in the reproductive age groups of 20-49 years.

Illegal abortion is another health risk area for Thai women. The Foundation for Women has estimated the number of unwanted pregnancy terminations to be 300,000 per year, many of which are among adolescent or young women. Since abortion is illegal in Thailand, no reliable statistics and services are available. A study by Keotswang *et al.* (1989, cited in Simmons, 1996) in five provincial hospitals, showed that among women admitted for post-termination abortion complications, only 17 per cent of abortions were performed by qualified doctors. Women undergoing unsafe abortions experienced severe complications, ranging from excessive bleeding, pelvic infection, hysterectomy, removal of the womb, and death.

Health hazards resulting from poor working conditions are another growing problem for women workers in both agriculture and industry. As indicated by some studies, widely used pesticides and insecticides in agriculture have caused serious health problems among farmers. For example, nearly 50 per cent of farm women were ill because of lack of knowledge on how to protect themselves from toxic substances. The ratio of women to men who suffer from pesticide poisoning was 10:31 and the death rate was 0.07:0.16. On the other hand, women who work in the industrial factories also suffer from worse working conditions even though the Labour Protection and Welfare Law intends to protect them from health hazard conditions. Many women are exposed to dust from textiles, lead, aluminum, trichloroethylene and other chemicals from their work. It is reported that a large number of women suffer because of lead poisoning which also has consequences for their reproductive health and health of their children, including spontaneous abortion, abnormal birth outcomes, and the delayed growth and mental development of the child (National Commission on Women's Affairs, 1994).

3. Cultural aspects of women's status

Historically, the status and roles of Thai women have been perceived differently in each

Kingdom: Sukhothai, Ayudhya, Ratanakosin. Detailed study of the issues concerning differential position of women in Thai society reveals that, in general, there have been some social, economic and cultural practices which promote and maintain an equal status of women to men in many respects. Some of the factors regarding the values and practices which promote gender equality and equity in Thai society are discussed below.

(a) Preference for sex of children

A daughter born into a Thai family is usually valued as much as a son. Compared with other Asian societies, a relatively less pronounced preference for a son is evident among Thais and this is associated with various factors, including religious beliefs, socio-economic conditions and traditional practices that are deep rooted in the society.

(b) Religious influence

Theravada Buddhism is predominant and accepted as the State religion in Thailand. More than 95 per cent of Thais identify themselves as Buddhists. Buddhism, in many respects, has long borne great influence over Thai ways of life. The pattern of social relations practised among Thais is much influenced by one of the Buddhist teachings on the principle of hierarchical order, characterized by a formalized superordinate-subordinate relationship among individuals. Based on this religious concept, the status inequalities within a family are defined in terms of relative ages of each family member (younger: older; children:parents; younger sibling: older sibling) rather than by the sex of a person (male: female). With this classification, the elderly are usually awarded the highest status and prestige and each family member has duties and obligations according to his or her own status within the family (Smith, 1979; Pongphit, 1988 cited in Limanonda, 1996). This religious concept and practice is conducive to reducing sex-biased attitudes and gives a certain status to female family members.

There are other religious practices and beliefs which provide an opportunity to women to maintain their importance as much as men in the family. In Buddhism, for instance, only a man could enter into monkhood, which is considered to be the most laudable act of children to gain great merit for the parents. It is also viewed as a gesture to repay the parents a debt of gratitude because they gave life to the child. This practice, however, does not explicitly suggest a superior status of a man over a woman. A daughter who is not allowed to enter the monkhood can also repay a debt of gratitude to parents in many other ways. For example, she could help parents by doing the household chores, working on the farm, earning income, supporting parents financially, looking after old parents, and obtaining a brideprice which is valued as a repayment for mother's milk (Rabibhadana 1984 cited in Limanonda, 1996). In fact, these obligations and practices place more burden on a daughter than a son. In this context, therefore, a daughter in the family could be a valuable asset in the eyes of the parents and also maintain a high status for daughters compared with sons.

(c)   Family lineage and inheritance system

In many east Asian societies, the patrilineal system and male heirs have played an important role in perpetuating the family name and lineage. In Thai society, in contrast, the importance of lineage is relatively low. The inheritance system is bilateral with a prevalence of matrilineal post-nuptial residence particularly in rural areas. This reflects a relatively greater importance of female members in the family. According to some anthropologists, it is apparent that among Thai families there exists little sense of lineage, little feeling of ancestry and little interest in descedents beyond living children or grandchildren. The lack of interest in ancestry or lineage is reflected in the fact that families have adopted surnames (or a family name) only recently as a result of a government decree, and that few rural families can trace their ancestry back for more than two or three generations (Prachuabmoh, Knodel and Alers 1974 cited in Limanonda, 1996). The bilateral inheritance system gives equal share of land and assets to the male and female children.

Marriage customs and patterns of post-nuptial residence in Thailand indicate the importance of females in many respects. The practice of paying a brideprice to a girl's parents is considered beneficial for the girl's family and increases the value of daughters. After marriage, the youngest daughter and her husband usually live with the woman's parents, caring for them in their old age. After the parents' death, this youngest daughter inherits the house and the land where the house is located. It is therefore, not necessary for Thais to rely predominantly on male heirs for old-age security. The practice of matrilocal post-nuptial residence is most pronounced among the rural population. Research findings on the attitudes towards the desired residence of sons and daughters have indicated that both male household heads and married women in rural areas are more likely to want their daughters than their sons to live with them. For the urban respondents, the reverse was true. (Prachuabmoh Ruffolo et al., 1996: Limanonda, 1979 cited in Limanonda, 1996).

(d)   Women's roles in decision making

As discussed earlier, Thai women have relatively high social status and an active economic role in the family. This gives them greater freedom to make their own decisions about domestic and social matters. Findings from the study on Status of Women and Fertility in Thailand (Chayovan, Wongsith and Prachuabmoh Ruffolo, 1995), indicate that about 88 per cent of currently married women aged 15-44 interviewed said that they felt free to purchase personal items, and 50 per cent felt free to purchase more expensive things like jewellery without having consulted their husbands. About 74 per cent of these women said that they felt free to study further (after marriage), and 79 per cent said that they had freedom to visit friends whenever they wanted to. In recent social surveys, a large proportion of married women indicated that joint decision-making between husband and wife occurs when it comes to important matters such as family investment, child care and child rearing, desired number of children, and children's education (Limanonda *et al.*, 1995 cited in Limanonda, 1996).

C. Women in politics

After the political transformation from the absolute monarchy to a constitutional monarchy in 1932, Thai women were granted the right to vote in 1933. Although more of the eligible and actual voters have been women, very few have been elected to various legislative bodies in the country. Hence, the share of women in political institutions at the national level (MPs or Senators) has been small. Statistics show that in the 1988 general election, women constituted only 2.8 per cent of MPs and 1.9 per cent of the Senate. In the 1996 general election, the percentage of women MPs increased to 5.6 per cent and for the Senate to 8.0 per cent.

In addition, statistics show that the number of female administrators in the State bureaucracy, is also negligible. The Local Administration Act of 1914 which originally did not allow women to hold administrative posts at either provincial or local (district and village) levels was revised in 1982 favouring women to participate in local administration. Since then, there has been an increasing number of women leaders at local levels holding various administrative posts. For the first time in 1993, a woman was designated to be the Governor of a province. In 1995, statistics showed that women constituted 2.7 per cent of all Governors in 75 provinces, 0.1 per cent of all Districts Heads in 774 districts and 0.2 per cent of Assistant District Heads out of 7,877 positions. At the lower levels, women constituted 6.3 per cent of Provincial Council Members, 8.2 per cent of Municipal Council Members, 1.4 per

cent of Heads of sub-districts and 1.8 per cent of Heads of village (National Statistical Office, 1997a).

The data on the composition of the judiciary for the year 1987 showed that women were only 7 per cent of the prosecution panel. Out of 1,048 judges, only 62 (6 per cent) were women and among 86 judge-trainees, 16 were women. Overall, women's participation in the judiciary was minimal as prosecutors, judges and judge-trainees (National Commission on Women's Affairs, 1994).

D. National commitment and responses to international concerns on women in development

The attempts to elevate the status of women and to provide them the opportunities to play more active roles in Thai society started in the 1940s through the effort of Thanpuying La-iad, the wife of Prime Minister Field Marshal P. Pibulsongkhram. During this period, the National Council of Women and Women's Culture Club were established. At the same time, laws were revised to eradicate various forms of sexual discrimination, giving equal opportunities to women to enter government services, etc. (Ekchai, 1984). In addition, through the efforts of the Women's Lawyers Association of Thailand (WLAT) and many other organizations, an equality clause, specifically guaranteeing women equal rights with men, was written into the 1974 Constitution (Section 28). This clause stated that: "All persons shall enjoy the rights and liberties under the Constitution. Men and women have equal rights. The restriction of rights and liberties in violation of objectives of the Constitution shall not be imposed" (Branch, 1982).

During the past three decades, policies in relation to women's development in Thailand have been influenced by the resolutions adopted at international conferences/meetings. As a response to the United Nations Declaration of the International Women's Year in 1975, and the 1976-1985 United Nations Decade for Women, the Thai Government established a National Executive Committee to implement the objectives of the International Women's Year.

The process of women in development started to gain more recognition from the government during the Fourth Five-year National Economic and Social Development Plan (1977-1981). In 1979, a sub-committee for the development of women's role and status was established to draft the Long-term Women's Development Plan (1982-2001), which was planned to be integrated into every five-year social and economic plan.

In the Fifth Five-year National Development Plan (1982-1986), there was an explicit emphasis on women as a special target group in social development. The areas to be developed included health, education, employment, and participation in politics and administration.

In 1989, the Long-term Women's Development Plan (1982) was reviewed and revised by the Sub-committee as a response to the rapid socio-economic changes occurring in the country. It was renamed as the Prospective Plan and Policies for Women's Development (1992-2011), and covered several areas for women's development with new guidelines for planning of women's development during the subsequent plans (National Commission on Women's Affairs, 1991; 1994:35).

In line with the Nairobi Forward-looking Strategies, the National Commission on Women's Affairs (NCWA) was established in 1989 as a central coordinating body to serve as a centre for information exchange for women's development activities. Since then, a number of non-governmental organizations (NGOs) have been established to enhance women's development activities in Thailand. The eight major NGOs include the Association for the Promotion of the Status of Women; the Foundation for Women (FFW); the Friends of

Women Foundation; Gender and Development Research Institute (GDRI); National Council on Social Welfare; the National Council of Women of Thailand under the Royal Patronage of Her Majesty the Queen (NCWT); Thai Women Culture Club; and Women Lawyers Association of Thailand (WLAT) under the Patronage of Her Majesty the Queen.

A comprehensive report on Women's Development was presented at the World Conference of the United Nations Decade for Women in Nairobi, Kenya in 1985. It specified that "The participation of women in development requires action at the national and local levels and within the family, based on changes in attitudes and in the roles of men and women. From the national point of view, there is much to be gained from a greater integration of women in development efforts, so long as this participation also leads to advances in women's status. Inequality as it pertains to the majority of women, is closely related to the problem of underdevelopment which itself is derived from inequitable national and international economic and political structures and relationships" (National Commission on Women Affairs, 1985:1).

The Thai Government also specified its commitment to women's development in the National Report prepared for the ICPD held in Cairo in 1994 which states that: "The country is committed to achieving several policy objectives related to developing women's fullest potential in every aspect. Efforts will be directed towards promoting a better quality of life for women, promoting equality between men and women and to eliminate discrimination against women both *de jure* and *de facto* especially for those who are employed and those in the disadvantaged groups. To achieve these goals, the networking between governmental, non-governmental organizations and other mechanisms responsible for women, as well as community and family should be further developed and strengthened" (Human Resource Planning Division, NESDB, 1994).

In joining the Beijing resolution in 1995, the National Commission on Women's Affairs set forth the forward-looking strategies for Thai women's development for the years 1995-2015, including the five-year plan of action (1996-2001) to promote the advancement of Thai women in various aspects, including realising their potential and improving their quality of life.

E. Problems and future prospects for women's development

It is generally perceived that women in Thailand are not seriously oppressed compared with women in many other countries of the region. As discussed earlier, Thai women's status has allowed them to play an active role in the family, community and society. The improvement in women's status over time is attributable to various factors, such as cultural practices allowing women to have freedom to develop themselves, the national economic and social development process, the commitment of the government to develop women's fullest potential, and the efforts made by NGOs, academic institutions and individuals in the area of women's development.

However, there are unresolved problems and issues which have hindered the smooth functioning of the women's development process and merit further attention. For instance, under the Family Law of the Civil and Commercial Code, many clauses discriminating against women can still be found. The Long-term Plan (1992-2011), therefore, proposed revisions in the law to provide protection to women in their roles as married women and mothers, and to encourage men as husbands and fathers to share more responsibilities in child rearing and household chores. The plan stated that all those laws that implicitly promote a double standard in treatment of women should be abolished. Moreover, the revision of marriage registration system was considered necessary to prevent a double-registered marriage. The plan further stated that women

need to be protected from being sexually abused, offended or harassed in various forms, including physical abuse, rape and domestic violence. Abortion laws need to be revised to suit the changing conditions of the society.

With respect to women's participation in the labour force, it is important that more women workers are covered under social insurance programmes and guaranteed workers compensation and severance pay. Laws should be reinforced on labour protection in relation to women's health and safety in working conditions (National Commission on Women's Affairs, 1991; 1994).

In the NCWA's Five-year Plan of Action (1995-2000), six problem areas in the process of women's development have been identified as follow:

1. Inequality of opportunity: Some women lack access to various economic and social services and other women are excluded as recipients of the resources and benefits of development;

2. Lack of participation by women in the decision making process and leadership roles;

3. There is still *de facto* and *de jure* discrimination against women;

4. Lack of protective measures for women as individuals and as female persons;

5. Negative attitudes and values are reflected in abuses, malpractices, and undesirable actions against women;

6. National development plans do not specifically mention women as a special target group.

Based on the available evidence and previous discussions, this section analyses the existing problems in each area that are expected to have an impact on the process of women's development. Where appropriate, recommendations for future actions are also made.

(a)   Educational attainment

Although most women in Thailand are literate and complete the primary level of education, a large number of girls especially in the lower social and economic groups of population, drop out at secondary level. Various reasons given for high drop out rates are poverty, limited educational facilities beyond the primary level in certain areas, and lack of law enforcement on receiving higher education. Lack of sufficient education and training for women forces them to take low-paid and low-status jobs, which has serious implications for national development.

Given this situation, it is important that the informal educational programmes such as vocational training, adult education, and skill development projects for income generation should be initiated as alternatives for girls who had left school at early ages. In addition, various kinds of occupational training programmes appropriate for agriculture and industry should be integrated into other ongoing development programmes in communities in both rural and urban areas. Such activities could be carried out at the grass-root level in collaboration with the Department of Community Development. For those women who are already in the labour market, it is necessary for them to receive apprenticeships and/or on-the-job training in order to develop and improve their working skills in accordance with the needs and demand of the labour market.

(b)   Female labour force participation

Statistics have indicated that a large number of women in the labour force are working in low-paid or unpaid jobs and face various kinds of discrimination in the labour market. It is unfortunate that many women in the informal sector work under adverse working conditions and only limited information is available to reflect their true situation regarding economic activities.

As job opportunities are greater in big cities and in the capital where the majority of factories are located, a large number of women migrate from rural areas to find work. Due to surplus labour and their low levels of education and skills, they get engaged in low-paid or informal type of economic activities with adverse working and living conditions. In order to uplift the status of these poor and migrant workers, it is suggested that there should be organizations providing them with knowledge and information necessary for job-seeking in places of destination, and utilize opportunities for skill development.

(c)   Family planning and reproductive health

The contraceptive prevalence rate (CPR) among currently married women in Thailand is quite high (about 75 per cent) and women's active role in the success of the programme is widely recognized. However, large gaps and problems still exist regarding the reproductive health and contraceptive use of women in various socio-economic groups and different geographical areas. The most disadvantaged groups of women are those in remote rural areas, in lower socio-economic classes, urban poor, slum dwellers, recent migrants and hilltribe women.

To remove these differentials, there is a need to improve the accessibility and availability of health services and contraception to these disadvantaged groups. Family planning knowledge and services should also be provided in the appropriate forms to unmarried adolescents to prevent unwanted pregnancies, and unsafe abortion.

Moreover, the growing threat of HIV/AIDS and high incidence of reproductive tract infections (RTIs) among the population, especially female adolescents and adults who are sexually active, is a matter of great concern in Thailand. According to one estimate, annually between 15 and 20 thousand pregnant women are found to be HIV positive, resulting in about 4,000 to 6,000 babies who receive the virus from their mothers (Bangkok Post, 13 July 1998). The rapid spread of HIV/AIDS and the high incidence of reproductive tract infections (RTIs) among women are largely due to the fact that many adolescents engage in unprotected sex activities at early ages.

To reduce the growing problem of HIV/AIDS and RTIs transmission, it is important that relevant systematic information about sexuality, health care and contraception be provided to women to create awareness about these problems. Clinics for treatment of RTIs and STDs and related services should be made available on a wider scale for both young married and unmarried women. With regard to the issue of illegal abortion, the NCAW (1994) has recommended that reform of the abortion law is necessary to conform to the changing social and sexual behaviour among adolescents in the society.

(d)   Commercial sex

One major problem related to women's position in Thailand is prostitution, which has shown an increasing trend over time. During the past two decades, the network of sex service businesses has expanded although no accurate data on the number of women entering this business are available. Many women from poor families and with low educational background are forced to engage in this job. Quite often, they have to travel illegally to engage in sex business for earning income and a source of livelihood for their family back home.

The problem of prostitution in Thailand has received great attention since the late 1980s when the AIDS epidemic spread rapidly, and female commercial sex workers have been blamed for the rapid HIV transmission. To help reduce the magnitude of this problem, it is important for the government and non-government agencies to give more serious consideration to this issue. Legal enforcement to check the problem has proved to be unsuccessful due to the complexities involved in

this illegal profession. However, the indirect measures suggested to rectify this situation include the provision of more education, occupational training and vocational skills for girls, which would improve their socio-economic status and could prevent them from engaging in the profession.

(e)   Female household heads

Another important area of concern regarding women's status in Thailand is the large number of women who are heads of households. These women are usually single parents who provide economic support and care to their family members, and undergo considerable social, economic and psychological pressures. The situation is worse for those who have low education and minimal occupational training. To improve the situation in this area, the government may have to take specific measures and provide economic alternatives in any form for this particular group of women.

(f)   Domestic violence

With regard to women's rights, domestic violence (especially wife beating) is a serious problem in Thai society. Due to the social stigma attached to the problem, it is speculated that the number of such cases is highly under-reported. Findings from a recent study on the Status of Women and Fertility in Thailand, that interviewed 2,800 women, have revealed that one-fifth (around 600 women) reported having been beaten by their husbands. The highest proportion of these women was in Bangkok. It is interesting to note that about 47 per cent of these women yielded to such violence without fighting back or running away (Chayovan, Wongsith and Prachuabmoh Ruffolo, 1995). This reflects that women's submission to men's violence in the family is either a result of women's dependence on men or the socialization to accept the man as the dominant person in the family. To protect women against this problem, it is important that social and media campaigns should be undertaken continuously in various forms to discourage and avoid such practice and make people realize its negative effects on the well-being of their family and children.

F. Concluding remarks

A review of statistics and available evidence on various aspects of women's development has shown that despite socio-economic changes and industrialization, there are many underprivileged or disadvantaged groups of women who lag behind in different spheres of life and deserve to be given attention. A substantial proportion of women still work in lower economic positions than their male counterparts and are prevented from fully participating in the development process. In an attempt to address women's problems, various policies and programmes of action have been proposed during the past few decades. Some measures have proved to be effective and successful, while some others need to be continued for a long term effect.

In order to achieve success in the proposed programmes of action for women's development, greater coordination and cooperation among the responsible organizations, both governmental and NGOs, as well as among individuals, are needed. The most important aspect is to see that all these planned programmes are implemented successfully and serve the needs of each target group. For this purpose, an efficient monitoring and evaluation of the impact of these programmes on the target population is required. In this regard, it is important that full support from high-level authorities (top-down) and an active participation at the grass-roots level (bottom-up) are attained for the execution of these programmes.

There is also a need to undertake research studies and collect data on issues for which information is still lacking. This would help in filling gaps for policy planning and setting up target plans to accelerate the process of implementation of women's development programmes.

One important dimension that has recently been considered important in facilitating the process of women's development is male participation and their role in sharing responsibilities in the family. The 1984 Mexico City Declaration on Population and Development emphasized the importance of men's role in women's development and stated that: "To achieve this goal to assist women in attaining full equality with men, it is necessary for men and women to share responsibilities jointly in areas such as family life, child-caring and family planning...". In the 1994 ICPD Programme of Action, it was recognized that to empower women without taking men into account would mean that the objectives would not be reached successfully. Men should be encouraged to take more responsibility for their parenthood, sexual behaviour, and social and family roles, so that men and women are equal partners in public and private life (United Nations, ICPD, 1994:20). As most of the planning in the past has focussed on women as a target group, it is time that men's participation and involvement are also taken into account in solving women's problems and in accelerating the process of national development.

REFERENCES

Bavornsiri, Varaporn (1982). Role, status and problems of women in education. In *Women in Development: Implications for Population Dynamics in Thailand,* Suchart Prasith-rathsint and Suwanlee, Piampiti, eds. Bangkok: Parbpim Ltd., Part. pp. 67-100.

Bennett, Anthony and others (1990). How Thailand's family planning programme reach replacement level of fertility: lessons learned. *Occasional paper No. 4. Population Technical Assistant Project.* Washington D.C.: Dual Associates Inc. and International Science and Technology Institute, Inc.

Branch, Betty (1982). Khunying Suphatra Singholka: Thailand's gentle equivalent of women's lib, *SWADDI Magazine* (March-April 1971) republished in *Women's Rights* by Khunying Suphatra Singholka. pp. 67-(Index). Bangkok: Ruen Keow Publishing Co.

Chamratrithirong, Apichat and others (1997). *Report on National Contraceptive Prevalence Survey 1996.* Bangkok: Institute for Population and Social Research, Mahidol University.

Chayovan, Napaporn, Malinee Wongsith, Vipan Prachuabmoh Ruffolo (1995). *A Study on Status of Women and Fertility in Thailand.* IPS Publication No. 229/95 (May). Bangkok: Institute of Population Studies, Chulalongkorn University.

Ekchai, Sanitsuda (1984). Thanpuying La-iad: gone but not forever *Bangkok Post Outlook.*

Kamnuansilpa, Peerasit and Apichat Chamratrithirong (1985). *Contraceptive Use and Fertility in Thailand: Results from the 1984 Contraceptive Prevalence Survey.* Bangkok: np.

Leo, John and Sandra Burton (1980). Cacophony in Copenhagen *TIMES International Magazine* August 4.

Limanonda, Bhassorn (1992). Nuptiality patterns in Thailand: their implications for further fertility decline. In *Fertility Transitions, Family Structure, & Population Policy,* Goldscheider, ed. Boulder: Westview Press.

_____ (1995). Families in Thailand: beliefs and realities. *Journal of Comparative Family Studies. Special Issue on Family in Asia: Beliefs and Realities* vol. XXVI No.1 (Spring). pp. 67-82.

_____ (1996) Preference for sex of children, determinants and implications: A case of Thailand. *Paper presented at the International Workshop on Fertility, Son Preference and Child Mortality of Koreans in Korea and China,* November.

Ministry of Public Health (1997). *Population Programme: Thailand 1996.* Leaflet .

National Commission on Women's Affairs (1985). *Women's Development in Thailand.* A report prepared by the National Committee for International Cooperation for the World Conference of the United Nations Decade for Women, Nairobi, Kenya (15-26 July, 1985). Bangkok: np.

_____ (1991). *Policies and Long-Term Plans for Women's Development (1992-2011). Sub-Committee for Long-Term Plan for Women's Development* (Draft). Bangkok: Office of the Civil Service Commission Printing House.

_____ (1994). *Thailand's Report on the Status of Women and Platform for Action 1994.* A report prepared for the Fourth World Conference on Women. Beijing, 1995.

National Economic and Social Development Board (1991). *Population Projections for Thailand 1980-2015.* Bangkok: NESDB.

_____ (1994). *Thailand: National Report on Population and Development.* Report prepared by Thailand Working Committee for preparation of the International Conference on Population and Development, September. Bangkok: NESDB.

National Statistical Office. *1960, 1970, 1980, 1990 Thailand Population and Housing Census: Whole Kingdom.*

_____ (1990b). *Report of the Labour Force Survey: Whole Kingdom (Round 3, August 1988)* Bangkok.

_____ (1991). *Report of the Labour Force Survey: Whole Kingdom (Round 3, August 1989).* Bangkok.

_____ (1992). *Survey of Migration into Surat Thani Province; Chiang Mai Province: Khon Kean Province, 1989.* Bangkok.

_____ (1995). *Report of the 1992 Migration Survey.* Bangkok.

_____ (1996). *Nuptiality of Thai Population: 1990 Population and Housing Census.* Subject Report No. 4. Bangkok.

_____ (1997a). *Statistical Booklet on Thai Women and Men.* Bangkok.

_____ (1997b). *Analysis of Households with Female Heads, 1997.* Bangkok.

Prachuabmoh Ruffolo, Vipan and others (1996). Thailand's Fertility Future: Phase II. Paper presented at the Annual Meeting of the Thai Population Association, November 21-22, 1996.

Simmons, Pam (1996). A case for legalizing abortion in Thailand. *The Nation.* September.

Tanothai, Sukdis, Pimsuda Teandum and Rachitta Na Pattalung (1982). Role, status and problems of Thai women in family planning. In *Women in Development: Implications for Population Dynamics in Thailand,* Suchart Prasitrathsin and Suwanlee Piampiti, eds. Bangkok.

United Nations, Department for Economic and Social Information and Policy Analysis (1994). *Population and Development. Programme of Action.* Adopted at the ICPD, Cairo 1994. vol. 1. New York: United Nations.

United Nations, Department of Public Information (1995). *Summary of the Programme of Action of the International Conference on Population and Development (ICPD, 1994)* March. New York: United Nations.

United Nations, ESCAP (1992). *Bali Declaration on Population and Sustainable Development. Fourth Asian and Pacific Population Conference, 19-27 August.*

_____ (1998). *1998 ESCAP Population Data Sheet.* Bangkok: ESCAP.

United Nations, Department for Policy Coordination and Sustainable Development (1998). *Report of the Fourth World Conference on Women.* Beijing, September, 4-15, 1995. Online document.

UNFPA. *A New Role for Men: Partners for Women's Empowerment.* New York: UNFPA. nd.

Van Griensven, Frits and Suwanee Surasiengsunk (1998). *The Use of Mortality Statistics as a Proxy Indicator for the Impact of the HIV Epidemic on the Thai Population.* Paper prepared for the AIDS Coordination Unit of the Delegation of the European Commission to Thailand. January.

Wongboonsin, Kua and Vipan Prachuabmoh Ruffolo (1995). Sex preference for children in Thailand and some other South-East Asian countries, *Asia-Pacific Population Journal* vol .10, No. 3. pp.43-62.

Wongboonsin, Pacharavalai and others (1997). *Human Resources Development and Migration Patterns among ASEAN Member States*. Working Paper for the AIPO ad-hoc committee on Human Resources Development. Bangkok: Institute of Population Studies, Chulalongkorn University.

Bibliothèque Université d'Ottawa Échéance	Library University of Ottawa Date Due